IMAGES
of America

St. Louis Radio and Television

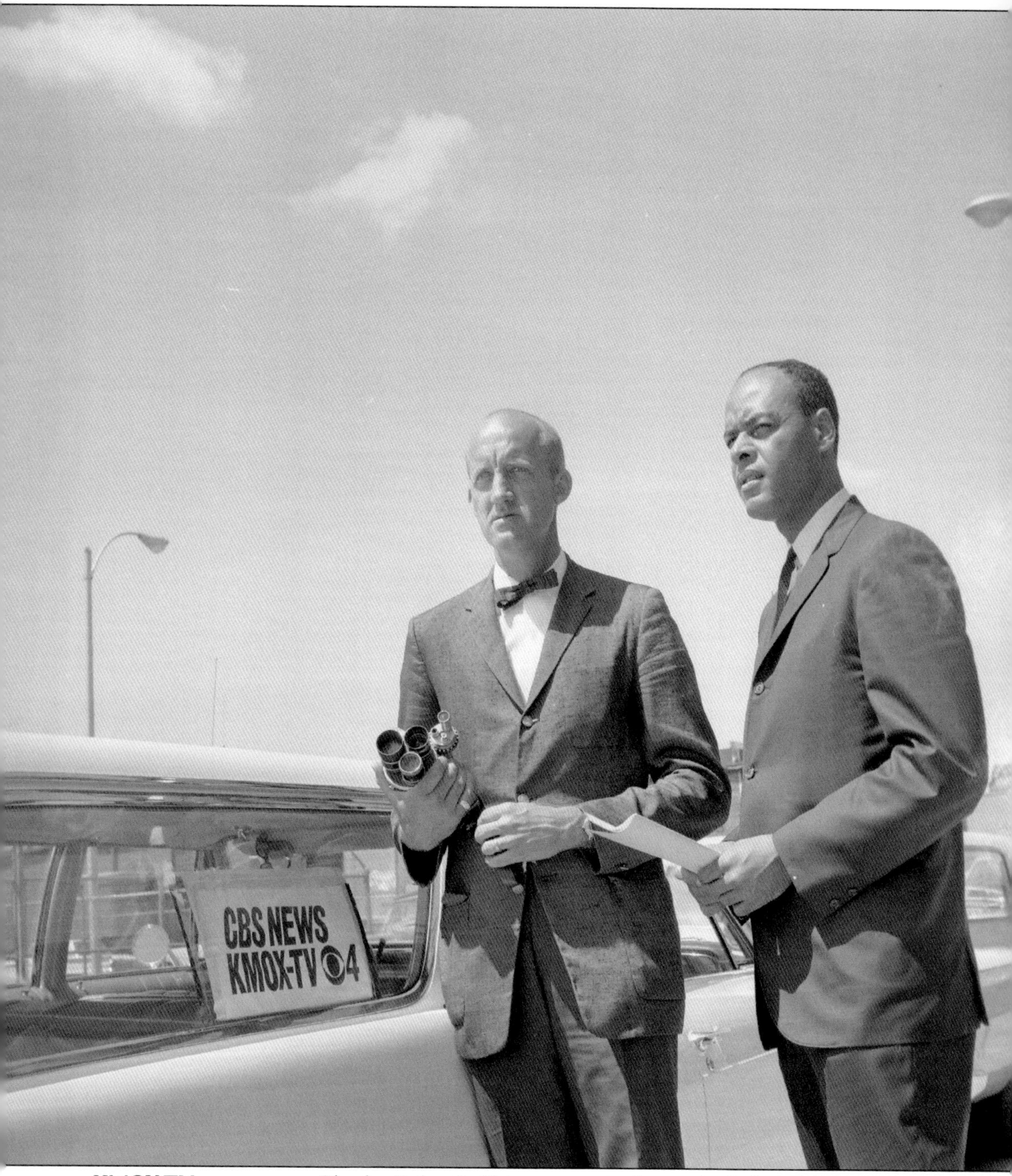

KMOX-TV cameraman Charles Bohn (left) is seen with the market's first African American anchor, Fred Porterfield. Porterfield served as an anchor at Channel 4 from 1965 to 1971. (KMOX-TV Collection, Missouri History Museum.)

On the Cover: St. Louis–born Harry Carabina, who adopted the air name "Harry Caray," is shown at the KXOK microphone, where it was said he worked for no pay just to gain broadcasting experience. (St. Louis Media Archive.)

IMAGES
of America

ST. LOUIS RADIO AND TELEVISION

Frank Absher

ARCADIA
PUBLISHING

ISBN 978-0-7385-9057-8

Published by Arcadia Publishing
Charleston, South Carolina

Printed in the United States of America

Library of Congress Control Number: 2012948048

For all general information, please contact Arcadia Publishing:
Telephone 843-853-2070
Fax 843-853-0044
E-mail sales@arcadiapublishing.com
For customer service and orders:
Toll-Free 1-888-313-2665

Visit us on the Internet at www.arcadiapublishing.com

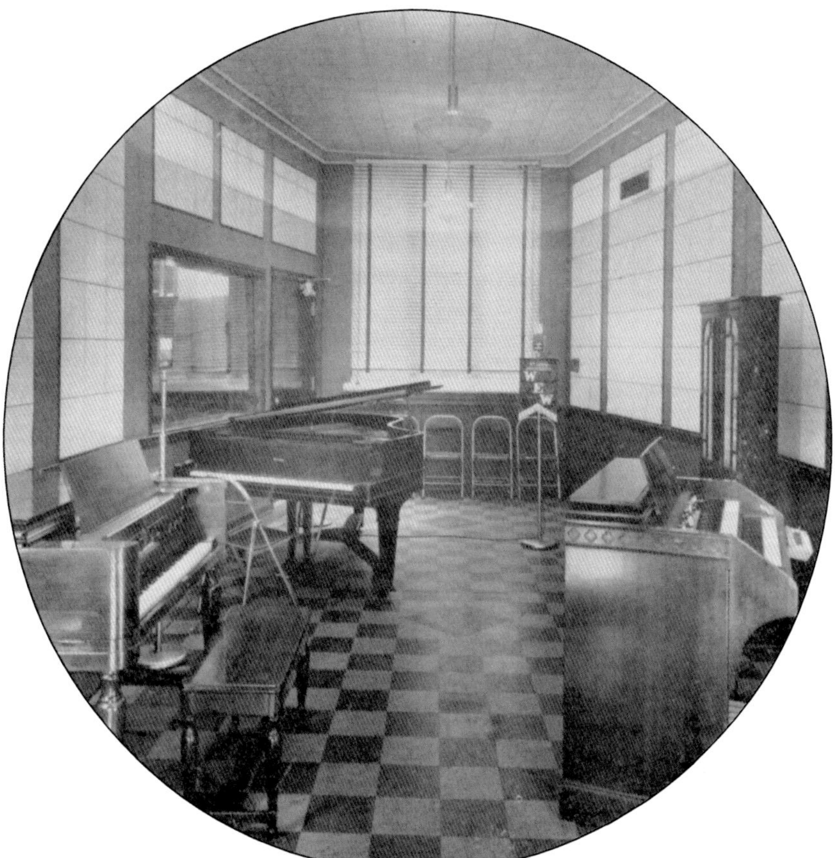

The studios of WEW are seen as they appeared in 1945. At that time, the station was still owned by Saint Louis University. (St. Louis Media Archive.)

Contents

Acknowledgments

From the time I was old enough to pay attention to what was on the radio, St. Louis media were in our home. My hometown was about 50 miles from the city, which meant some lower-power radio stations were hard to pull in, but in my young life, everything important came from a St. Louis radio or television station.

Working at a St. Louis radio or television station became a professional goal in college, and I was fortunate to work at several. In my later years, I set out to preserve the history of St. Louis media, so this book is a logical step.

Regrettably, there are many holes in the photographic history of St. Louis broadcasting. This means many people or developments deserving of mention in this book were left out. Still, you are in for a fascinating trip into the past browsing these pages.

Thanks to Jean Gosebrink and Amanda Bahr-Evola, St. Louis Public Library Media Archive; Charles Brown, St. Louis Mercantile Library; Allen Cohen, KMOV-TV; Joe Sonderman; Dr. Wayne Brasler; the Spencer Allen family; Amanda Claunch, Missouri History Museum; Dick Ulett; Kathy Corey; Bobby Day; Suzi Mahe, KPLR-TV/KTVI-TV; Don Rockwell; Matt Huelskamp, KETC-TV; Michael Henry, Library of American Broadcasting-University of Maryland; Sue Dorn; Phil Donato, KWMU; Jack LeChien; Howard DeMere; and the St. Louis Media History Foundation.

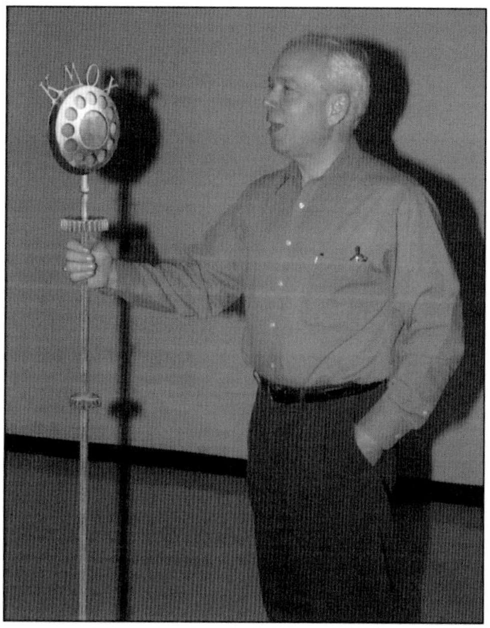

The author is pictured behind the mic. (Courtesy Dhimitri Zonia.)

INTRODUCTION

Although it is not well known outside the community of broadcast historians, St. Louis was host to a significant event in the development of radio broadcasting. It took place on March 1, 1893, on the 1300 block of Olive Street where the St. Louis Public Library's Central facility is now located. Back then, it was the site of the Exposition Center, where the National Electric Light Association was meeting.

On the stage, Nikola Tesla demonstrated the transmission of electricity, without the use of wires, sending it through the air from one side of the stage to the other to light a tube similar to a fluorescent light.

This first demonstration of "wireless" eventually led to the wireless transmission of telegraph signals and then of the human voice. Unfortunately, Guglielmo Marconi is generally credited with this, although his "invention" came two years later.

Fast-forward to November 1920, when two young electrical whizzes from St. Louis broadcast results of the Harding-Cox presidential election using transmitters they had constructed in the basements of their respective homes in South St. Louis. William E. Woods and Lester Arthur Benson had formed the Benwood Company, which would later manufacture transmitters for the city's first licensed radio stations. But on the night of November 2 of that year, the two sent out the area's first radio voice transmissions, relaying election information to those listeners who had assembled receivers. For decades, though, the Westinghouse Electric Corporation claimed to have been first to do this on the same evening on their company station, KDKA, in Pittsburgh. But Woods and Benson did something that KDKA did not: they stayed on the air and correctly reported that Warren G. Harding had won the election; KDKA had shut down its operation earlier in the evening and concluded that James Cox had won.

Less than two years after that broadcast, St. Louis had two licensed radio stations on the air. KSD and WEW received their licenses within days of each other in 1922: KSD on March 14 and WEW on March 22. Both had been broadcasting experimentally for several weeks prior to licensing.

The history of television in St. Louis may also surprise some people—because it began in the late 1920s. The Convey family, owners of radio station KWK, conducted experimental television broadcasts from their studios in the Chase Hotel. These broadcast experiments were reportedly a success, but the Conveys were using what is now known as a disc scanning system to break down the pictures. The television industry settled on a linear scan system developed by a young man who envisioned the principles of the system while still in high school in Utah. Philo Farnsworth had filed for a patent for his system before turning the age of 22.

In St. Louis, the first television station was owned by the daily newspaper, the *St. Louis Post-Dispatch*. Joseph Pulitzer's second in command, George Burbach, is credited with persuading Pulitzer to invest in the construction of KSD-TV after Burbach had seen a demonstration of the medium in Europe. After having seen a closed-circuit broadcast demonstration of his station, Pulitzer reportedly declared that television would be the death of radio.

When KSD-TV went on the air on February 8, 1947, there were only four sets in St. Louis that could receive the broadcasts, and Burbach had one in his office. It was a fluke in Washington, DC, that made KSD-TV profitable.

Shortly after the station signed on, the Federal Communications Commission was flooded with applications to build television stations all over the nation. The commission was not equipped to process the huge number of applications, so a freeze was placed on new television-station construction. During the six years the freeze was in place, KSD-TV was the only game in town, and more and more people were buying television sets.

At about the time KSD-TV was making its debut, a new form of radio was also hitting St. Louis. Touted as "staticless radio," FM was supposed to be the next big thing—it was not. KWK-FM, KFUO-FM, KXLW-FM, WIL-FM, KSLH-FM, KSD-FM, KXOK-FM, and WEW-FM all went on the air; WTMV-FM was also broadcasting in the market from East St. Louis. It was a time for experimenting. Two of the stations, KFUO-FM and KSLH-FM, were non-commercial. The others ran into problems as the decade wound down. WEW-FM pulled its plug as 1950 arrived, with a spokesman saying the new medium had not been accepted by the public. KSD-FM ceased operation in November 1949 because of what was called a "business decision." WIL-FM shut down the same month for what owner Lester Benson called "obvious reasons." KWK-FM owner Robert T. Convey said, "Public acceptance of the medium has not been widespread" when he shut down in April 1950. In short, there was not any money to be made in FM broadcasting in the 1940s and early 1950s.

But it was the broadcasters' mistake that doomed early FM in St. Louis. The stations broadcast exactly the same programming that was being heard on AM frequencies, thus listeners had no real incentive to go out and buy new radios that could pick up FM stations since they could already hear the same shows on radios they already owned.

This meant broadcasters had spent money for all the additional transmitting equipment, as well as the additional expense of electricity to power the transmitters, but were realizing no additional income for the investment. So, the plug was literally pulled on the market's earliest commercial FM stations within five years of their births. When Harry Eidelman began offering unique commercial programming on his stand-alone KCFM in the mid-1950s, he gave St. Louis a new form of radio entertainment that grew, very slowly, into what later became the dominant audio medium of the nation.

The pages of this book provide the reader with a photographic trip through the history of St. Louis broadcasting. These are the faces of the people who helped make it happen.

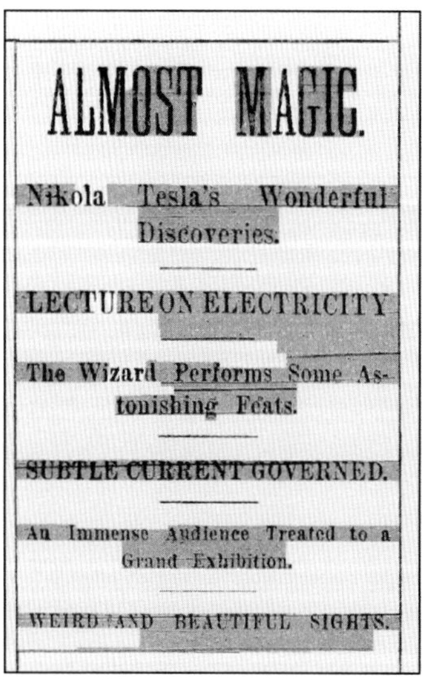
ALMOST MAGIC.

Nikola Tesla's Wonderful Discoveries.

LECTURE ON ELECTRICITY

The Wizard Performs Some Astonishing Feats.

SUBTLE CURRENT GOVERNED.

An Immense Audience Treated to a Grand Exhibition.

WEIRD AND BEAUTIFUL SIGHTS.

The *St. Louis Republic* gave extensive coverage to the Tesla appearance. The article's headline is seen at left, and the accompanying caricature of him is on the right.

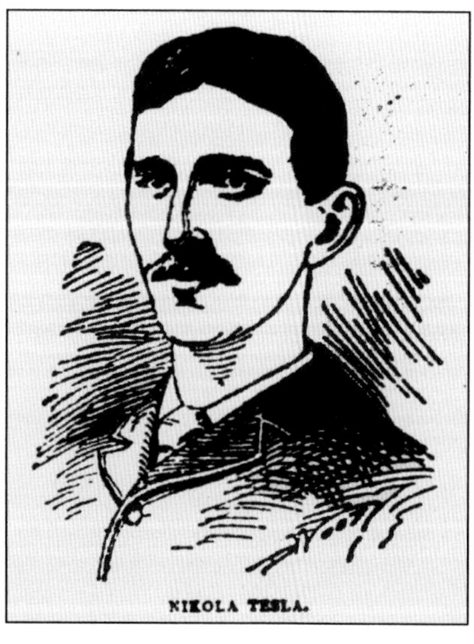

One

THE BEGINNINGS OF BROADCASTING

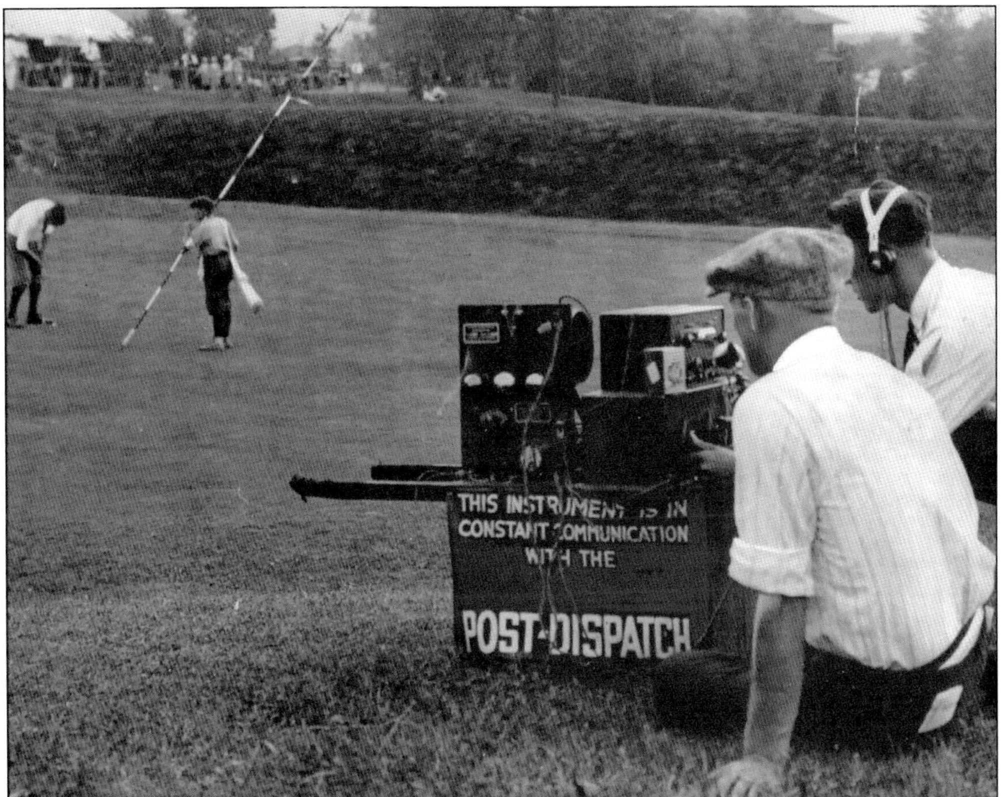

There was no organized development of radio; instead, people all over the world experimented with homemade equipment. In 1921, during this experimental period, the *Post-Dispatch* radio station tested wireless equipment at the National Amateur Golf Tournament at the St. Louis Country Club. Sportswriter J. Roy Stockton, in front wearing the cap, sent reports via radio back to the newspaper's offices downtown, where the writers turned those reports into newspaper write-ups immediately. (St. Louis Media Archive.)

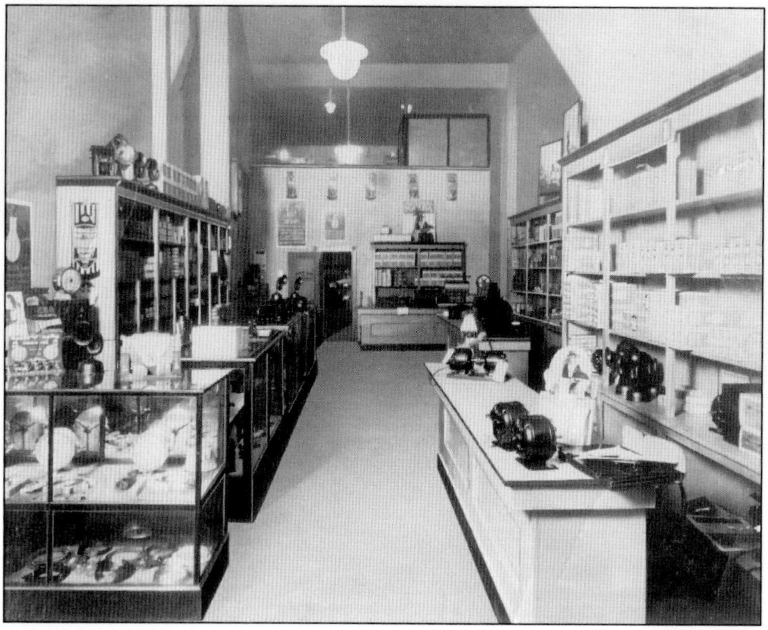

Transmitters for several of St. Louis's early radio stations, including KSD, were built by Lester Benson and William Woods at their Benwood Electronics Store on Olive Street downtown. The two men were responsible for the first radio broadcast originating in St. Louis in 1920. (Sue Batterson.)

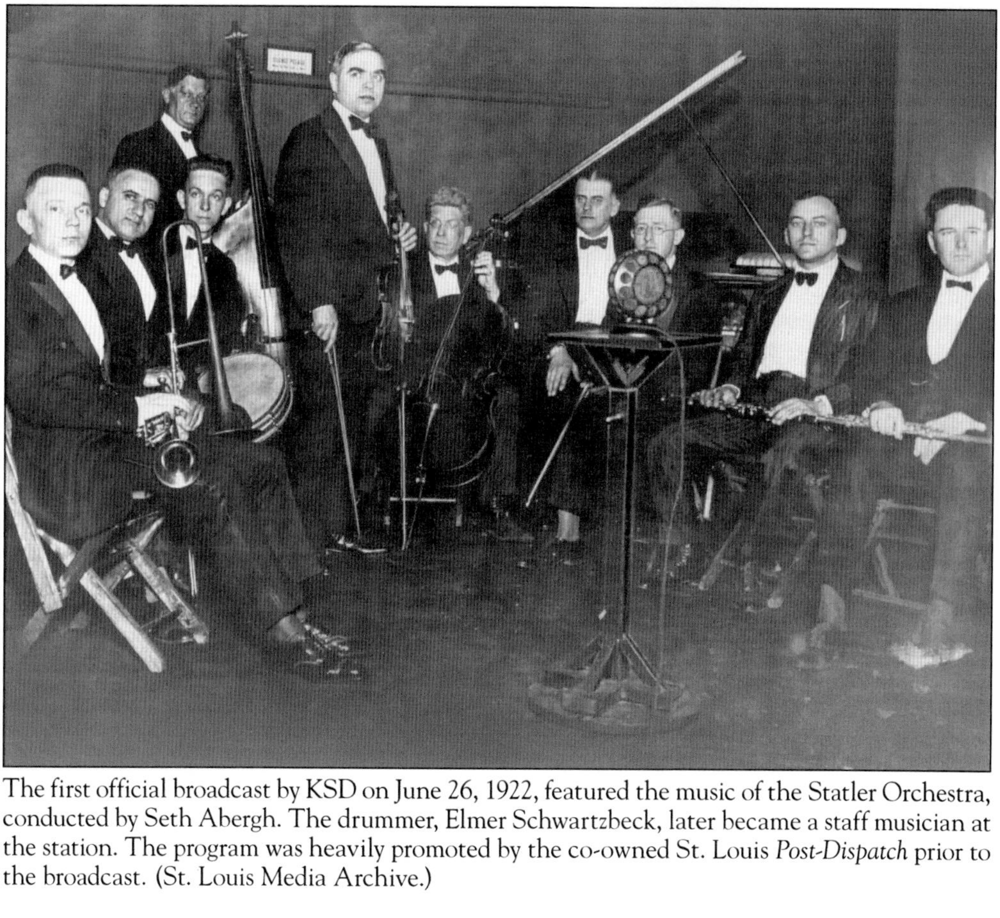

The first official broadcast by KSD on June 26, 1922, featured the music of the Statler Orchestra, conducted by Seth Abergh. The drummer, Elmer Schwartzbeck, later became a staff musician at the station. The program was heavily promoted by the co-owned St. Louis *Post-Dispatch* prior to the broadcast. (St. Louis Media Archive.)

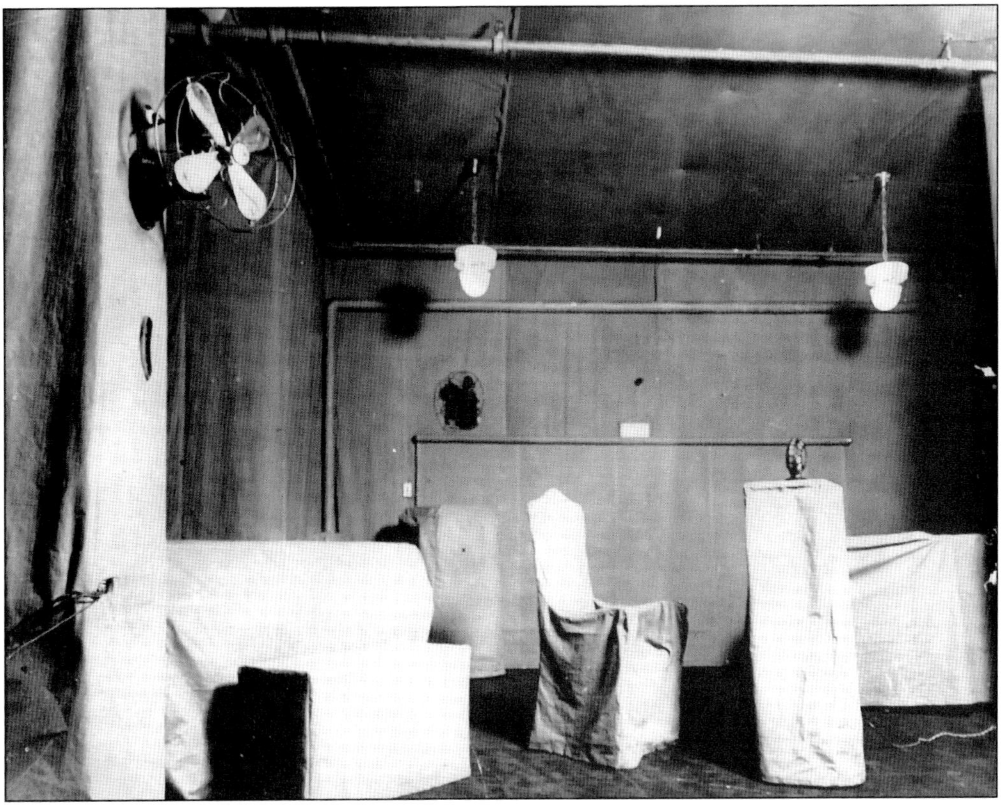

Furniture in KSD's first broadcasting studio in the Post-Dispatch Building at Twelfth and Olive Streets was draped in fabric to deaden the sound and eliminate all echoes. The microphone was placed on the tall table to the right in the photograph. (St. Louis Media Archive.)

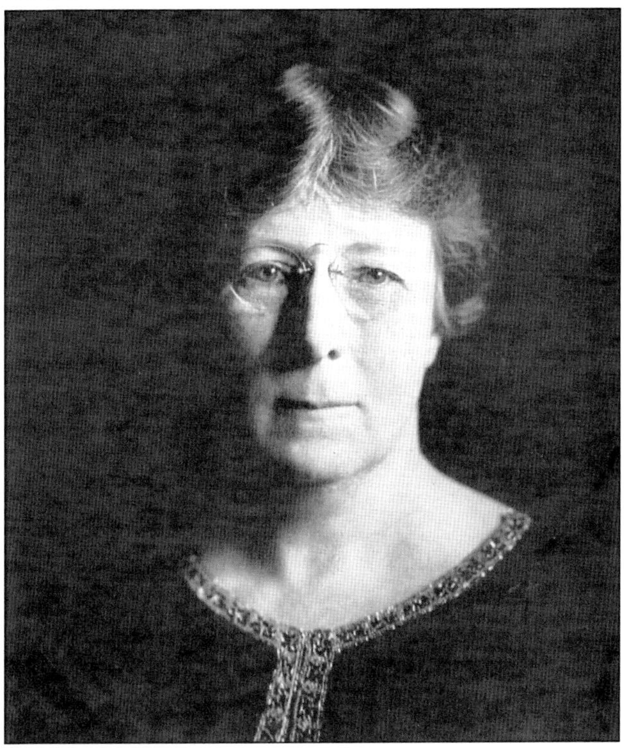

Virginia "Val" Jones was the first lady of St. Louis radio, having worked as a program director and announcer at KSD when the station signed on in 1922. Legend has it that hers was a deep, distinguished voice, and listeners occasionally mistook her for a man while on the air. (St. Louis Media Archive.)

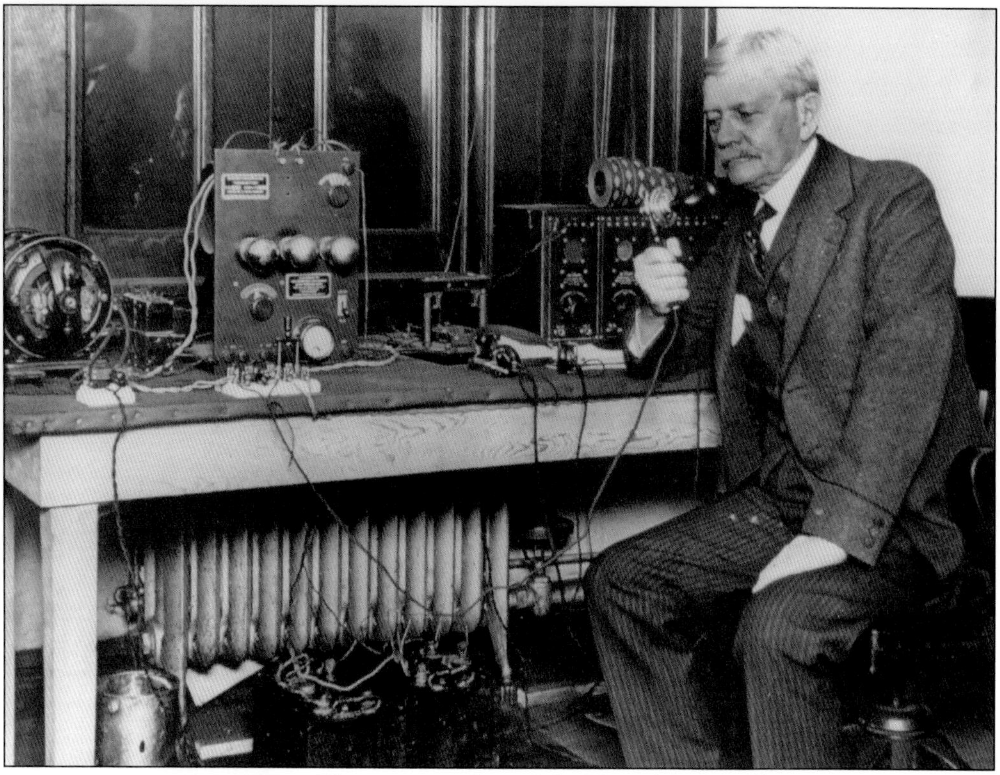

The vice president of the United States, Thomas Marshall, broadcast from the studios of KSD on April 25, 1922. (St. Louis Media Archive.)

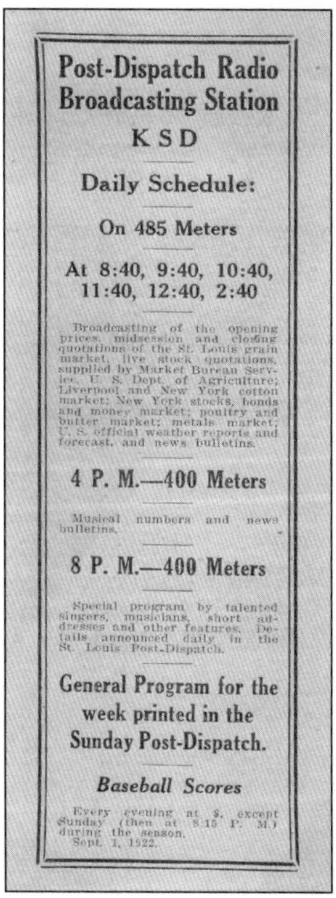

Post-Dispatch Radio Broadcasting Station

KSD

Daily Schedule:

On 485 Meters

At 8:40, 9:40, 10:40, 11:40, 12:40, 2:40

Broadcasting of the opening prices, midsession and closing quotations of the St. Louis grain market, live stock quotations, supplied by Market Bureau Service, U. S. Dept. of Agriculture; Liverpool and New York cotton market; New York stocks, bonds and money market; poultry and butter market; metals market; U. S. official weather reports and forecast, and news bulletins.

4 P. M.—400 Meters

Musical numbers and news bulletins.

8 P. M.—400 Meters

Special program by talented singers, musicians, short addresses and other features. Details announced daily in the St. Louis Post-Dispatch.

General Program for the week printed in the Sunday Post-Dispatch.

Baseball Scores

Every evening at 8, except Sunday (then at 8:15 P. M.) during the season.

Sept. 1, 1922.

In radio's earliest days, stations did everything they could to lure listeners. In addition to publishing their broadcast schedule in the *Post-Dispatch*, KSD distributed cards to the public. (St. Louis Media Archive.)

Other stations printed up small booklets. WCK was the radio station owned by the Stix, Baer & Fuller department store. The store's owners believed the public would be prompted to buy radios at the store if there were more stations available. Later, the station's call letters were changed to WSBF. (St. Louis Media Archive.)

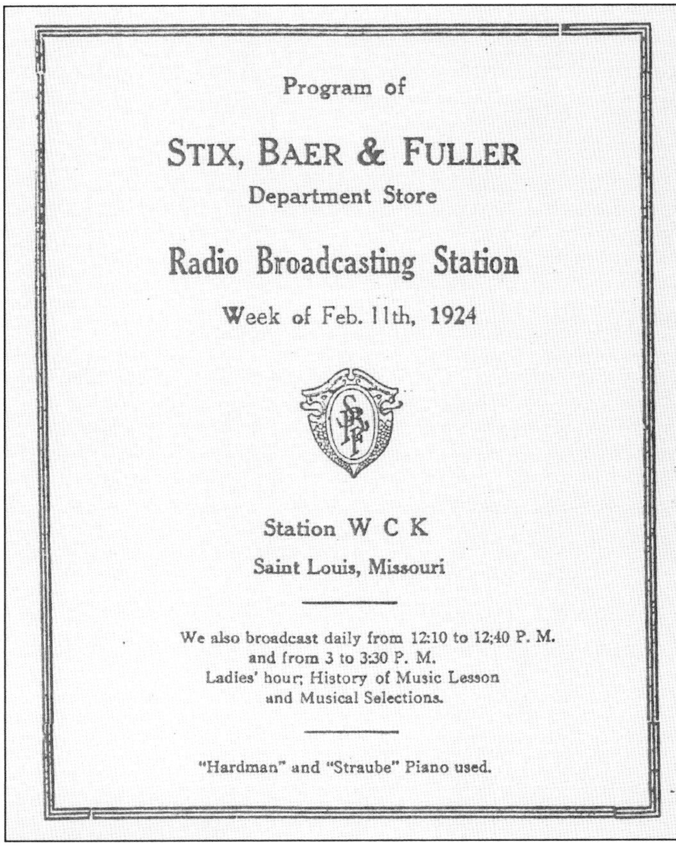

Program of

STIX, BAER & FULLER

Department Store

Radio Broadcasting Station

Week of Feb. 11th, 1924

Station W C K

Saint Louis, Missouri

We also broadcast daily from 12:10 to 12:40 P. M.
and from 3 to 3:30 P. M.
Ladies' hour; History of Music Lesson
and Musical Selections.

"Hardman" and "Straube" Piano used.

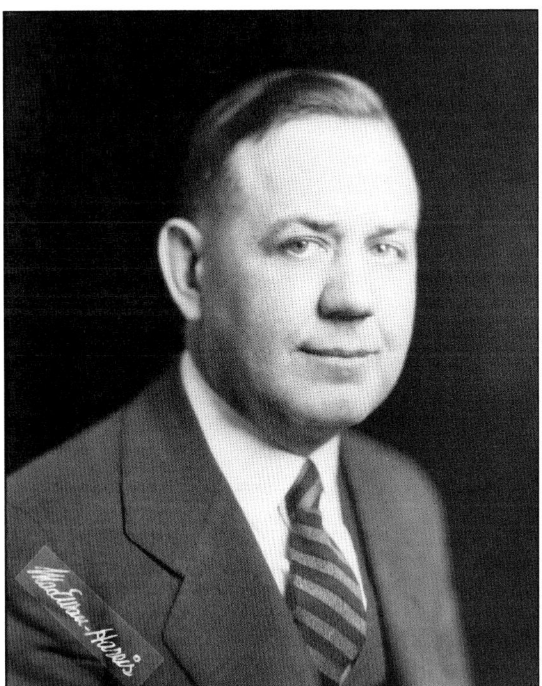

Promoter Thomas Patrick Convey approached community leaders in 1925 with the idea of pooling their financial resources to build a radio superstation in St. Louis. The group adopted the corporate name of "The Voice of St. Louis, Incorporated," and by the end of that year, their radio station, KMOX, was on the air, and Convey was the station manager. (St. Louis Media Archive.)

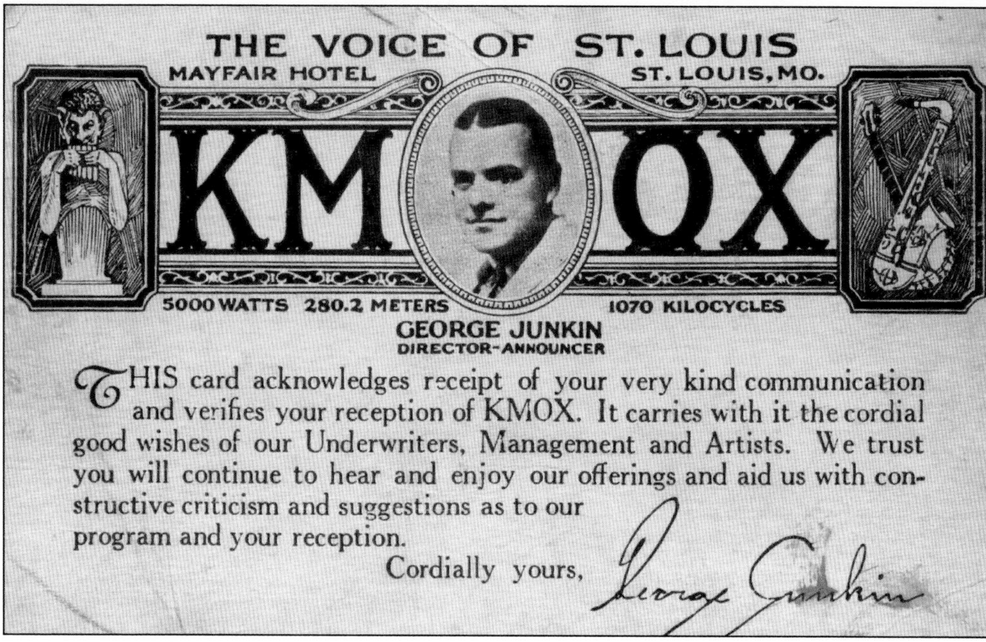

THE VOICE OF ST. LOUIS
MAYFAIR HOTEL ST. LOUIS, MO.

KMOX

5000 WATTS 280.2 METERS 1070 KILOCYCLES

GEORGE JUNKIN
DIRECTOR-ANNOUNCER

THIS card acknowledges receipt of your very kind communication and verifies your reception of KMOX. It carries with it the cordial good wishes of our Underwriters, Management and Artists. We trust you will continue to hear and enjoy our offerings and aid us with constructive criticism and suggestions as to our program and your reception.

Cordially yours,
George Junkin

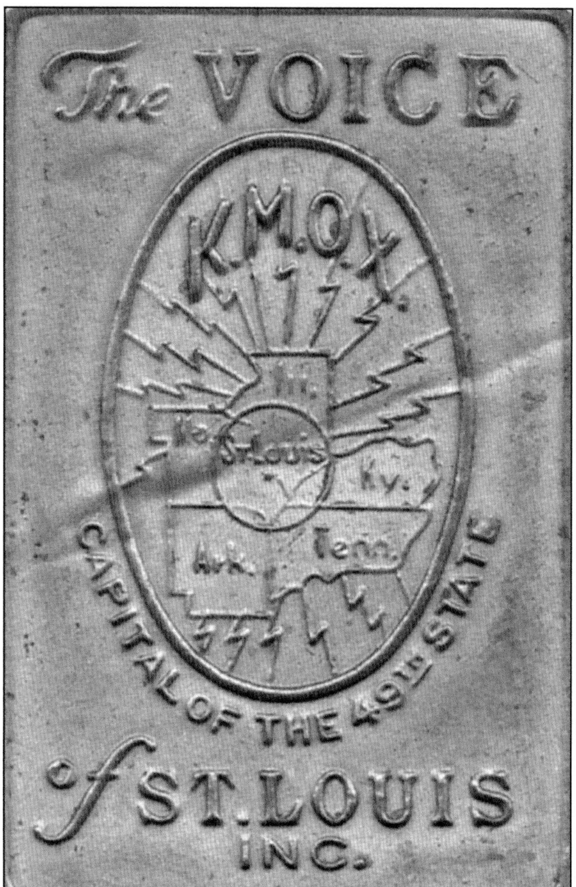

In the 1920s, radio stations were anxious to acknowledge listeners in faraway places. The card shown above, known as a QSL card, was sent to listeners who sent mail to the station describing what they had heard, along with the time and date of reception. The small stamp at left (enlarged) was a collector's item known as an EKKO stamp. Radio listeners kept special albums of stamps from radio stations they had heard. (St. Louis Media Archive.)

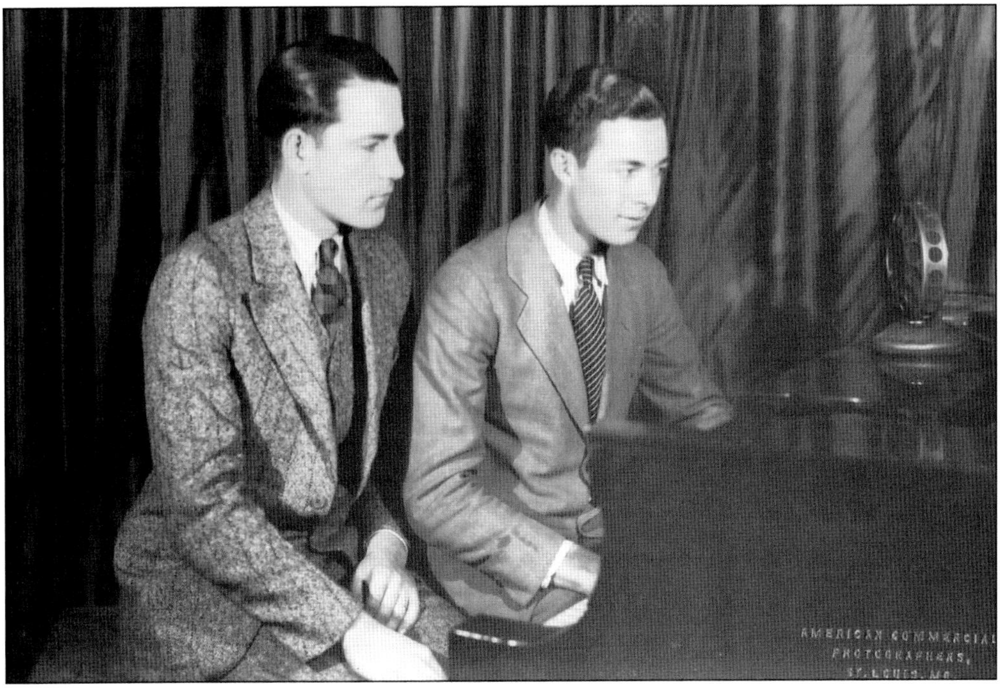

The musical duo known as "Red and Gold" presented a musical show on KMOX sponsored by Stark Brothers' Nursery, one of the station's shareholders. All corporate shareholders were given radio programs in the station's early days. (St. Louis Media Archive.)

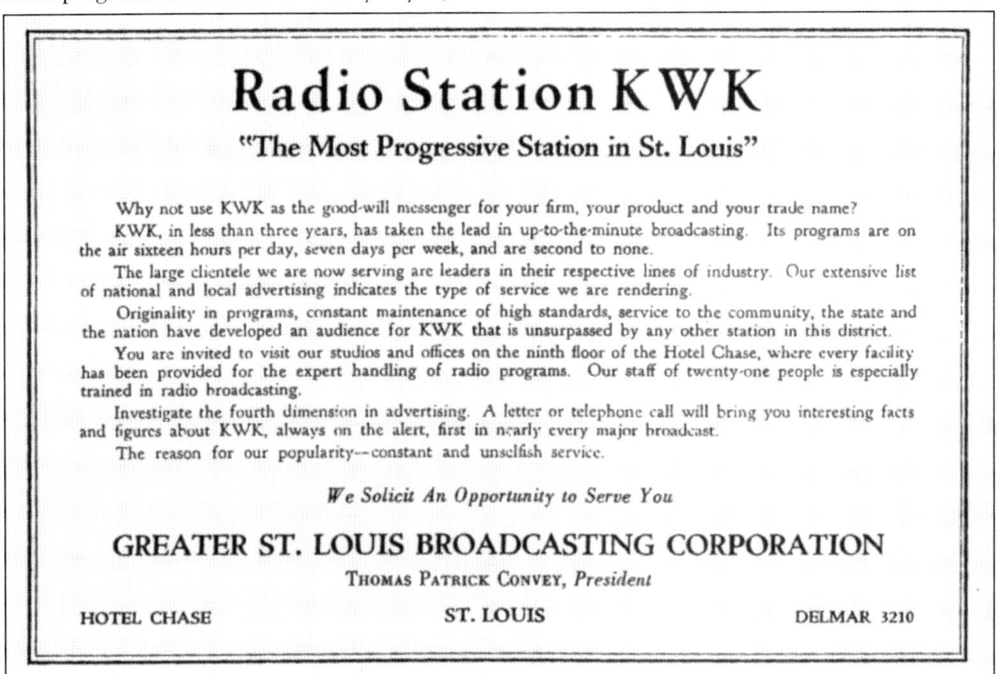

Radio Station KWK

"The Most Progressive Station in St. Louis"

Why not use KWK as the good-will messenger for your firm, your product and your trade name?

KWK, in less than three years, has taken the lead in up-to-the-minute broadcasting. Its programs are on the air sixteen hours per day, seven days per week, and are second to none.

The large clientele we are now serving are leaders in their respective lines of industry. Our extensive list of national and local advertising indicates the type of service we are rendering.

Originality in programs, constant maintenance of high standards, service to the community, the state and the nation have developed an audience for KWK that is unsurpassed by any other station in this district.

You are invited to visit our studios and offices on the ninth floor of the Hotel Chase, where every facility has been provided for the expert handling of radio programs. Our staff of twenty-one people is especially trained in radio broadcasting.

Investigate the fourth dimension in advertising. A letter or telephone call will bring you interesting facts and figures about KWK, always on the alert, first in nearly every major broadcast.

The reason for our popularity--constant and unselfish service.

We Solicit An Opportunity to Serve You

GREATER ST. LOUIS BROADCASTING CORPORATION

Thomas Patrick Convey, *President*

HOTEL CHASE | ST. LOUIS | DELMAR 3210

Radio competition began to heat up in St. Louis in the late 1920s, which was quickly followed by the Great Depression. Stations often pursued advertising dollars by running advertising in print media. (St. Louis Media Archive.)

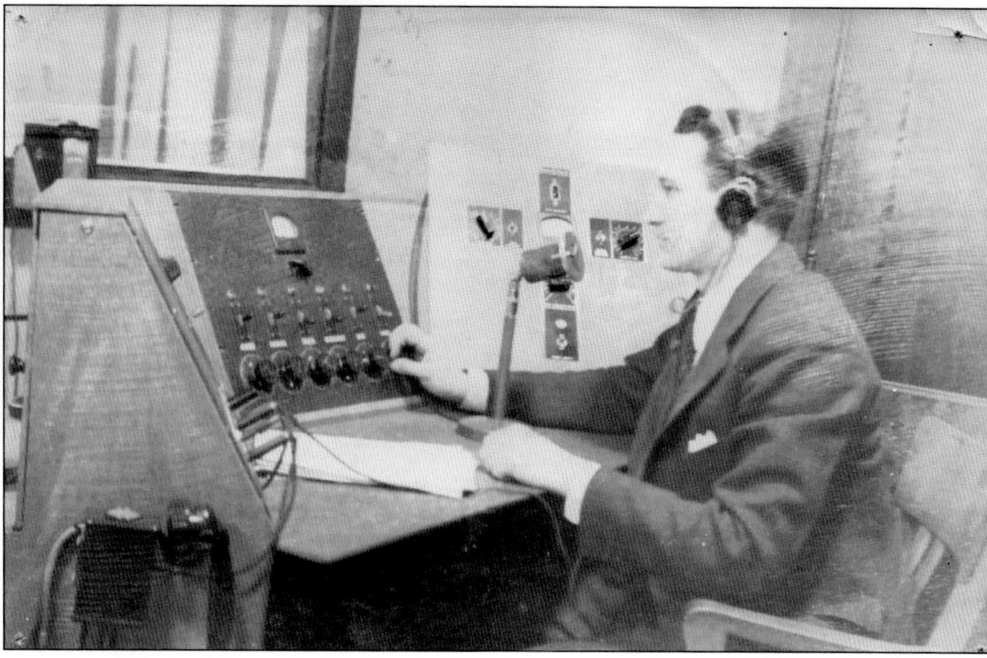

Announcer/engineer Lewis Sieck is shown at the KFUO microphone in 1934. The station, owned by the Lutheran Church Missouri Synod, was located at the Concordia Seminary. (St. Louis Media Archive.)

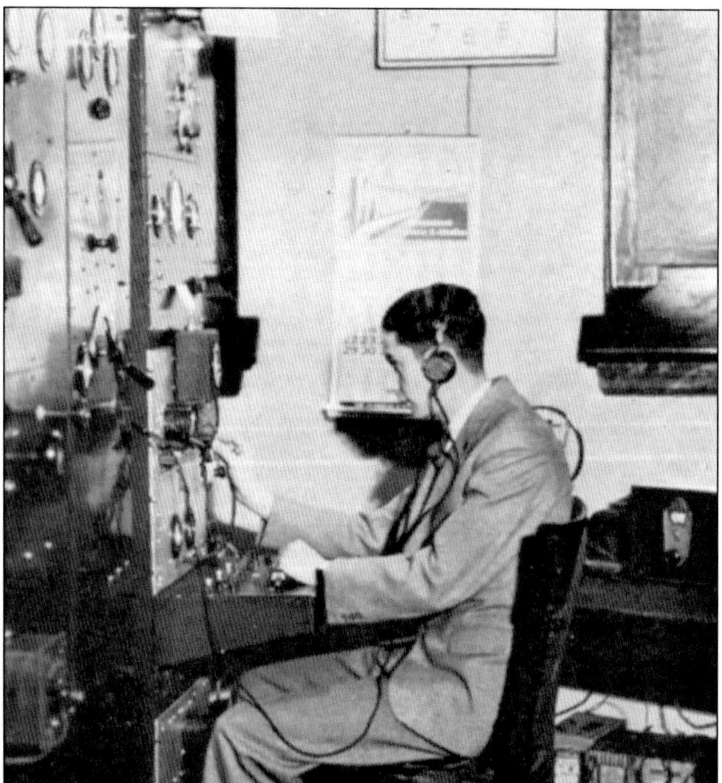

Gordon Sherman, the "chief operator" at WEW, is seen working at the station's control board in 1933. WEW was owned and operated by Saint Louis University. (St. Louis Media Archive.)

During the Great Depression, radio provided entertainment for the masses in its broadcasts and, occasionally, produced external events to showcase talent or encourage audience participation. (St. Louis Media Archive.)

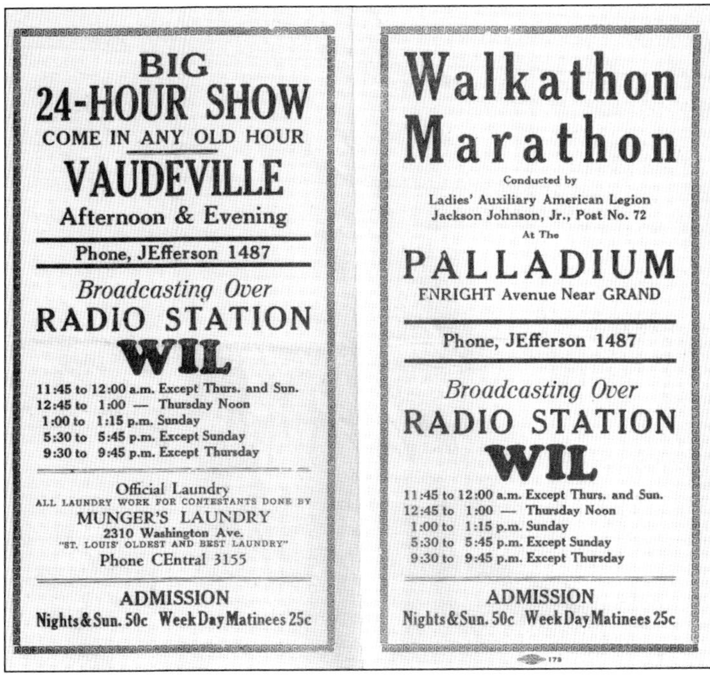

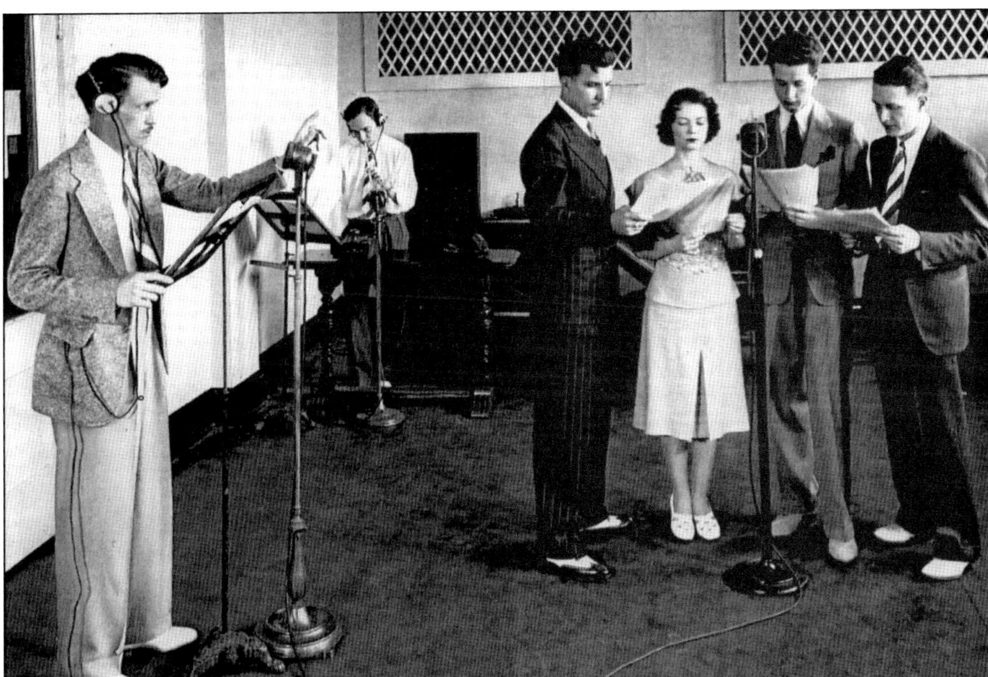

Every radio station produced live dramatic programs. For this broadcast, WIL's Portal Players have gathered at the microphones, while a sound-effects man stands in the background. (St. Louis Media Archive.)

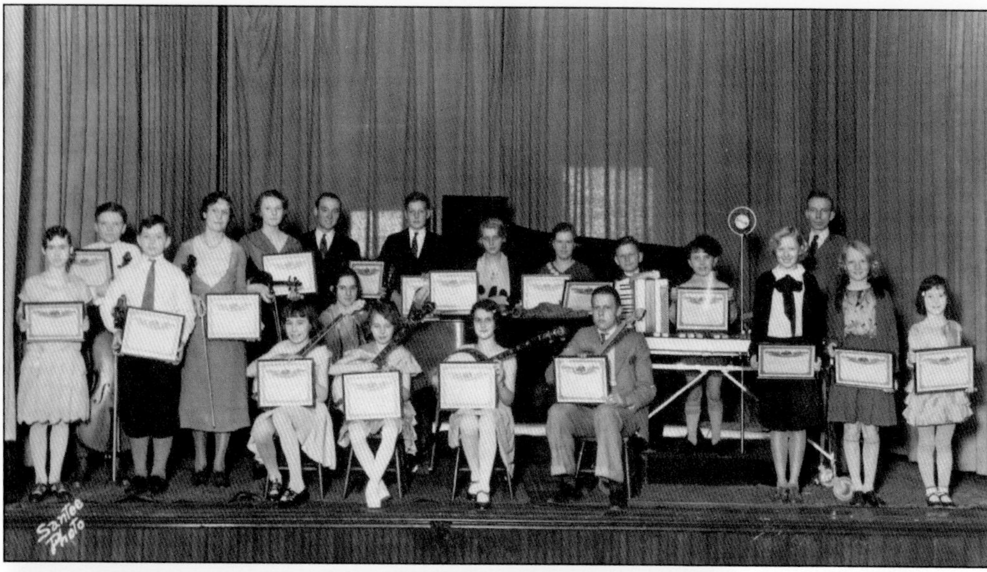

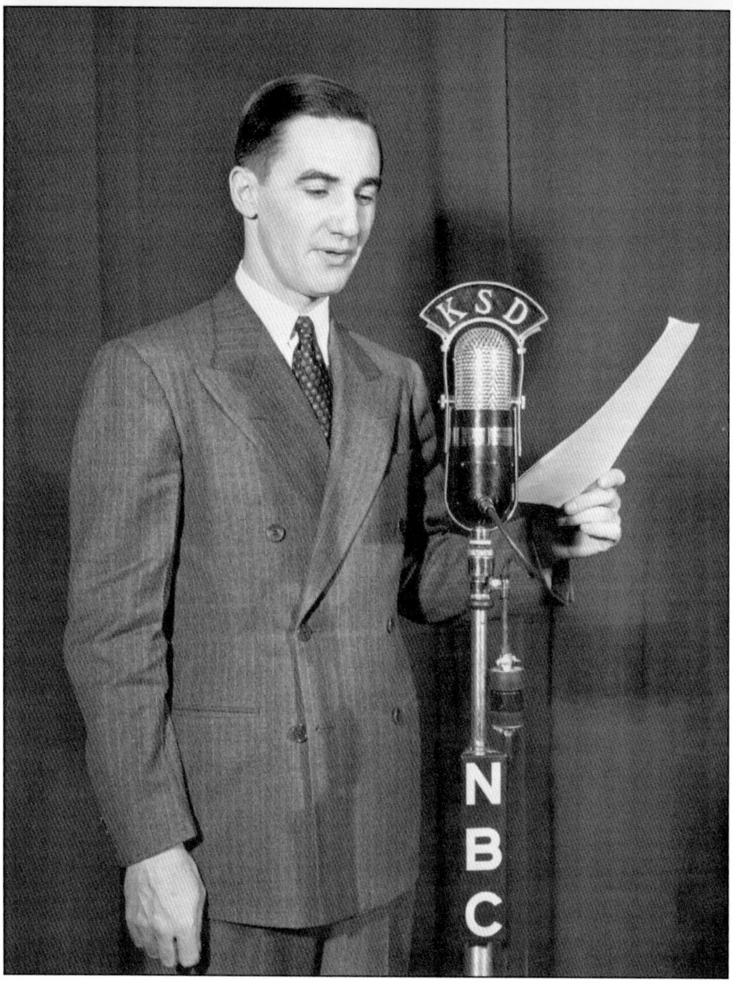

Because of the constant need to fill airtime with live broadcasts, stations were always searching for new talent. Some, like KSD, used program time to audition possible broadcasters. (St. Louis Media Archive.)

Harold Grams, who started working as an announcer at KSD in 1938, rose to the position of corporate vice president of broadcast operations before retiring. (St. Louis Media Archive.)

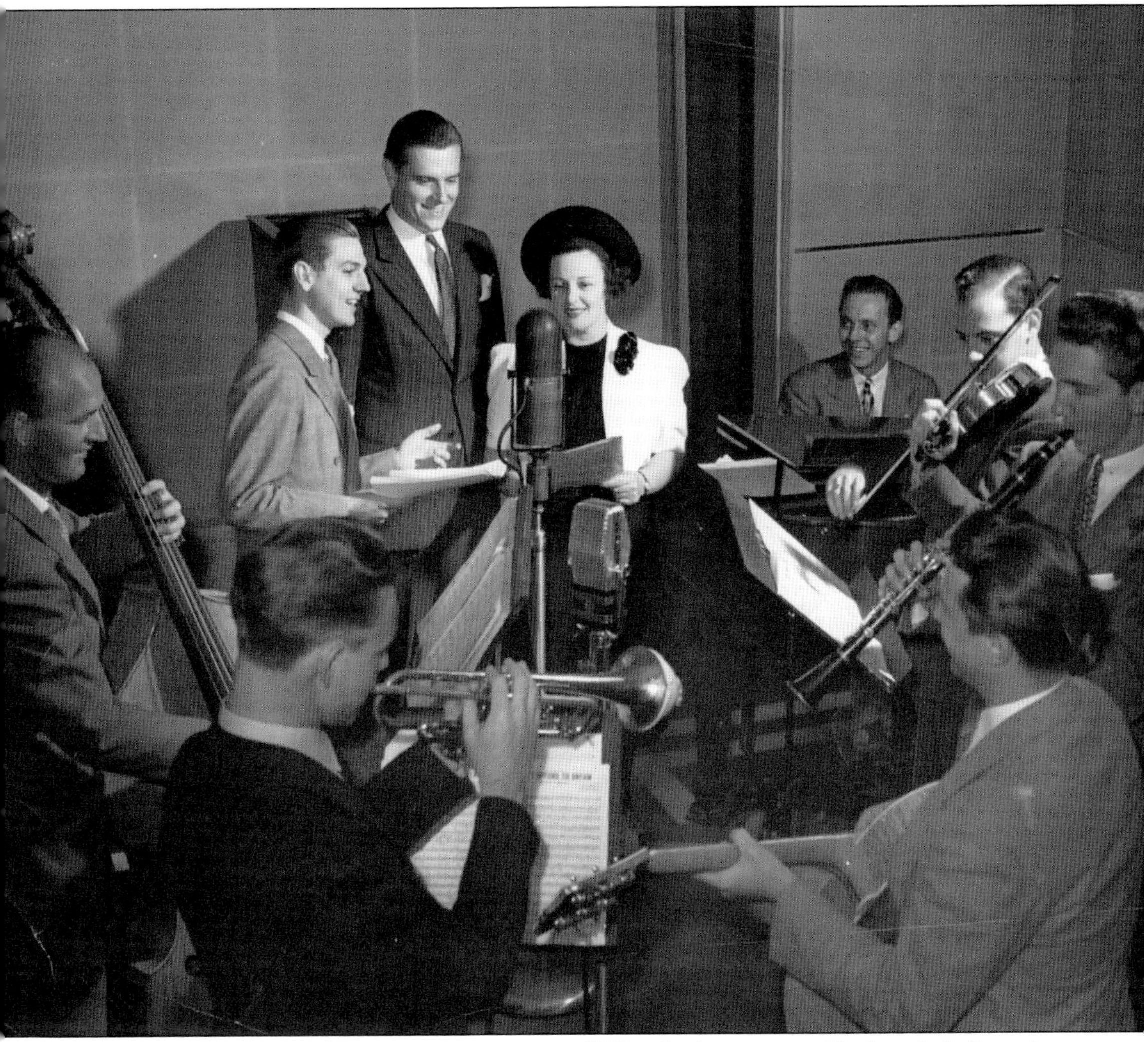

This photograph shows a dramatic presentation at KSD, which was owned by Joseph Pulitzer. It highlights a major difference in broadcast operations when compared to the WIL photograph on page 17. Pulitzer had very deep pockets via corporate funding, which meant the station had a full-time studio orchestra and musical director/arranger, Russ David (at the piano on the right). (St. Louis Media Archive.)

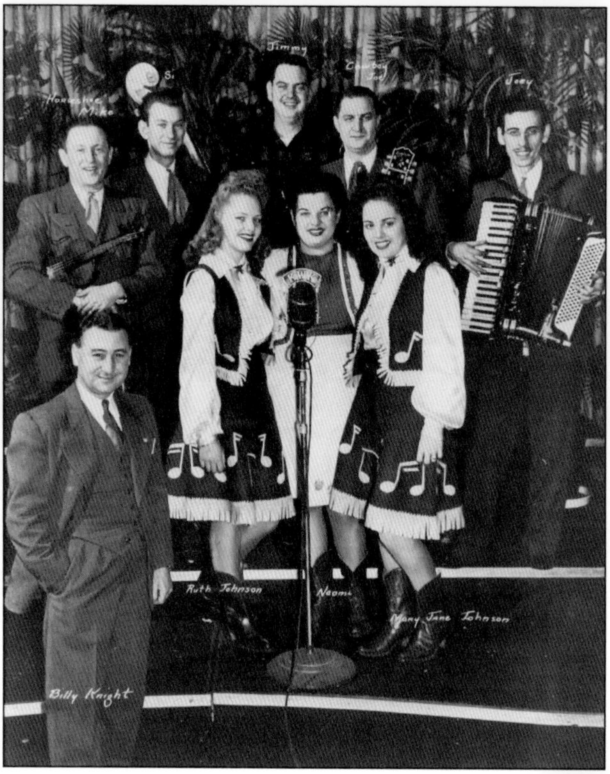

Billy Knight and his orchestra were mainstays in St. Louis hotel ballrooms and were heard regularly in remote broadcasts on KWK. (St. Louis Media Archive.)

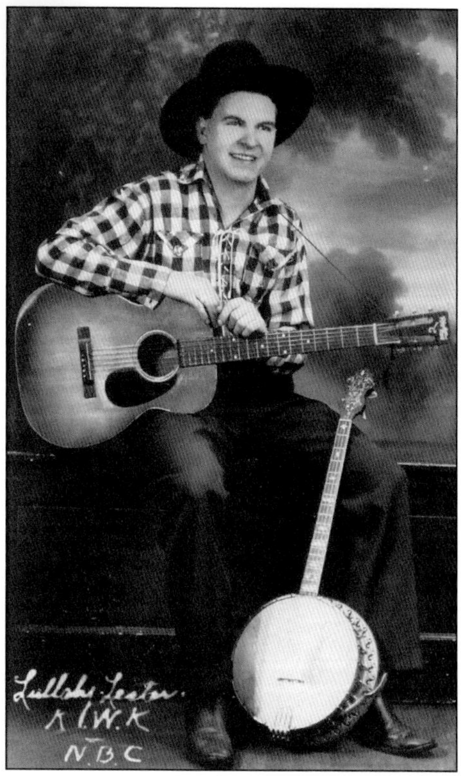

"Lullaby Lester" Mayberry came to town as a teenager from Iron County, Missouri, and was hired to the musical staff at KMOX. He later moved on to KWK before leaving the market. (St. Louis Media Archive.)

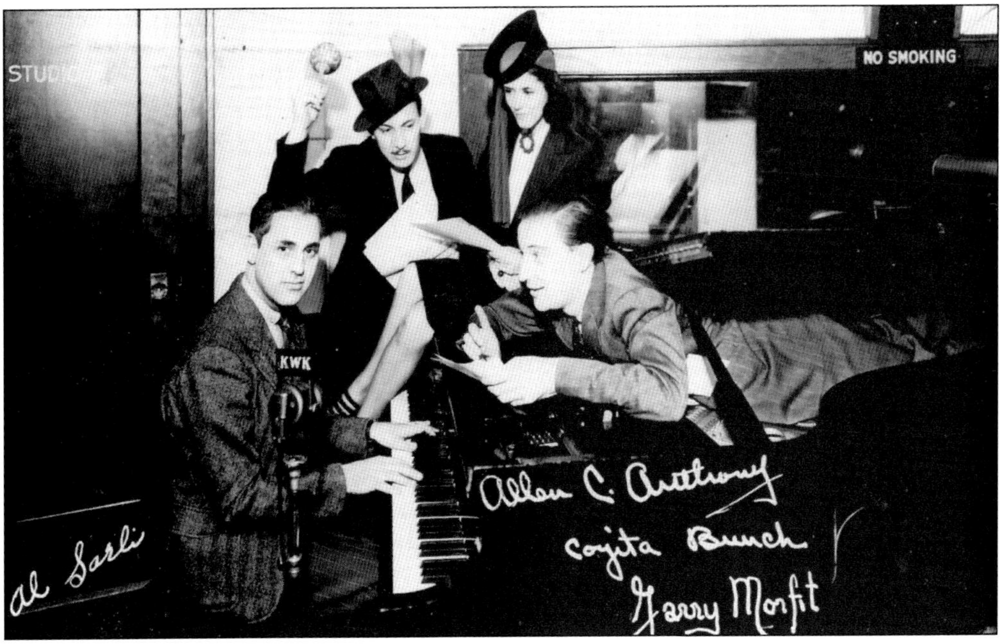

Musical staffers at KWK in the late 1930s included Garry Morfit (lying on the piano). He pursued opportunities elsewhere and later became known as national television personality Garry Moore. (St. Louis Media Archive.)

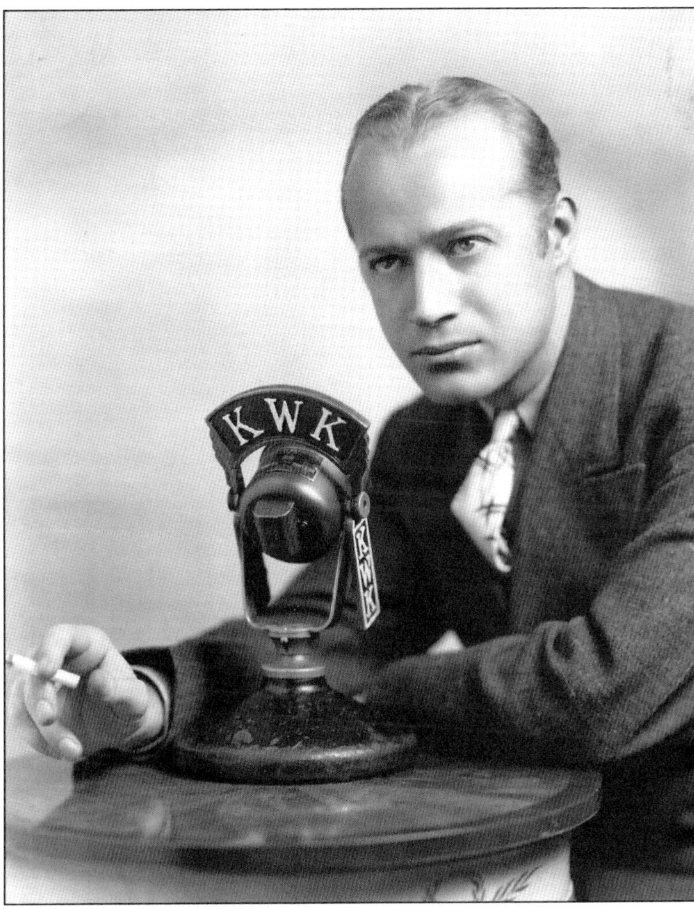

Throughout the 1930s, several radio stations broadcast Cardinals and Browns baseball games from Sportsman's park. Johnny O'Hara did the play by play for KWK from 1936 to 1943, moving with the team franchises to other St. Louis stations from 1944 to 1947. (St. Louis Media Archive.)

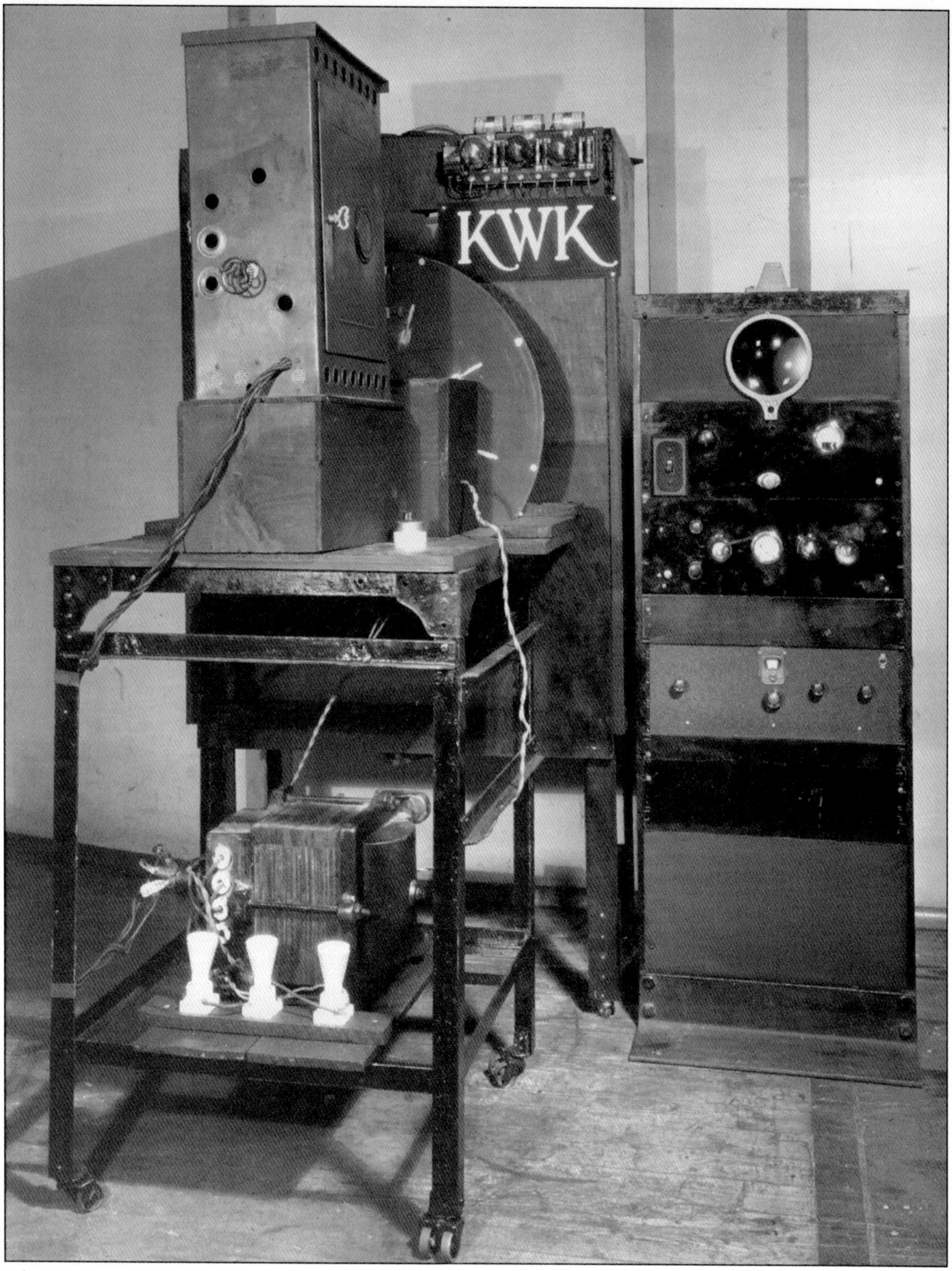

There were already rumblings about a new invention, television, that would allow people to watch programs broadcast over the airwaves. Thomas Patrick Convey, one of KWK radio's owners, began experimental broadcasts with this television equipment from the radio studios in the Chase Hotel in 1928. This equipment was used to turn the images into a format for electronic transmission. (St. Louis Mercantile Library Association.)

Two

Radio Comes Alive

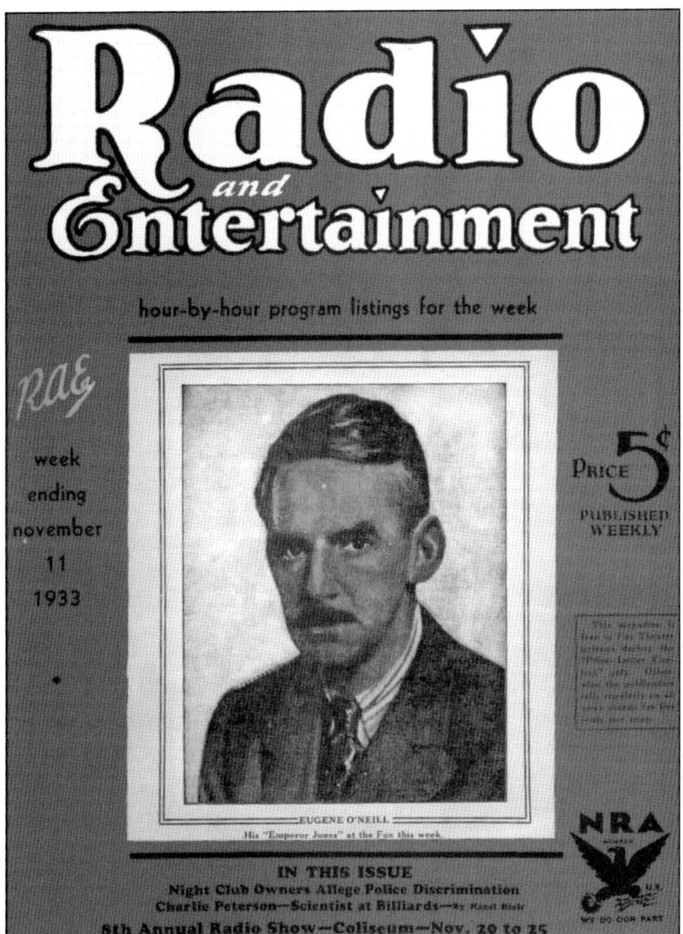

As the 1920s came to an end, a large portion of US homes had a radio. The Depression economy was bad, but radio provided "free" entertainment. In the late 1920s, St. Louisans could subscribe to the weekly magazine *Radio & Entertainment* (later *RAE*) for a complete listing of all shows on local stations along with news features and photographs of their favorite stars. (St. Louis Media Archive.)

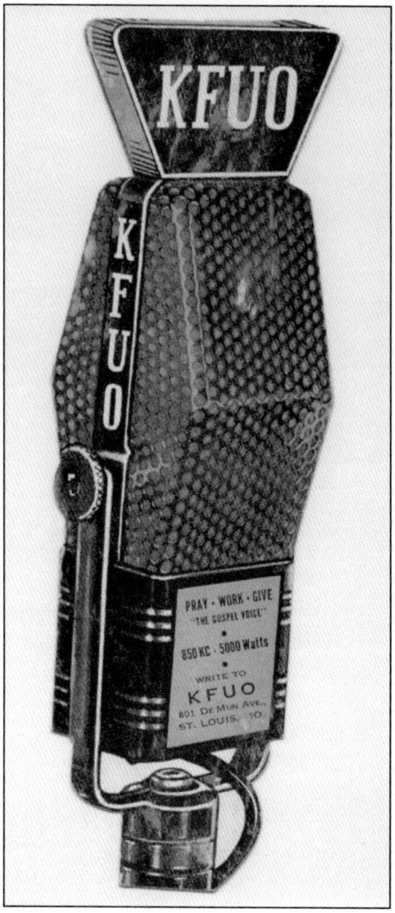

KFUO, the religious station owned by the Lutheran Church Missouri Synod, distributed this promotional bookmark in the early 1930s. Throughout its history, the station relied on public donations to cover its expenses. (St. Louis Media Archive.)

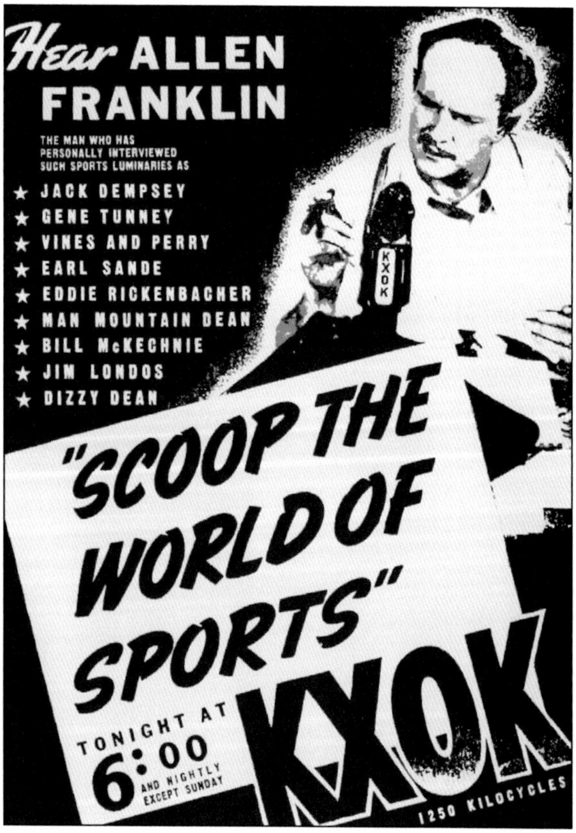

Allen Franklin played a major role in the development of KXOK. In addition to being an announcer and personality from the station's beginning, he was involved in the hiring and training of the on-air staff. (St. Louis Media Archive.)

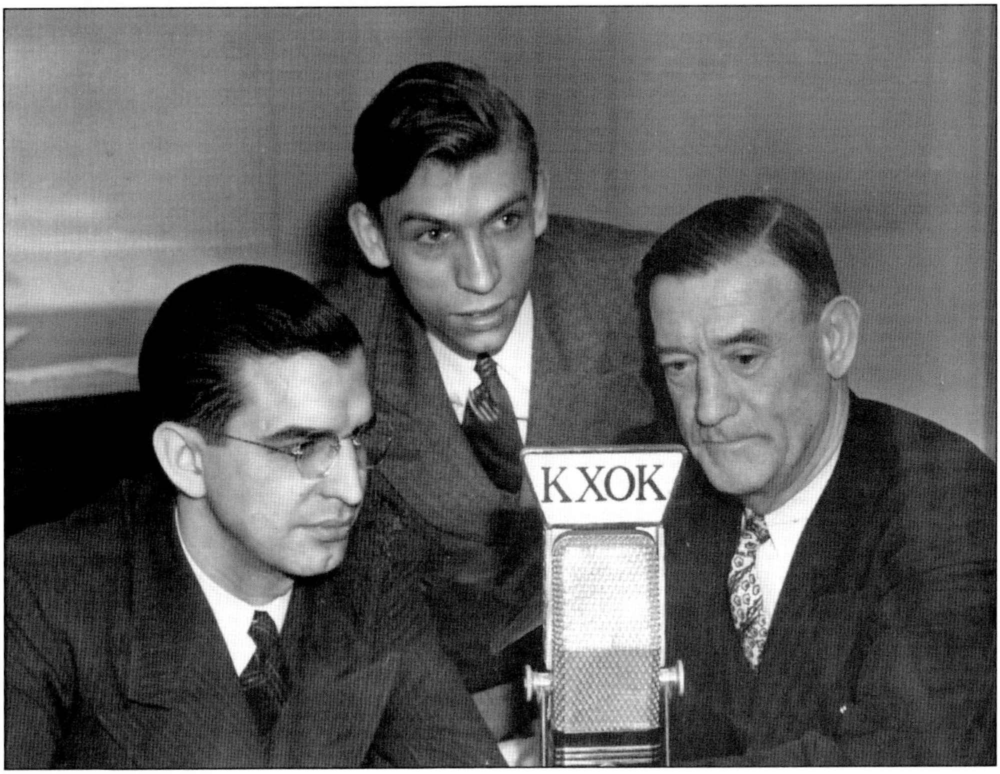

Pictured here from left to right, Ray Schmidt, Alex Buchan, and Gabby Street made up KXOK's baseball broadcast team during the 1940 season. (St. Louis Media Archive.)

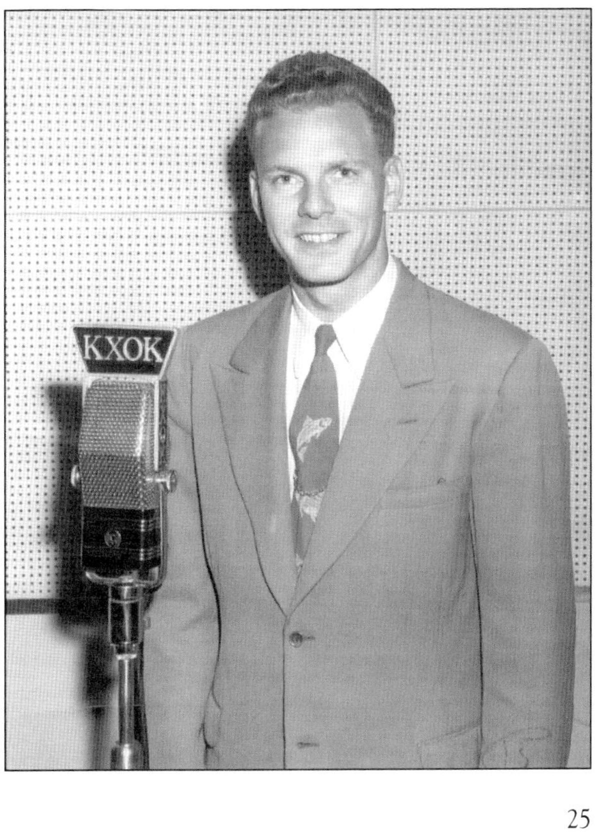

Bob Hille went to work at KXOK when it signed on shortly after he had graduated from high school. He later moved to KSD-TV and Radio as an announcer/newsman. (St. Louis Media Archive.)

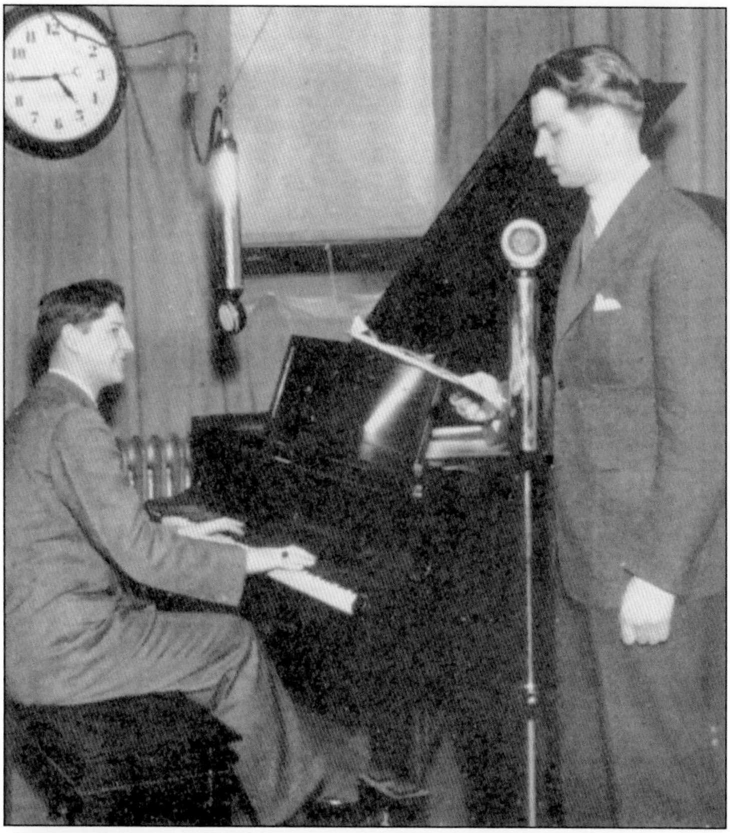

The Saint Louis University radio station WEW continued its successful non-commercial operation. Dick Cross is seen in this photograph with an unidentified piano player. (St. Louis Media Archive.)

The university student body provided plenty of free labor for WEW, from on-air talent to engineers and writers. (Saint Louis University Archives.)

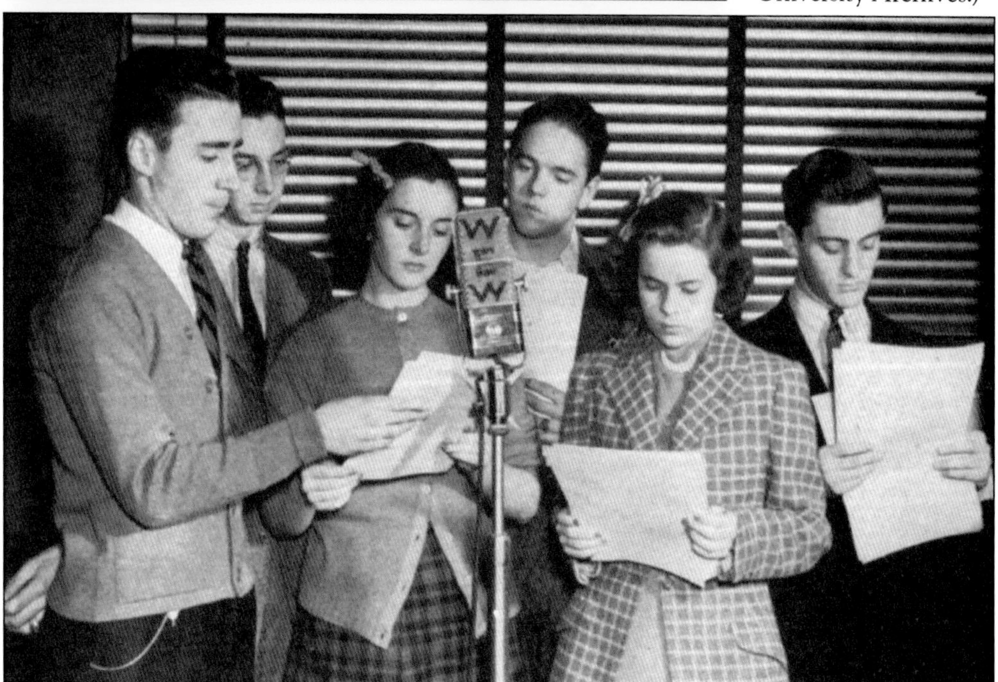

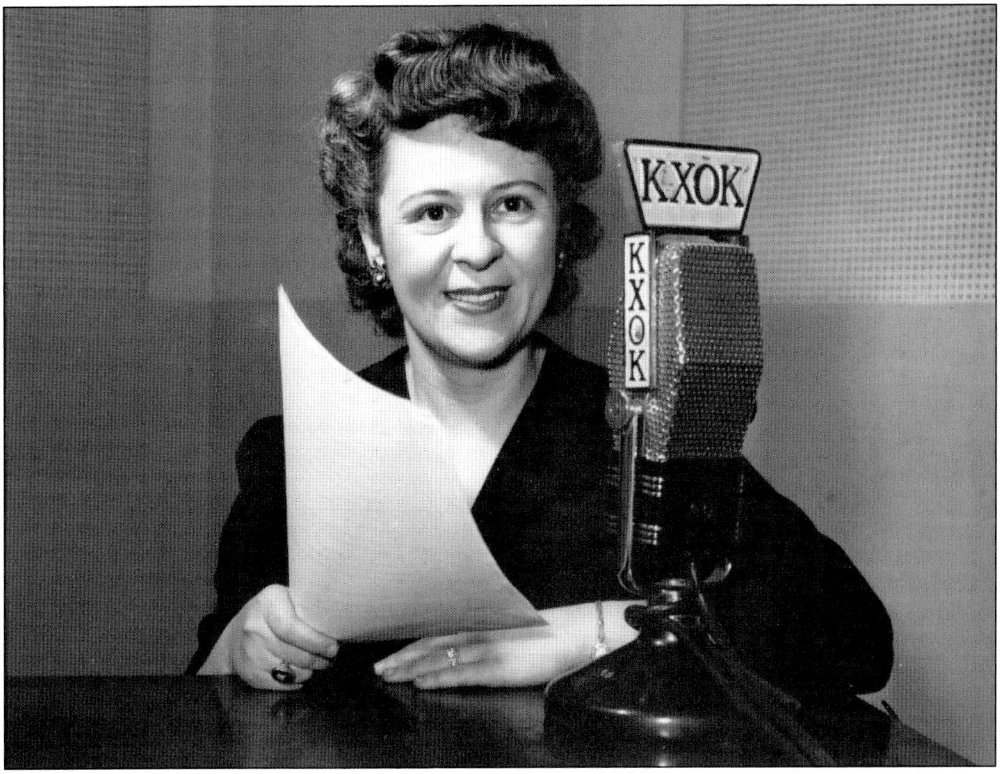

Kay Morton got her start in radio when she went to work at WTMV while a student at Washington University. She hosted women's shows on several radio stations and on television under several different air names. She is shown here at KXOK in 1943. (St. Louis Media Archive.)

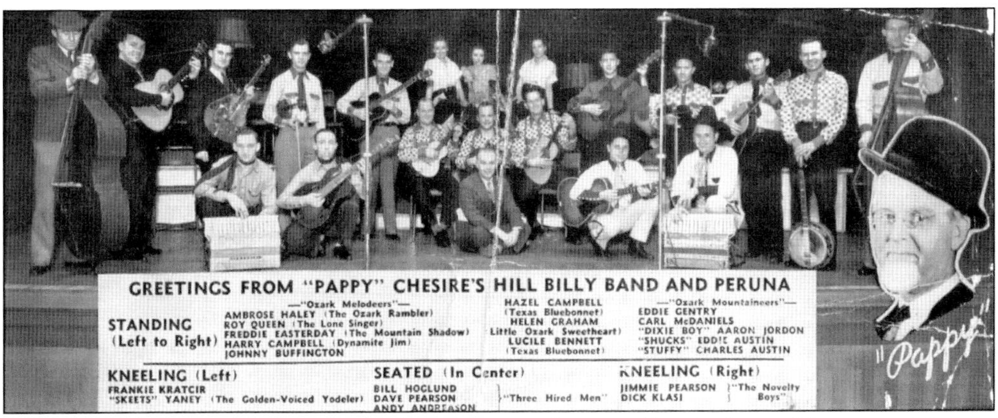

KMOX, which was owned by CBS, had the biggest radio payroll in St. Louis. The station's largest musical ensemble was led by Pappy Cheshire (seen in the bottom right corner). His programs were sponsored by Uncle Dick Slack's furniture stores. (St. Louis Media Archive.)

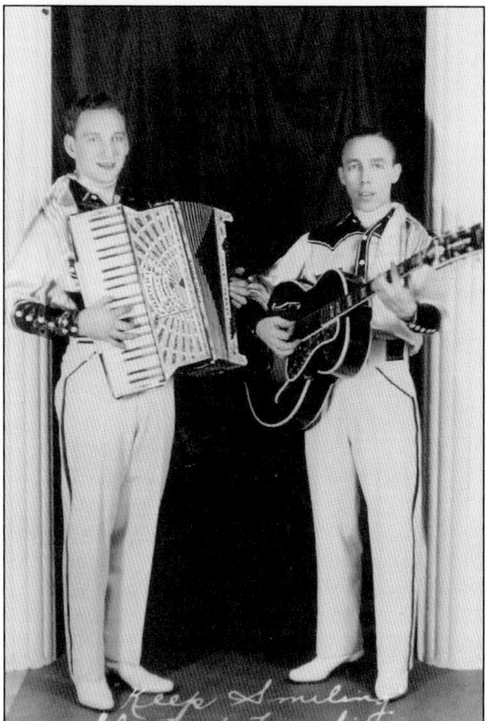

These popular hillbilly performers, Frankie (left) and Skeets, had their own programs and also participated in ensemble shows. (St. Louis Media Archive.)

To compete with Pappy Cheshire, Carson's Melody Roundup group was formed to represent Carson's furniture store. At one point, the group was heard on three different stations in St. Louis: KWK, WEW, and KSD. (St. Louis Media Archive.)

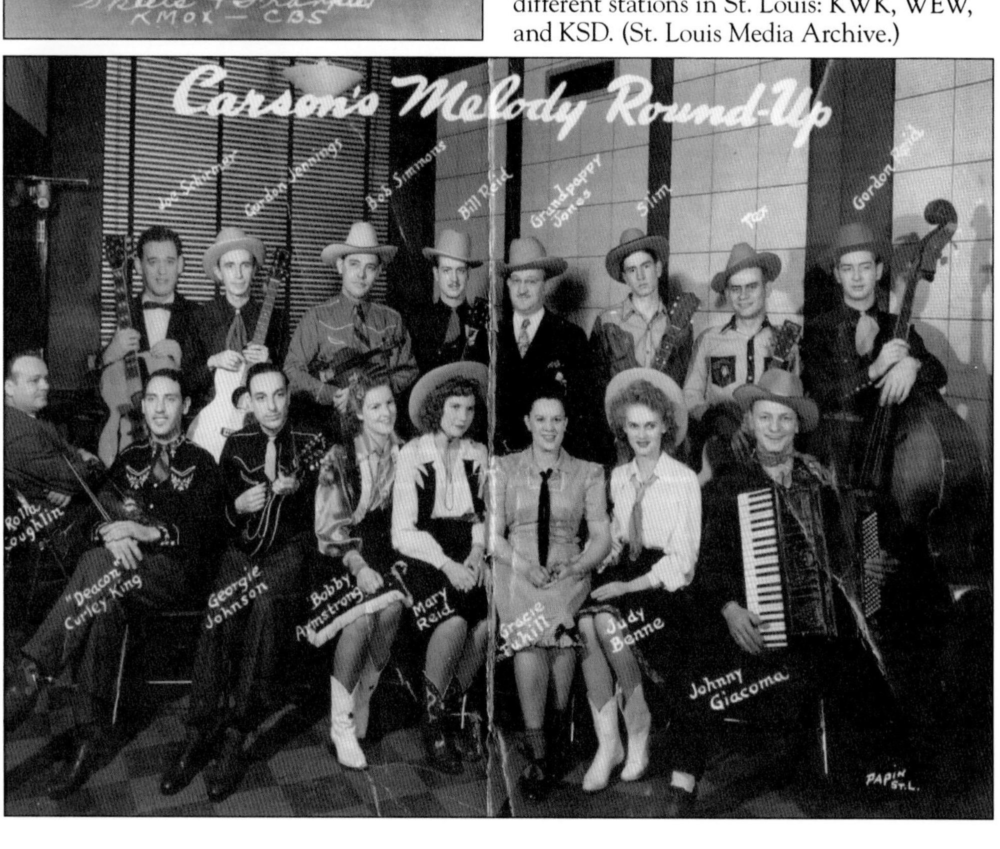

It seemed every radio station had its own hillbilly group. Front man Ambrose Haley is seen standing between the Miccolis Sisters. (St. Louis Media Archive.)

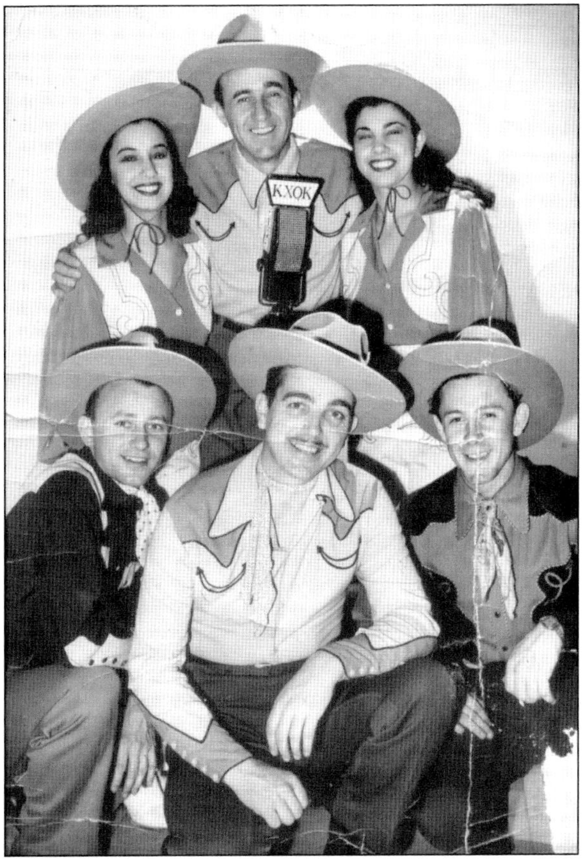

At the Chase Hotel in St. Louis, the KWK studios were home to the Coon Crick Boys. (St. Louis Media Archive.)

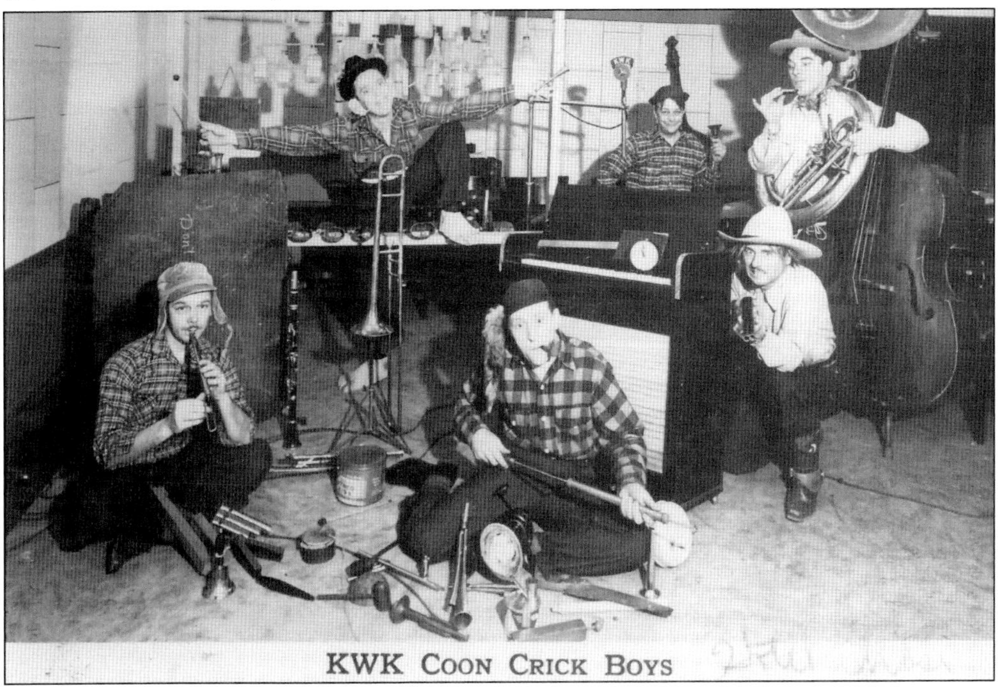

KWK COON CRICK BOYS

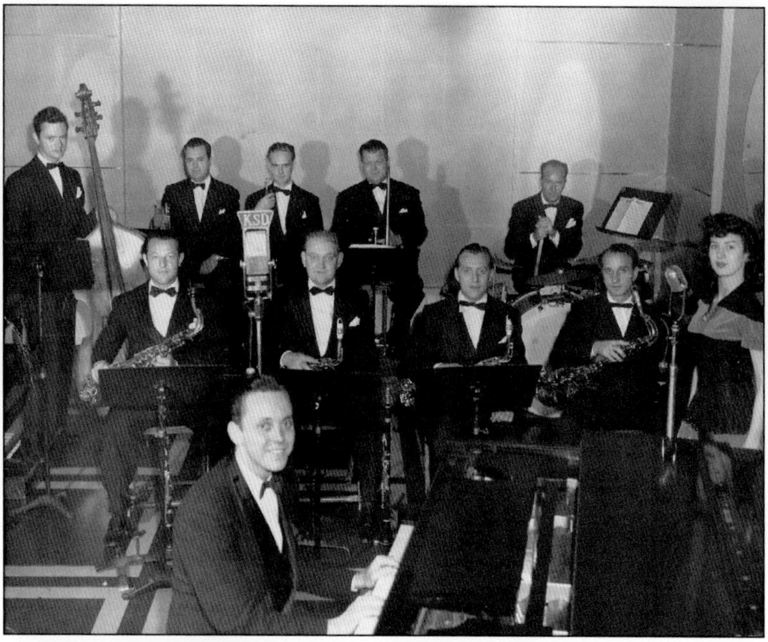

Live music was an integral part of the daily programming at KSD. The station's music director, Russ David, is at the piano. (St. Louis Media Archive.)

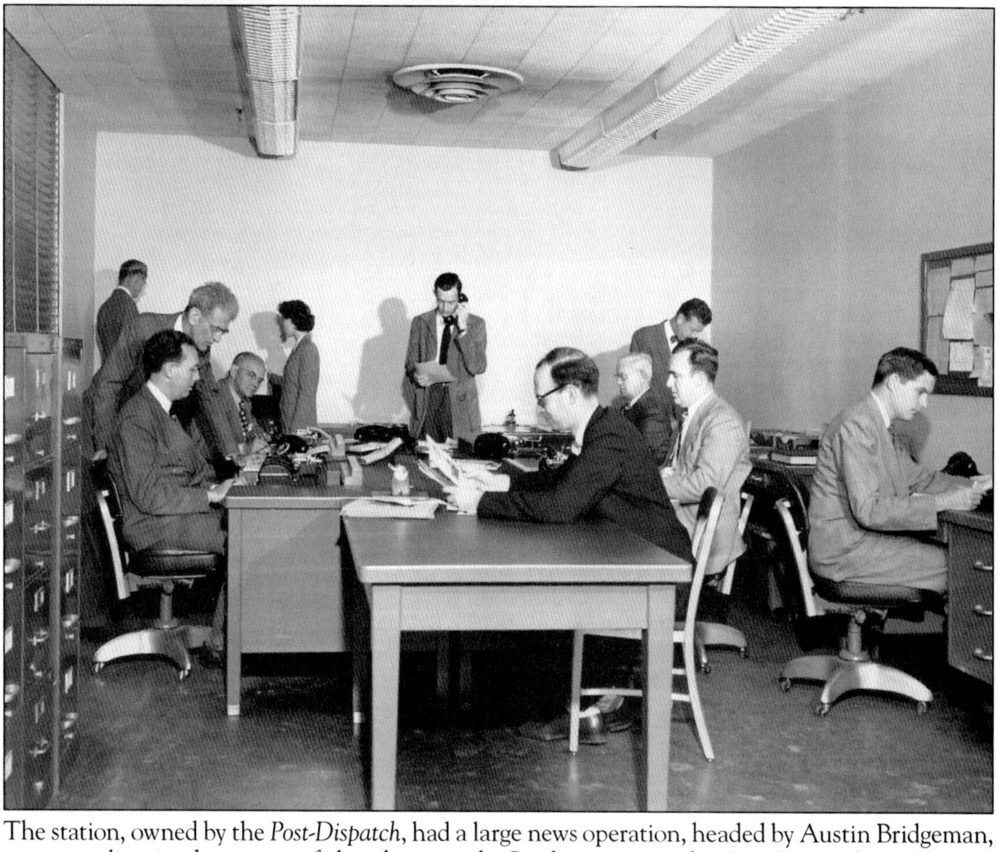

The station, owned by the *Post-Dispatch*, had a large news operation, headed by Austin Bridgeman, seen standing in the center of the photograph. Studios were in the Post-Dispatch Building at Twelfth and Olive Streets. (St. Louis Media Archive.)

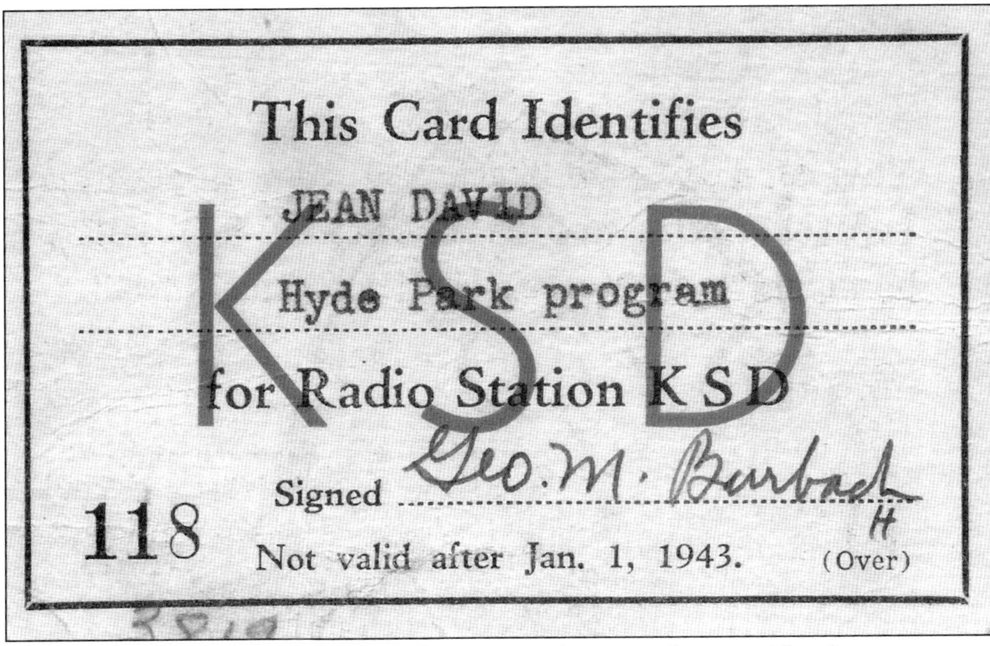

This Card Identifies

JEAN DAVID

Hyde Park program

for Radio Station KSD

KSD

Signed Geo. M. Burbach

118

Not valid after Jan. 1, 1943. (Over)

During World War II, security was very tight at major radio stations because of fear that enemy agents might try to commandeer communications facilities. Even the wives of well-known personalities were required to present station-issued identification cards to enter the building. (Sue Dorn.)

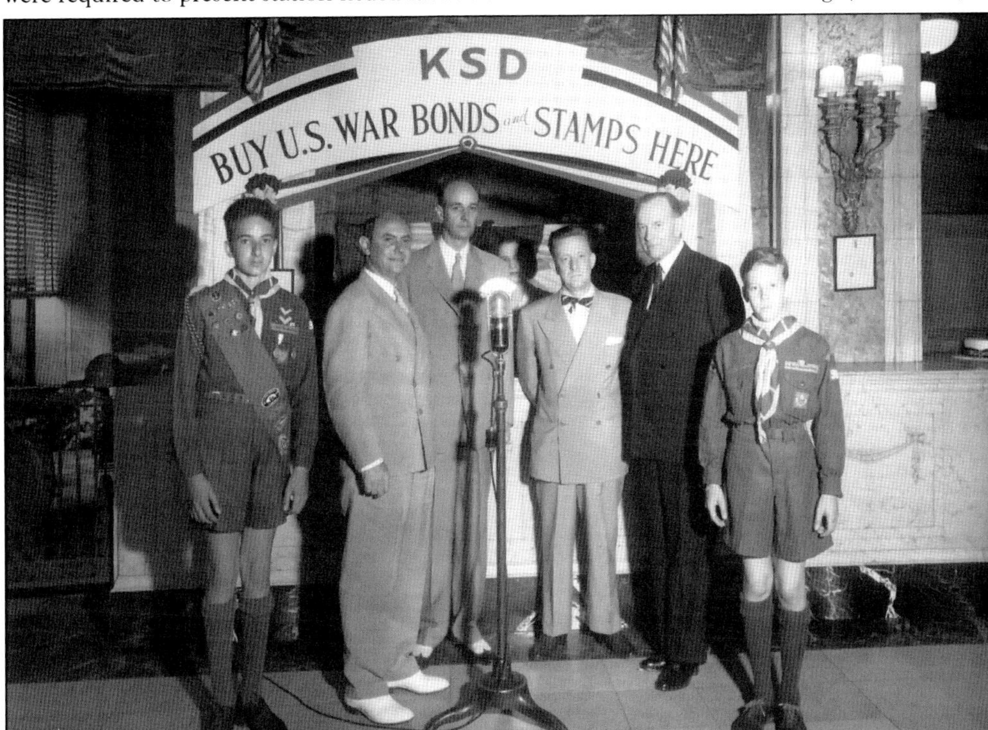

All stations were encouraged to do what they could to support the war effort and drum up patriotism. (St. Louis Media Archive.)

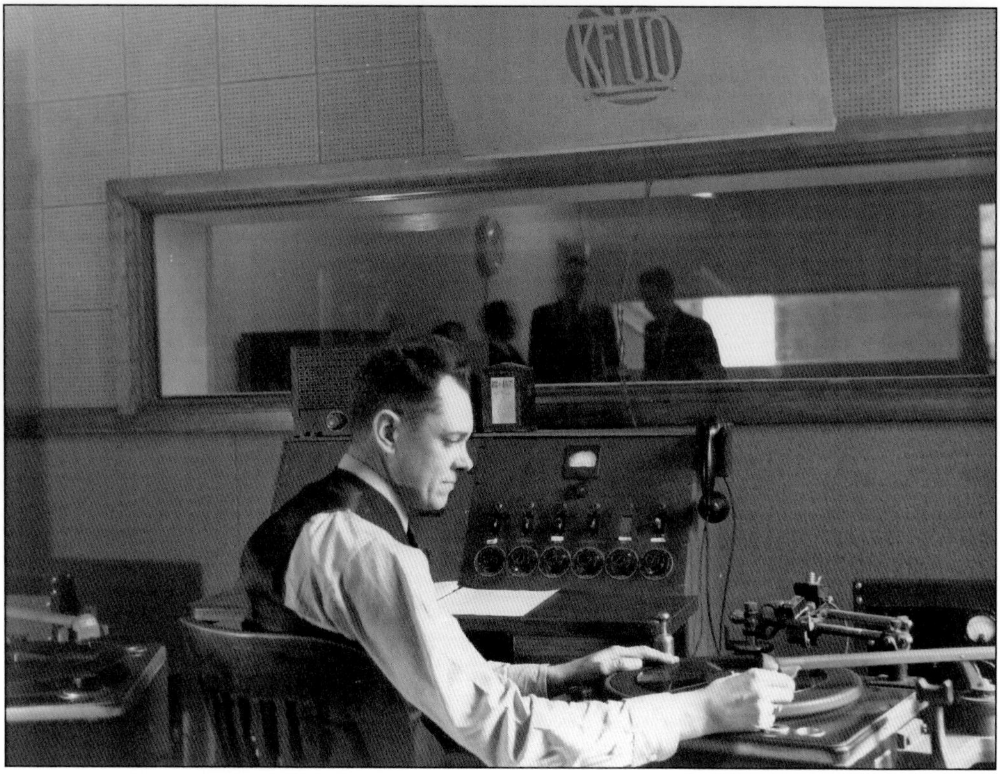

A seldom-seen insider's view shows audio production facilities at KFUO. The turntable on the right was used to make electronic transcriptions (audio recordings) on special lacquered discs and was the preferred method of preserving audio. Recording tape had not yet been invented. (St. Louis Media Archive.)

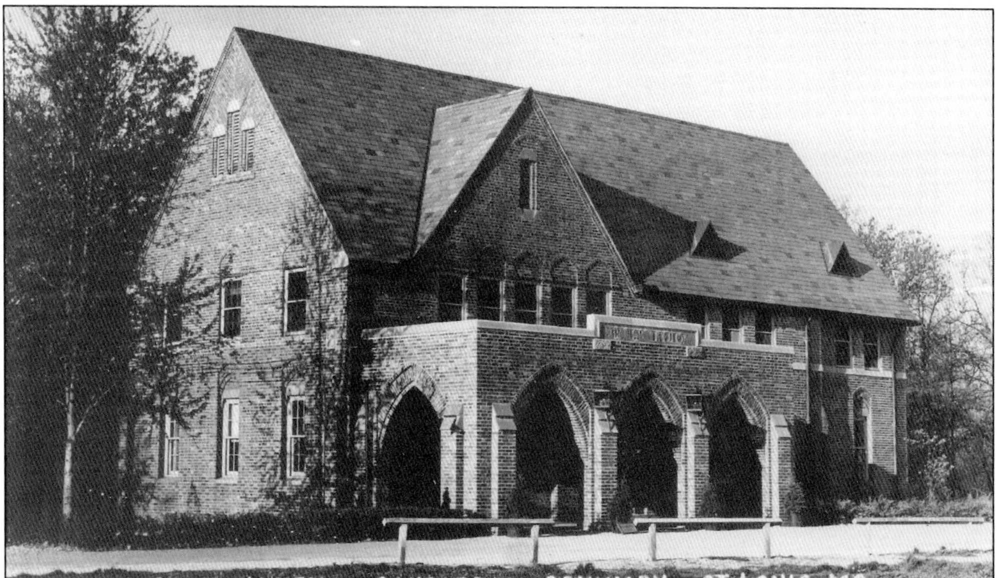

KFUO's studio building was located on the grounds of Concordia Seminary in Clayton. (St. Louis Media Archive.)

Three

Television Enters the Picture

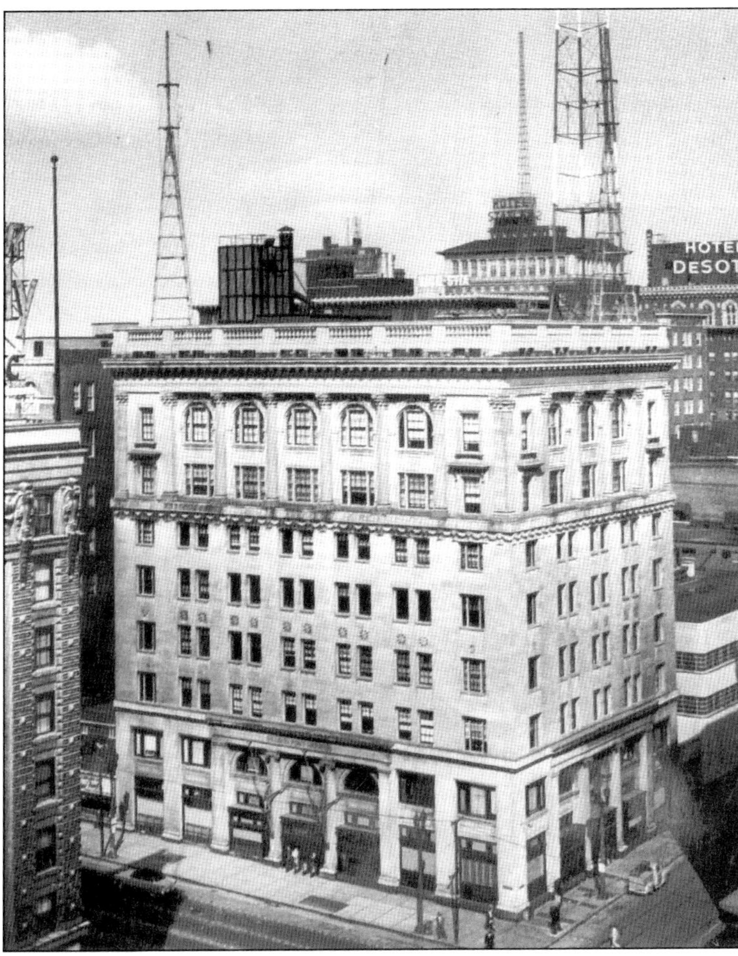

All technical development in broadcasting stopped when the United States entered World War II. This freeze ended when the war concluded, and in St. Louis, KSD-TV signed on in February 1947, becoming the eighth television station in the United States. The Post-Dispatch Building at Twelfth and Olive Streets was the site of the first studios of KSD Radio and KSD-TV. Broadcast towers, which were 70 feet high, can be seen on the building's roof in this image. (St. Louis Media Archive.)

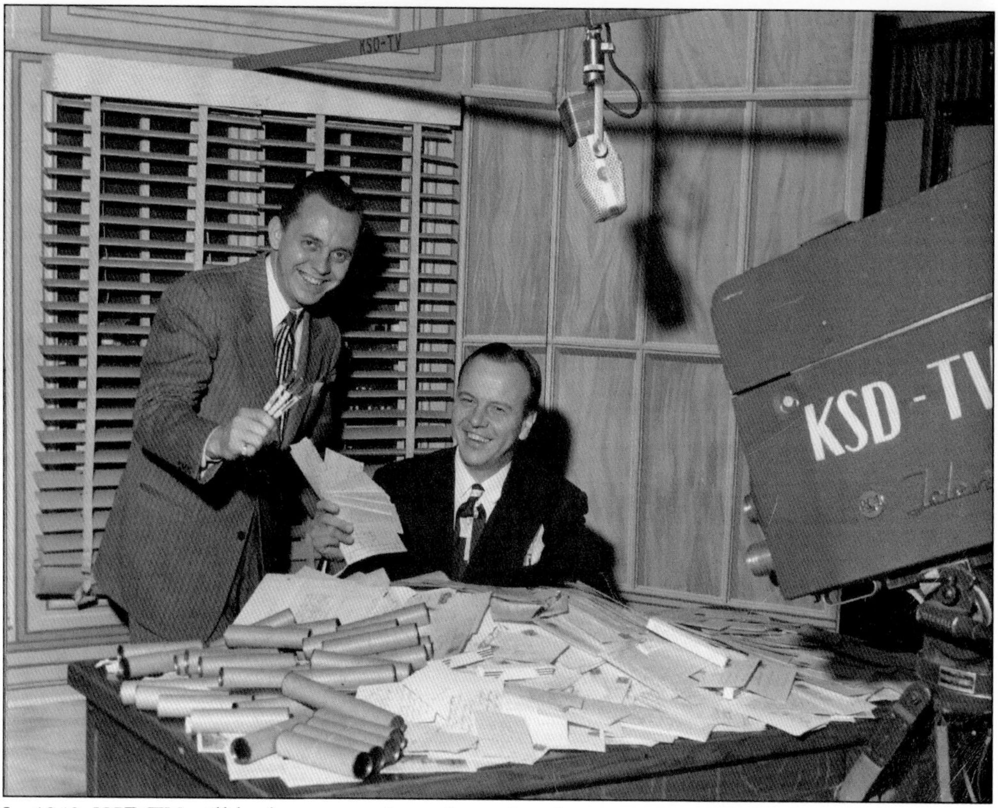

In 1949, KSD-TV still had a monopoly as the only television station in St. Louis. The station's music director and program host, Russ David (left), poses here with an executive of a local pen manufacturer that had sponsored a station promotion. The mail on the table represents the viewer response. (St. Louis Media Archive.)

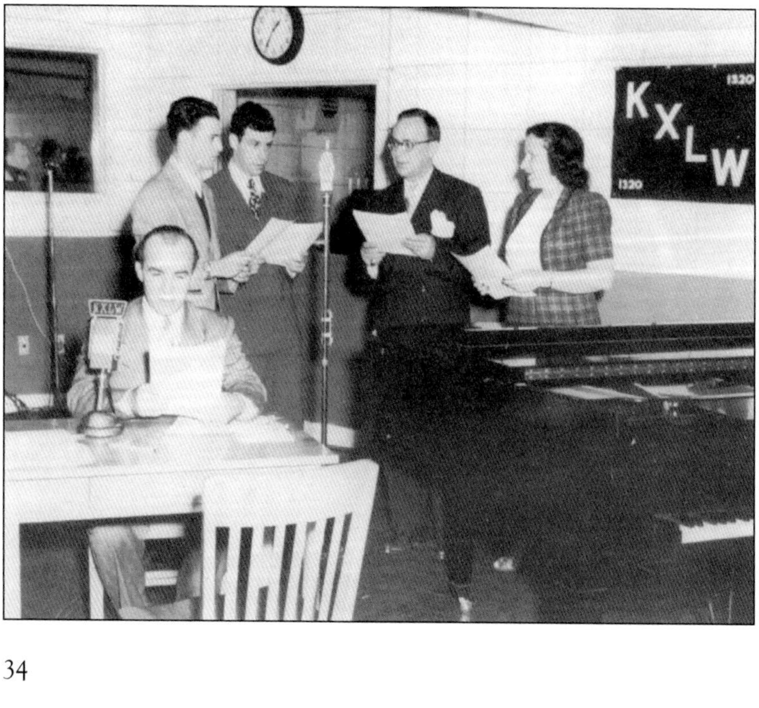

This radio production took place in the relatively small KXLW studios. The station signed on in 1947, broadcasting from downtown Clayton. (St. Louis Media Archive.)

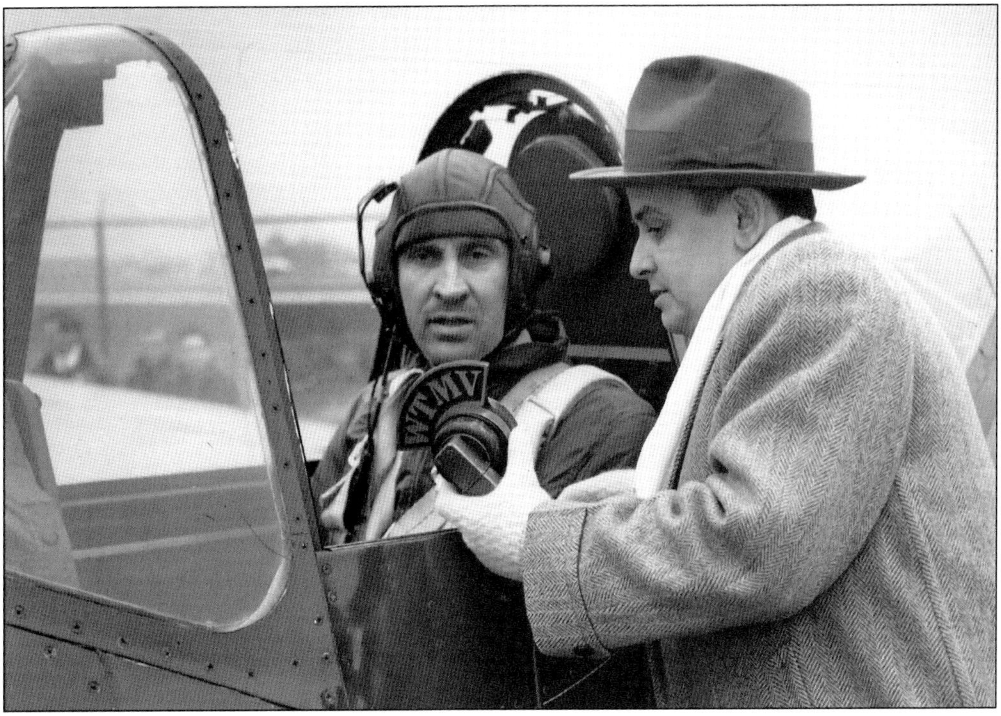

WTMV newsman Gayton Talks is seen on the right interviewing an unidentified pilot. (St. Louis Media Archive.)

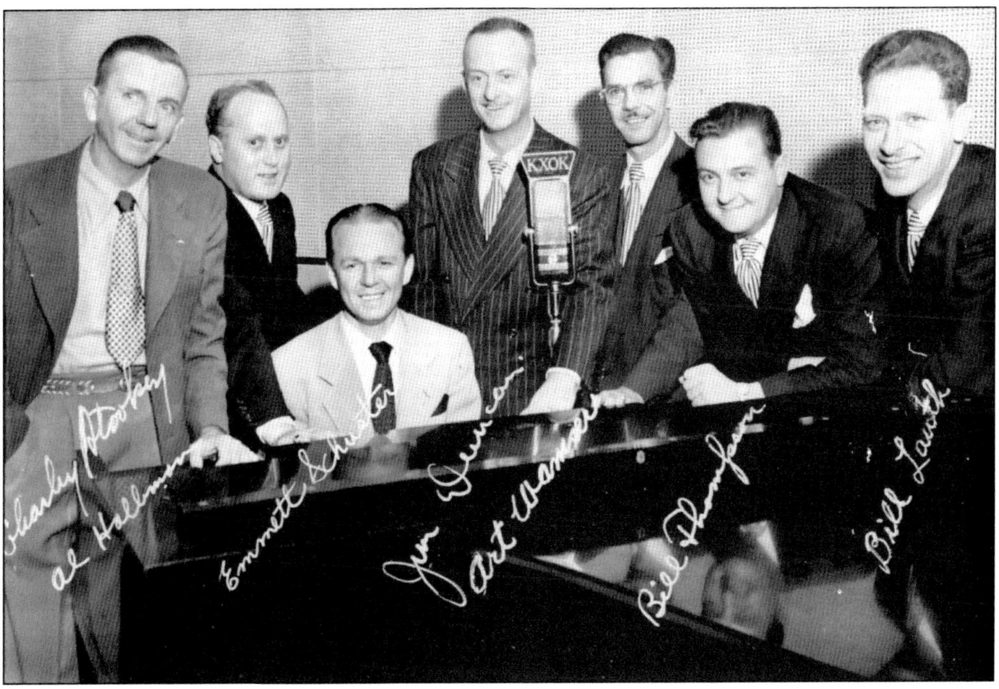

Members of KXOK's announcing staff is seen posing for this group shot in 1946. The station was owned by the *St. Louis Star-Times*, whose print reporters often supplemented the station's news-gathering efforts. (St. Louis Media Archive.)

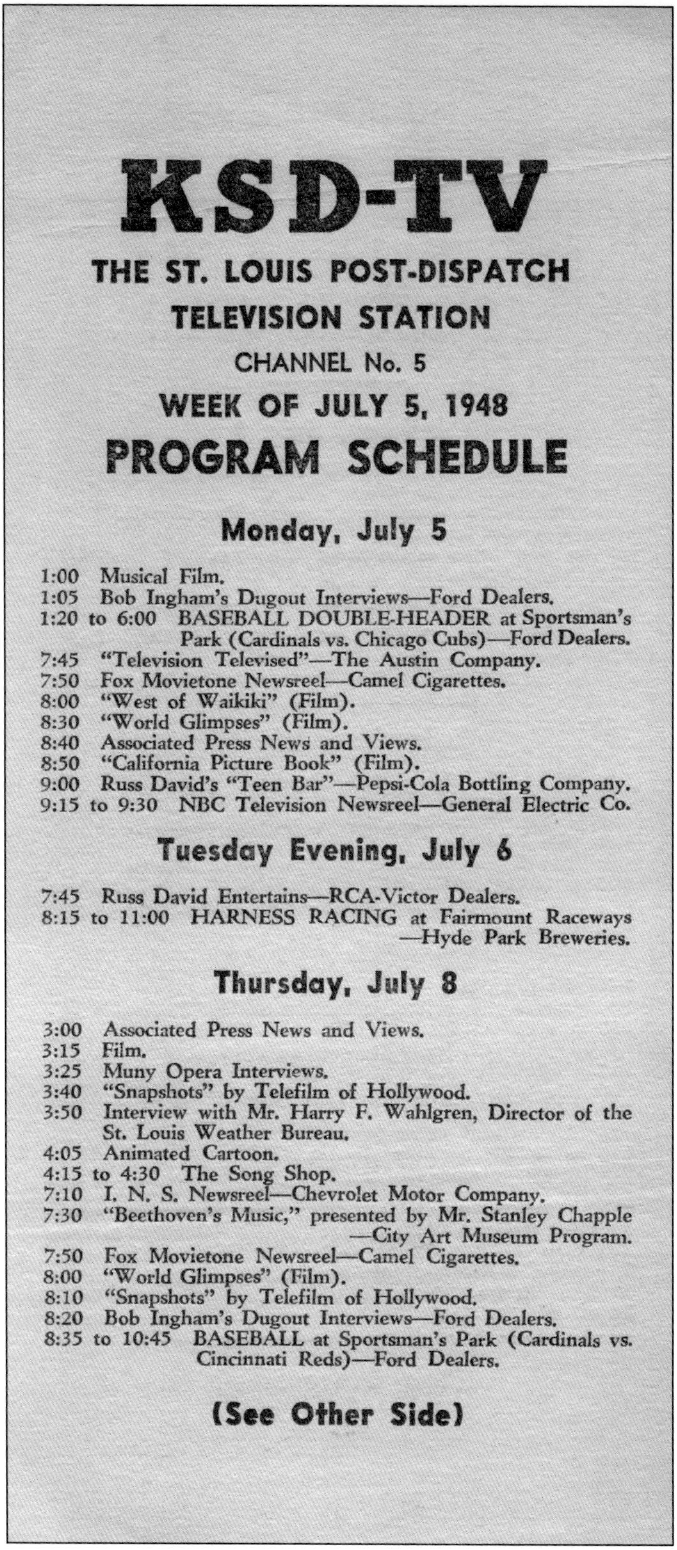

KSD-TV

THE ST. LOUIS POST-DISPATCH
TELEVISION STATION

CHANNEL No. 5

WEEK OF JULY 5, 1948

PROGRAM SCHEDULE

Monday, July 5

1:00 Musical Film.
1:05 Bob Ingham's Dugout Interviews—Ford Dealers.
1:20 to 6:00 BASEBALL DOUBLE-HEADER at Sportsman's Park (Cardinals vs. Chicago Cubs)—Ford Dealers.
7:45 "Television Televised"—The Austin Company.
7:50 Fox Movietone Newsreel—Camel Cigarettes.
8:00 "West of Waikiki" (Film).
8:30 "World Glimpses" (Film).
8:40 Associated Press News and Views.
8:50 "California Picture Book" (Film).
9:00 Russ David's "Teen Bar"—Pepsi-Cola Bottling Company.
9:15 to 9:30 NBC Television Newsreel—General Electric Co.

Tuesday Evening, July 6

7:45 Russ David Entertains—RCA-Victor Dealers.
8:15 to 11:00 HARNESS RACING at Fairmount Raceways —Hyde Park Breweries.

Thursday, July 8

3:00 Associated Press News and Views.
3:15 Film.
3:25 Muny Opera Interviews.
3:40 "Snapshots" by Telefilm of Hollywood.
3:50 Interview with Mr. Harry F. Wahlgren, Director of the St. Louis Weather Bureau.
4:05 Animated Cartoon.
4:15 to 4:30 The Song Shop.
7:10 I. N. S. Newsreel—Chevrolet Motor Company.
7:30 "Beethoven's Music," presented by Mr. Stanley Chapple —City Art Museum Program.
7:50 Fox Movietone Newsreel—Camel Cigarettes.
8:00 "World Glimpses" (Film).
8:10 "Snapshots" by Telefilm of Hollywood.
8:20 Bob Ingham's Dugout Interviews—Ford Dealers.
8:35 to 10:45 BASEBALL at Sportsman's Park (Cardinals vs. Cincinnati Reds)—Ford Dealers.

(See Other Side)

As the parent company had done for its radio station in the earliest days of radio broadcasting, KSD-TV published a weekly schedule of its television programs to mail to the relatively small group of people who owned receivers. (St. Louis Media Archive.)

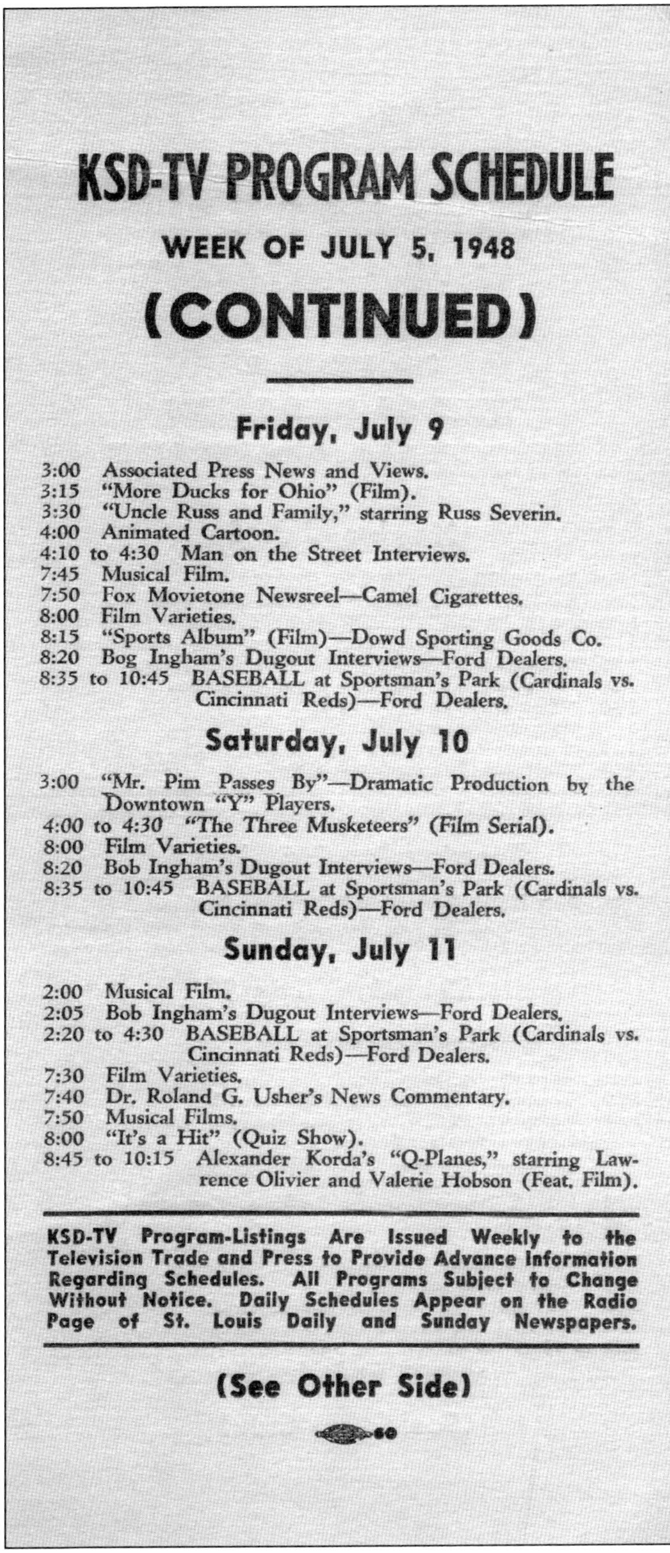

KSD-TV PROGRAM SCHEDULE

WEEK OF JULY 5, 1948

(CONTINUED)

Friday, July 9

3:00 Associated Press News and Views.
3:15 "More Ducks for Ohio" (Film).
3:30 "Uncle Russ and Family," starring Russ Severin.
4:00 Animated Cartoon.
4:10 to 4:30 Man on the Street Interviews.
7:45 Musical Film.
7:50 Fox Movietone Newsreel—Camel Cigarettes.
8:00 Film Varieties.
8:15 "Sports Album" (Film)—Dowd Sporting Goods Co.
8:20 Bog Ingham's Dugout Interviews—Ford Dealers.
8:35 to 10:45 BASEBALL at Sportsman's Park (Cardinals vs. Cincinnati Reds)—Ford Dealers.

Saturday, July 10

3:00 "Mr. Pim Passes By"—Dramatic Production by the Downtown "Y" Players.
4:00 to 4:30 "The Three Musketeers" (Film Serial).
8:00 Film Varieties.
8:20 Bob Ingham's Dugout Interviews—Ford Dealers.
8:35 to 10:45 BASEBALL at Sportsman's Park (Cardinals vs. Cincinnati Reds)—Ford Dealers.

Sunday, July 11

2:00 Musical Film.
2:05 Bob Ingham's Dugout Interviews—Ford Dealers.
2:20 to 4:30 BASEBALL at Sportsman's Park (Cardinals vs. Cincinnati Reds)—Ford Dealers.
7:30 Film Varieties.
7:40 Dr. Roland G. Usher's News Commentary.
7:50 Musical Films.
8:00 "It's a Hit" (Quiz Show).
8:45 to 10:15 Alexander Korda's "Q-Planes," starring Lawrence Olivier and Valerie Hobson (Feat. Film).

KSD-TV Program-Listings Are Issued Weekly to the Television Trade and Press to Provide Advance Information Regarding Schedules. All Programs Subject to Change Without Notice. Daily Schedules Appear on the Radio Page of St. Louis Daily and Sunday Newspapers.

(See Other Side)

The station concentrated on late afternoon/early evening programming because that was when the maximum potential audience was available. (St. Louis Media Archive.)

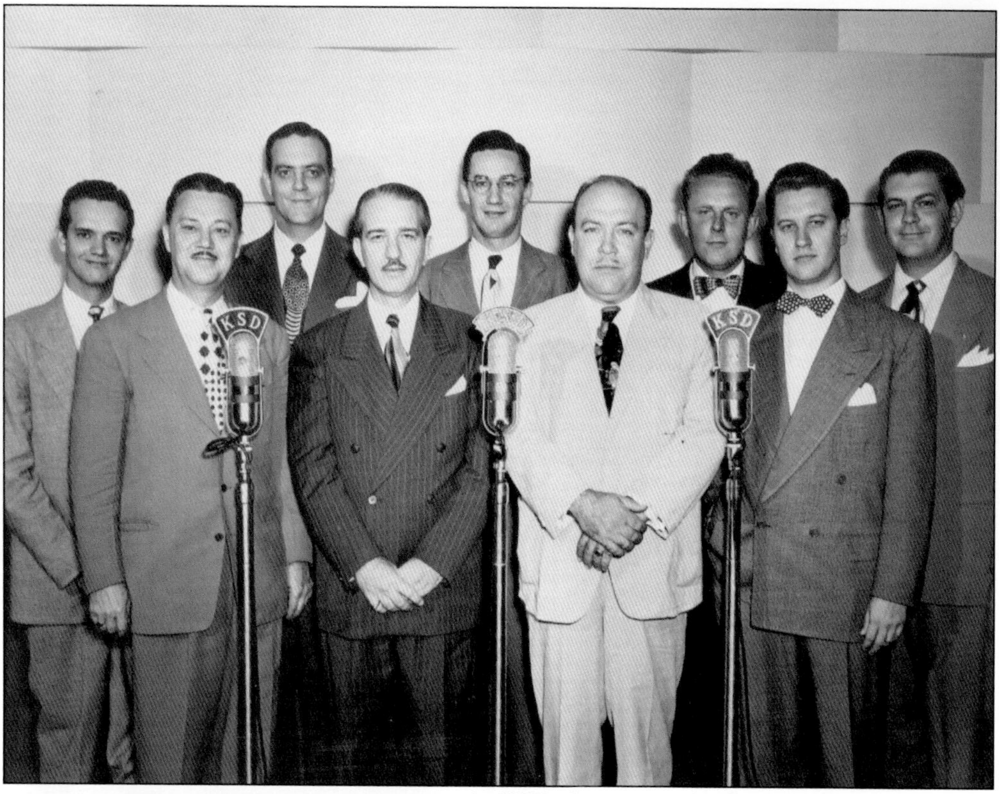

At KSD, this group of radio announcers was also tapped to work on the television side. Posing here, they are from left to right, Alan Post, Sterling Harkins, Jack Garrison, Del King, Harold "Hod" Grams, Frank Eschen, George Abel, Carl McIntire, and John Roedel. (St. Louis Media Archive.)

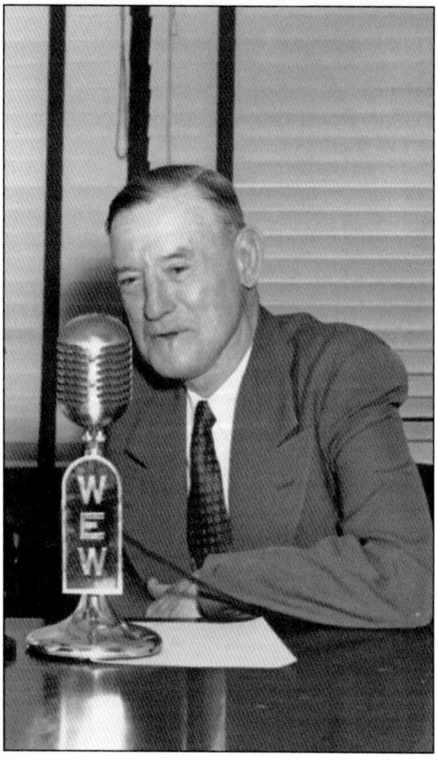

Baseball announcer Gabby Street was part of the Cardinals broadcasting team in the 1940s, which meant he was an announcer of whichever station owned the broadcast rights. Thus, he was heard on both WEW and WTMV for three seasons, beginning in 1946. (St. Louis Media Archive.)

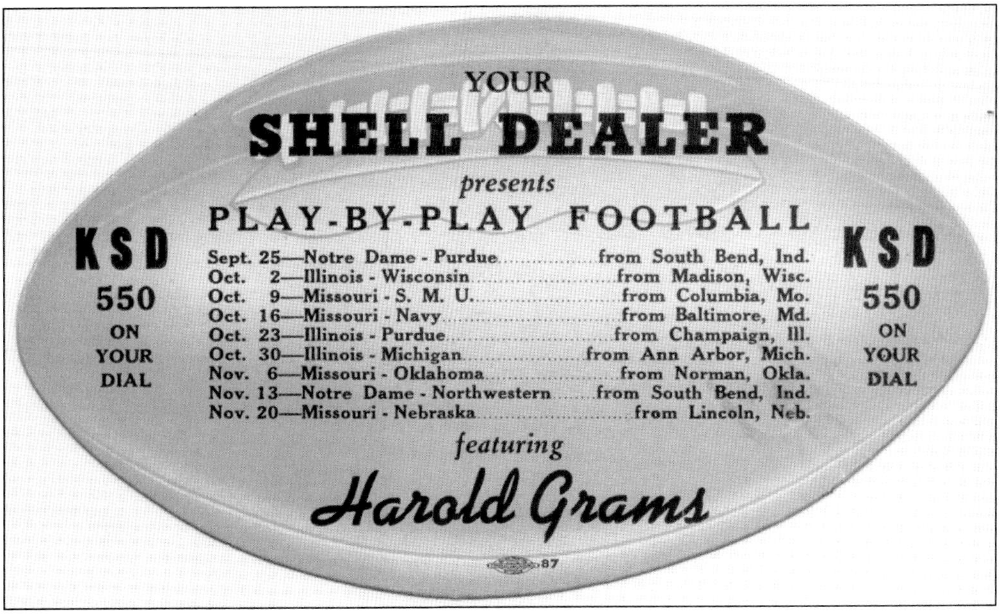

The St. Louis–area Shell gasoline dealers association distributed this printed schedule of college football broadcasts in 1948. (St. Louis Media Archive.)

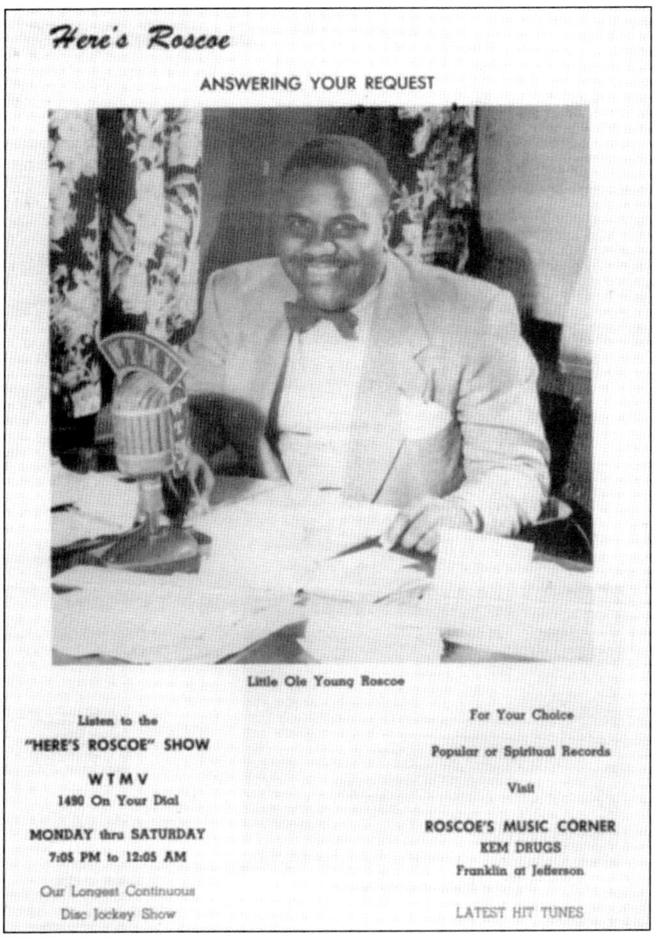

In the latter part of his life, Roscoe McCrary was known for his barbecue restaurant. Few of his patrons knew he had a previous successful career as a radio announcer. (St. Louis Media Archive.)

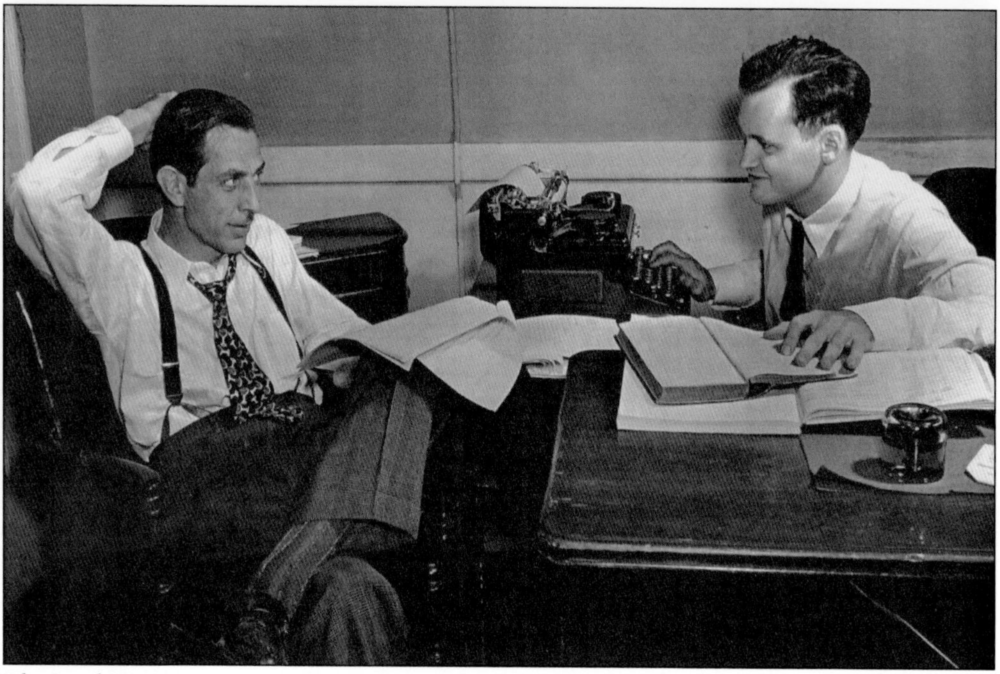

The Land We Live In was the longest-running radio drama in St. Louis. Director Ted Westcott (left) and writer Kensinger Jones worked together on the program for most of its 25 years. The show, sponsored by Union Electric, was first heard on KMOX and later on KSD. (St. Louis Media Archive, Kensinger Jones Collection.)

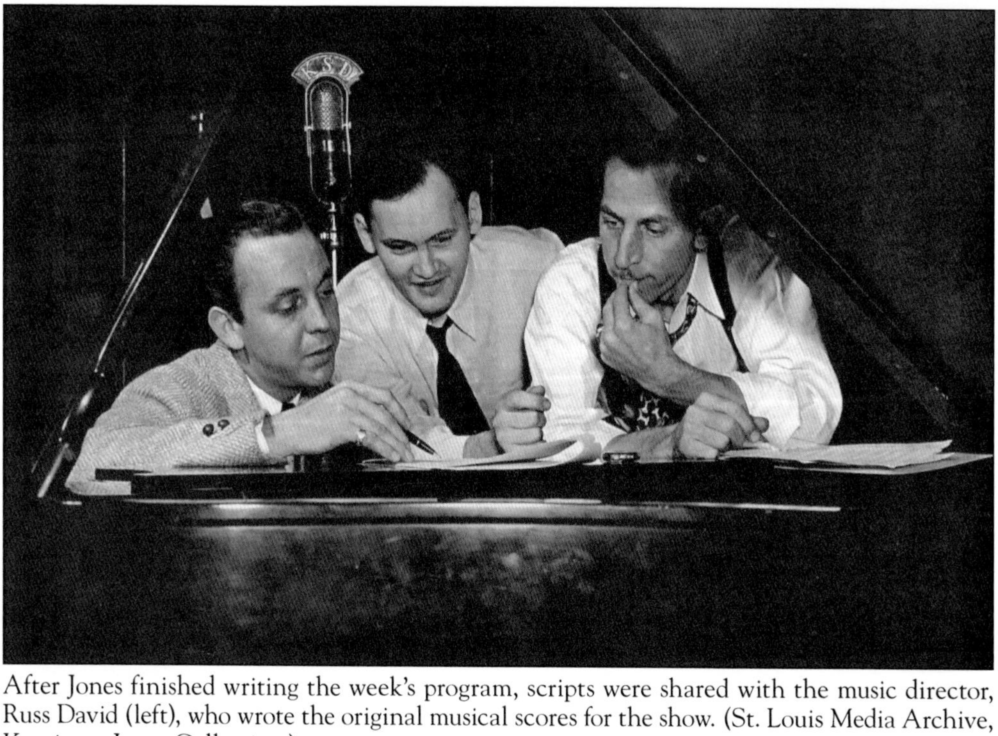

After Jones finished writing the week's program, scripts were shared with the music director, Russ David (left), who wrote the original musical scores for the show. (St. Louis Media Archive, Kensinger Jones Collection.)

Seen at rehearsal, Westcott (back to camera) and Jones coach actors (from left to right) Elliot Bergfeld, Emily Coleman, and Bruce McFarlane, along with announcer Del King. (St. Louis Media Archive, Kensinger Jones Collection.)

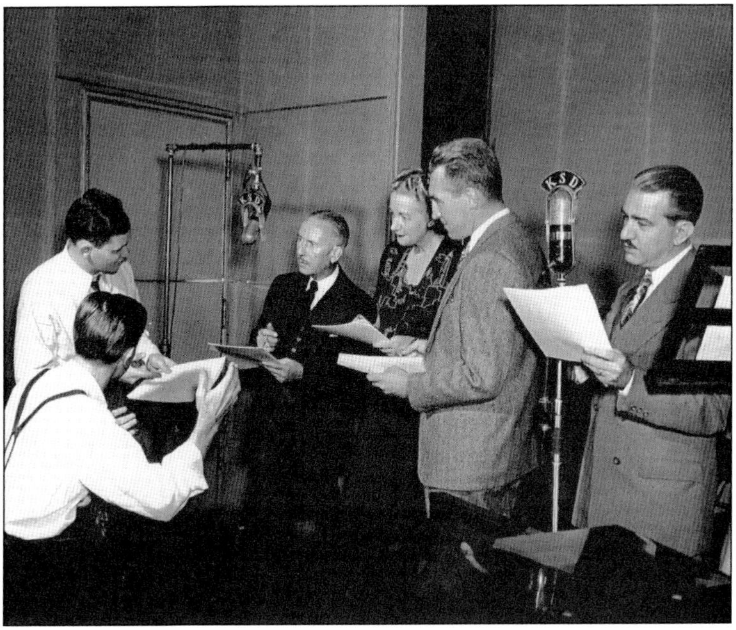

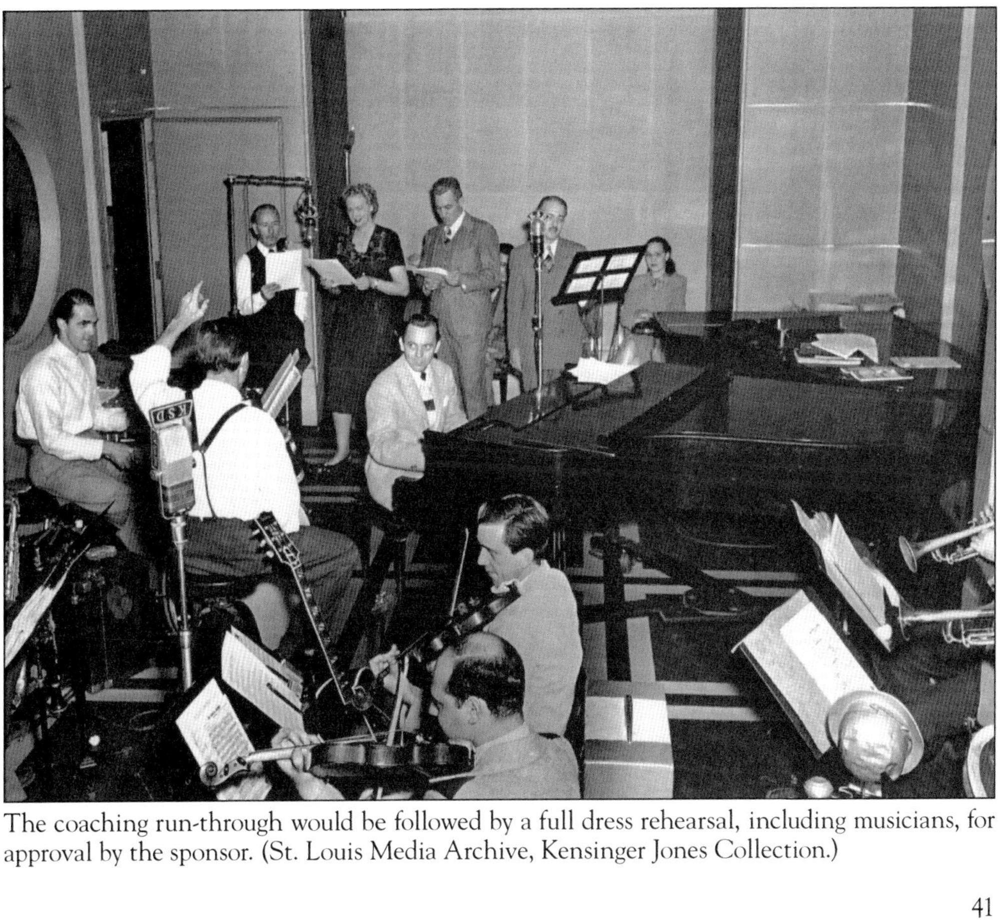

The coaching run-through would be followed by a full dress rehearsal, including musicians, for approval by the sponsor. (St. Louis Media Archive, Kensinger Jones Collection.)

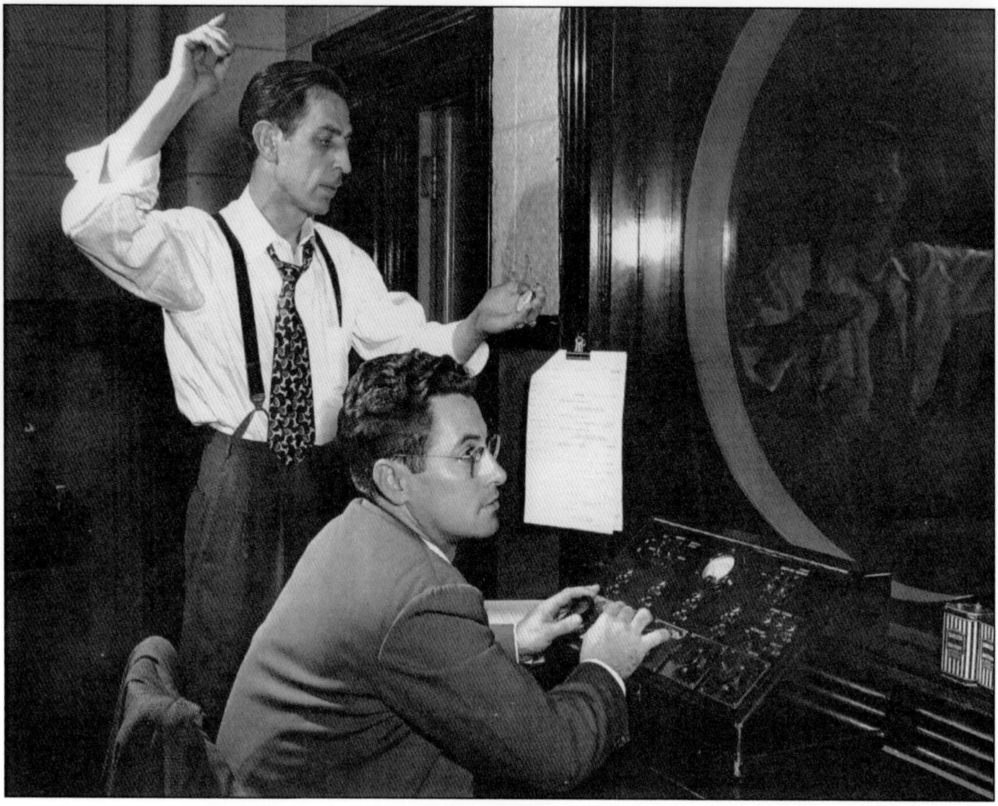

For the actual broadcast, Ted Westcott (left) would take his place in the engineering booth. (St. Louis Media Archive, Kensinger Jones Collection.)

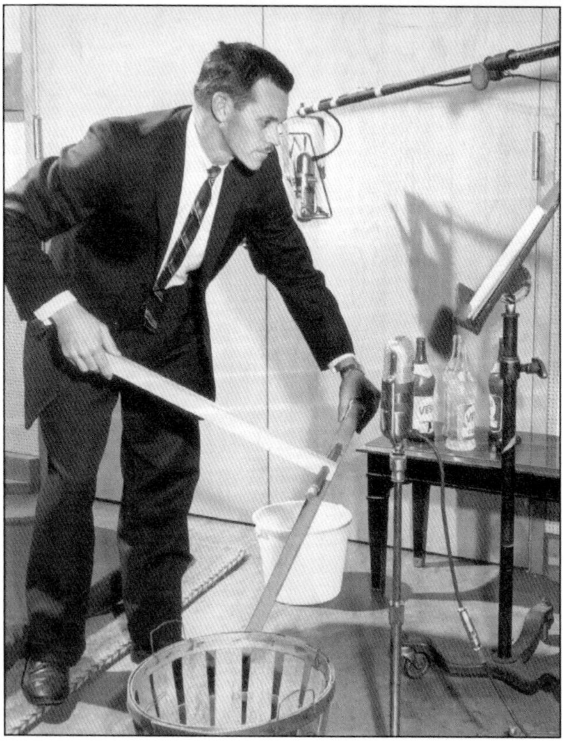

Every radio production worth its salt included a sound-effects man to help provide what was termed "theater of the mind"—mental images of what was happening in the program's plot. KSD's Harold Wright is shown here with some of his props. (St. Louis Media Archive.)

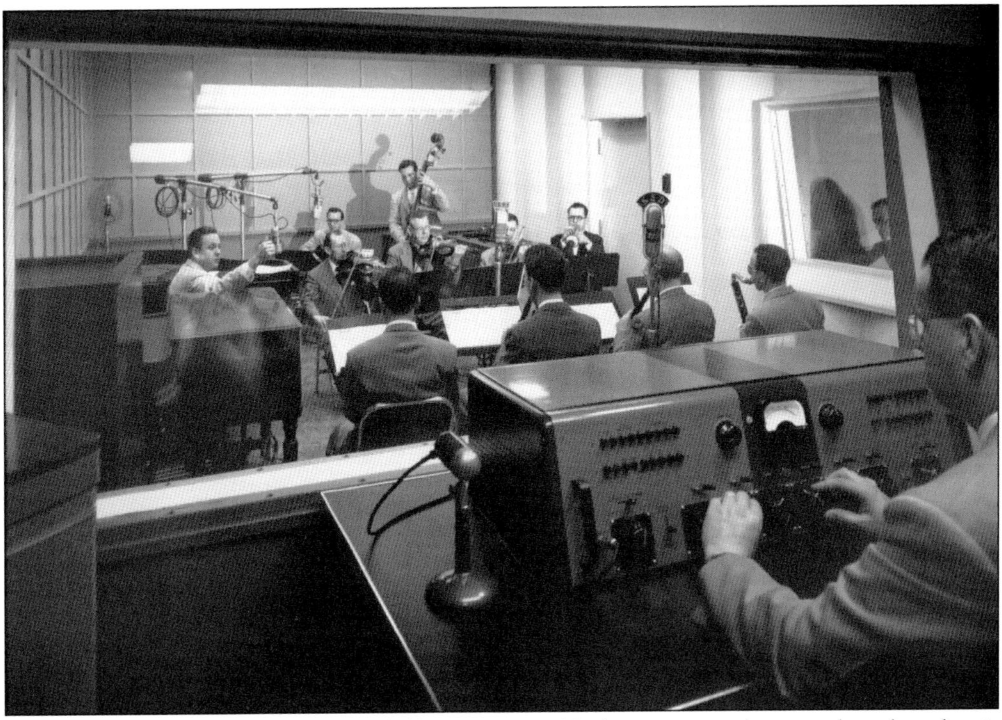

KSD's music director Russ David (far left) was responsible for arranging the tunes heard on the air and scheduling performers. In addition, he often hosted programs. (St. Louis Media Archive.)

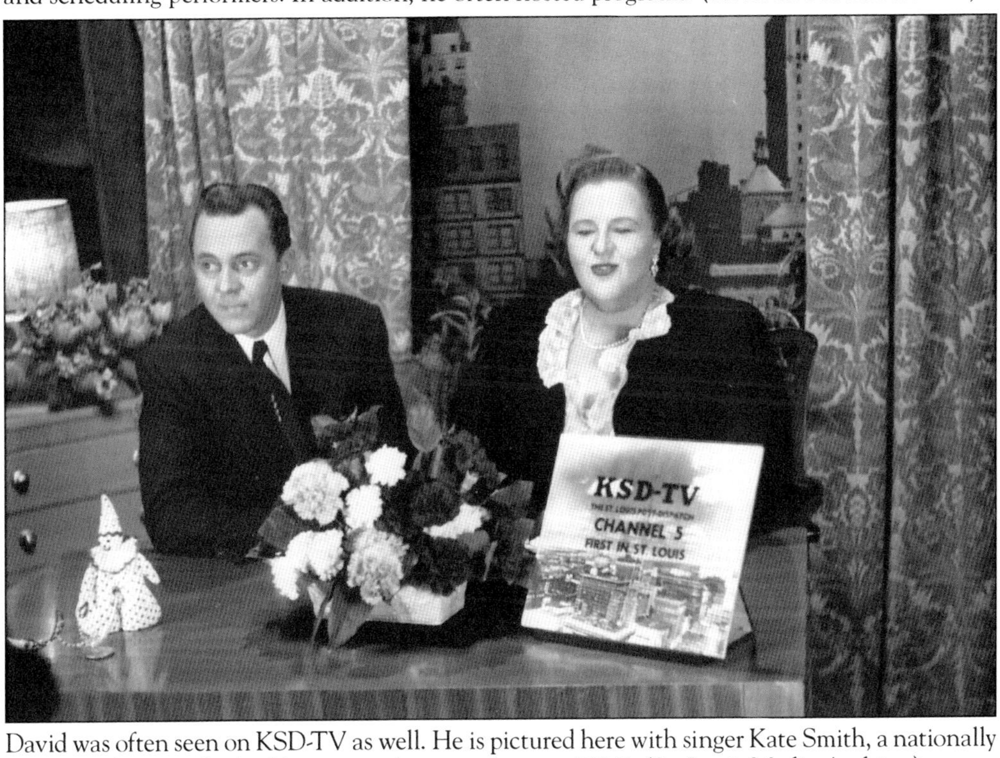

David was often seen on KSD-TV as well. He is pictured here with singer Kate Smith, a nationally known radio star who had her own television show on NBC. (St. Louis Media Archive.)

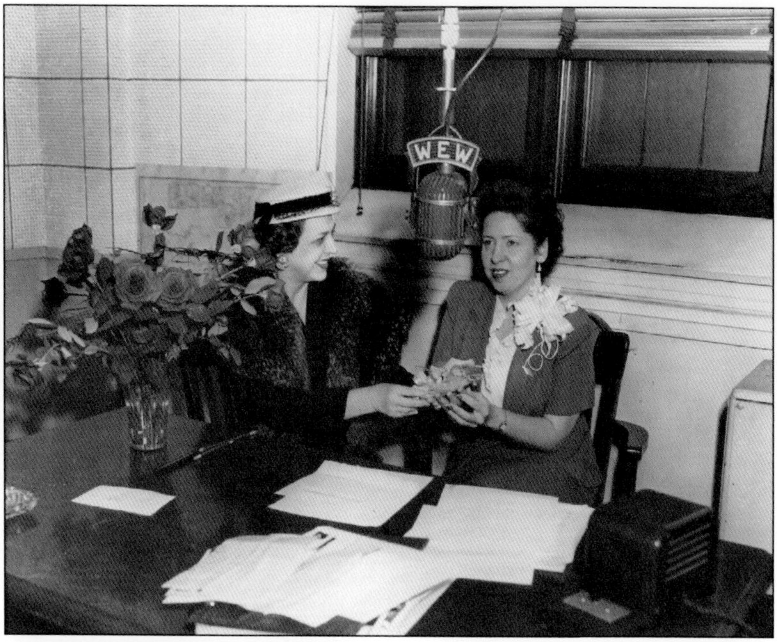

Louise Dopking was hostess of WEW's *Just for Women* program. She is shown here (right) in 1953 interviewing Edna Emme, who had been the first guest on the program 10 years earlier. (St. Louis Media Archive.)

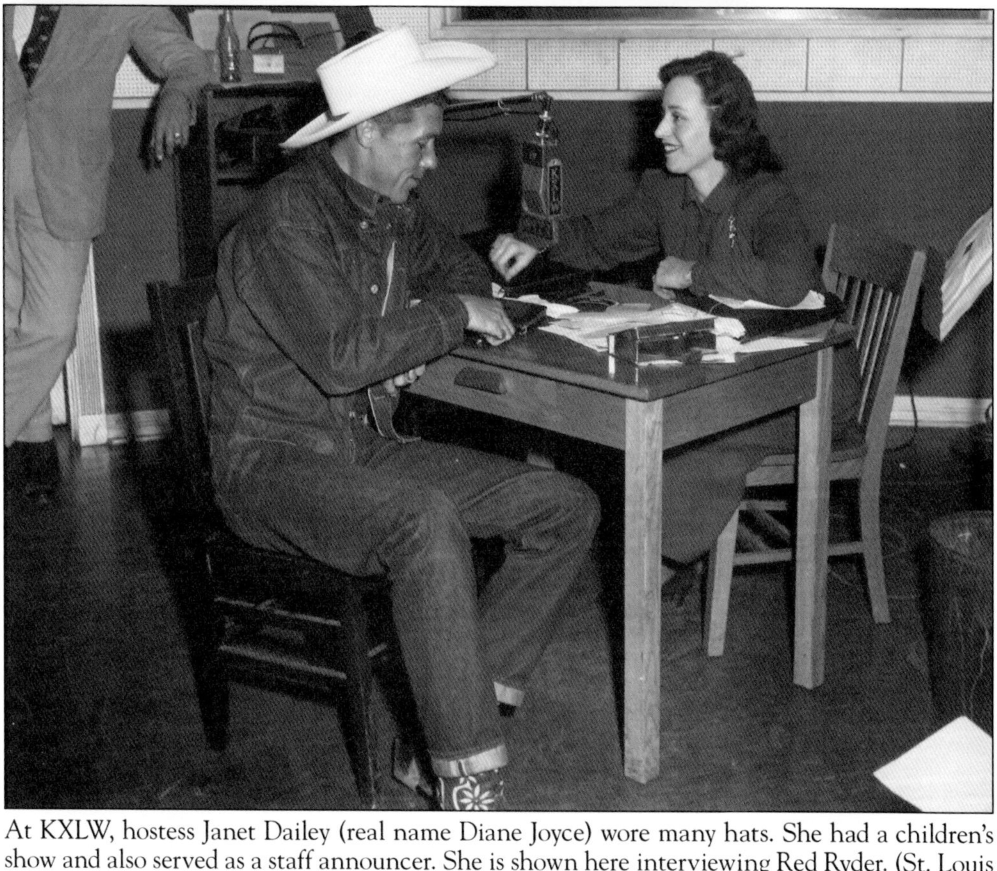

At KXLW, hostess Janet Dailey (real name Diane Joyce) wore many hats. She had a children's show and also served as a staff announcer. She is shown here interviewing Red Ryder. (St. Louis Media Archive.)

This postcard was sent out to promote Janet's children's program. (St. Louis Media Archive.)

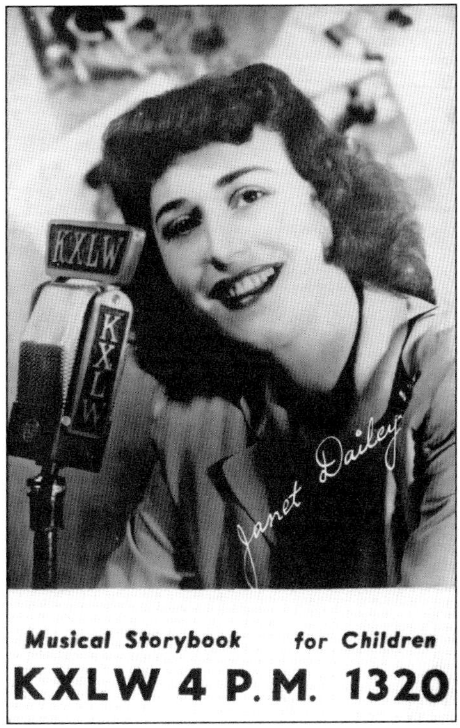

Kids' shows were also popping up on television. Elf Genevieve Bierman is shown helping KSD-TV's Santa. (St. Louis Media Archive.)

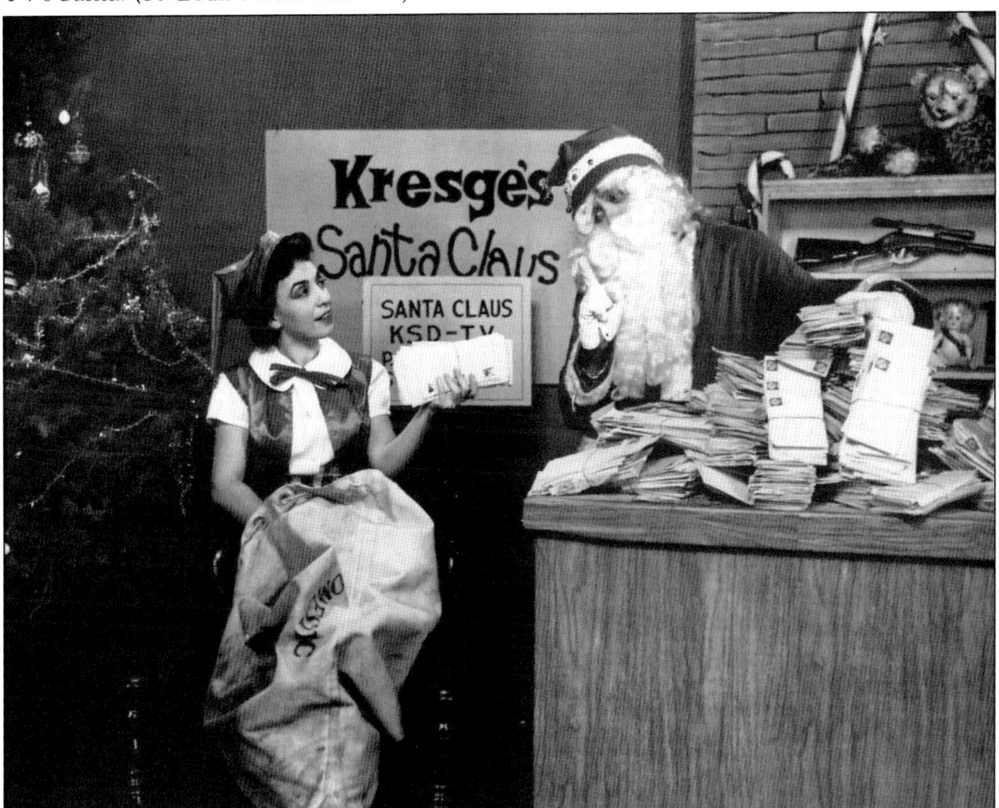

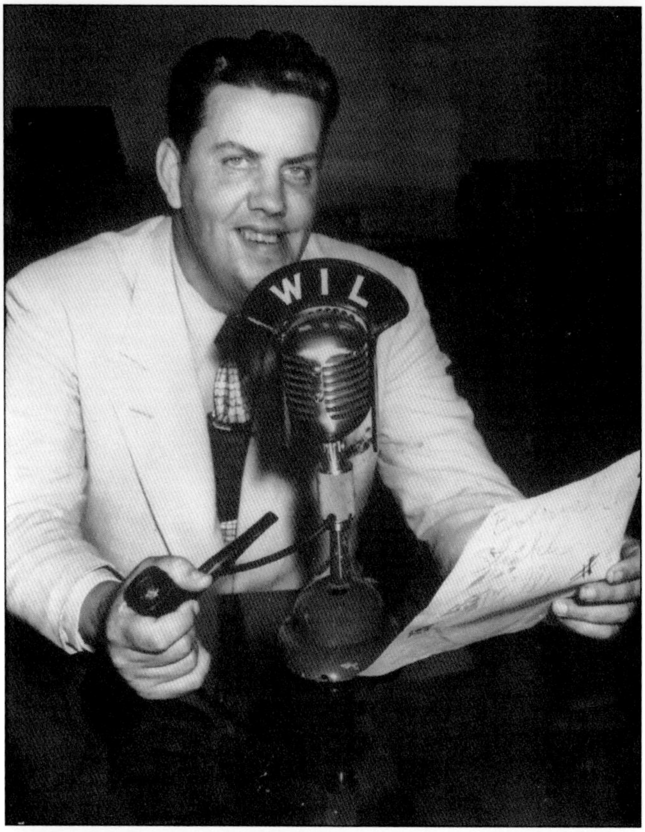

Campbell A. Miller was a very popular sports announcer in St. Louis from the mid-1940s to the mid-1950s. On the air, he was known as "Stretch" Miller. He was also seen occasionally on local television. (St. Louis Media Archive.)

As KSD-TV became even more successful, the station's owner constructed a new facility at 1111 Olive Street to house the television and radio stations. (St. Louis Media Archive.)

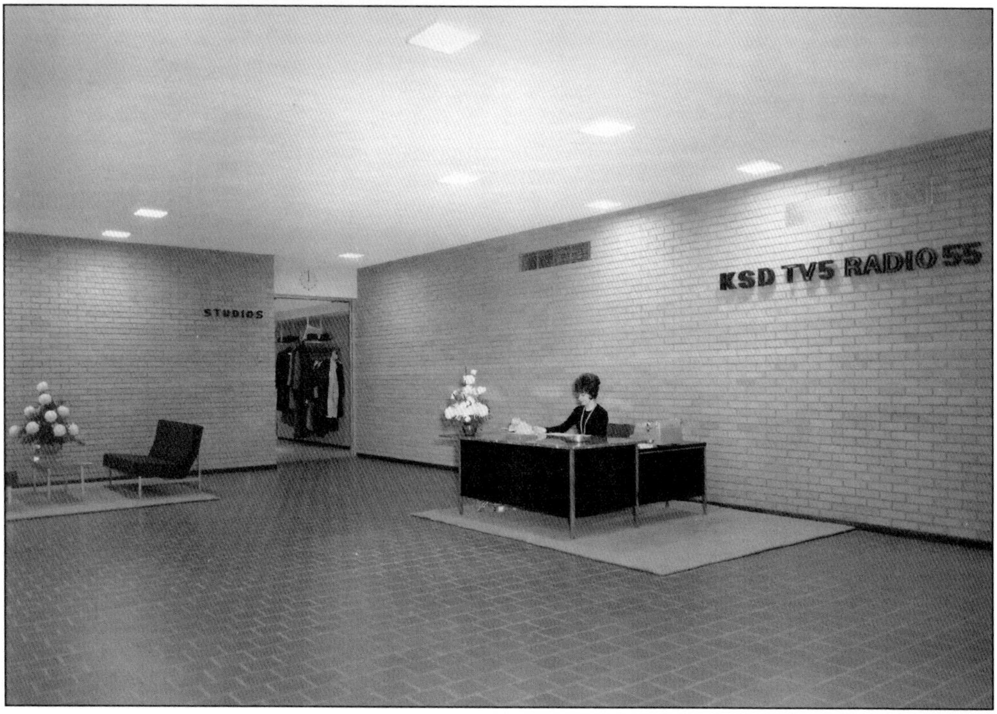

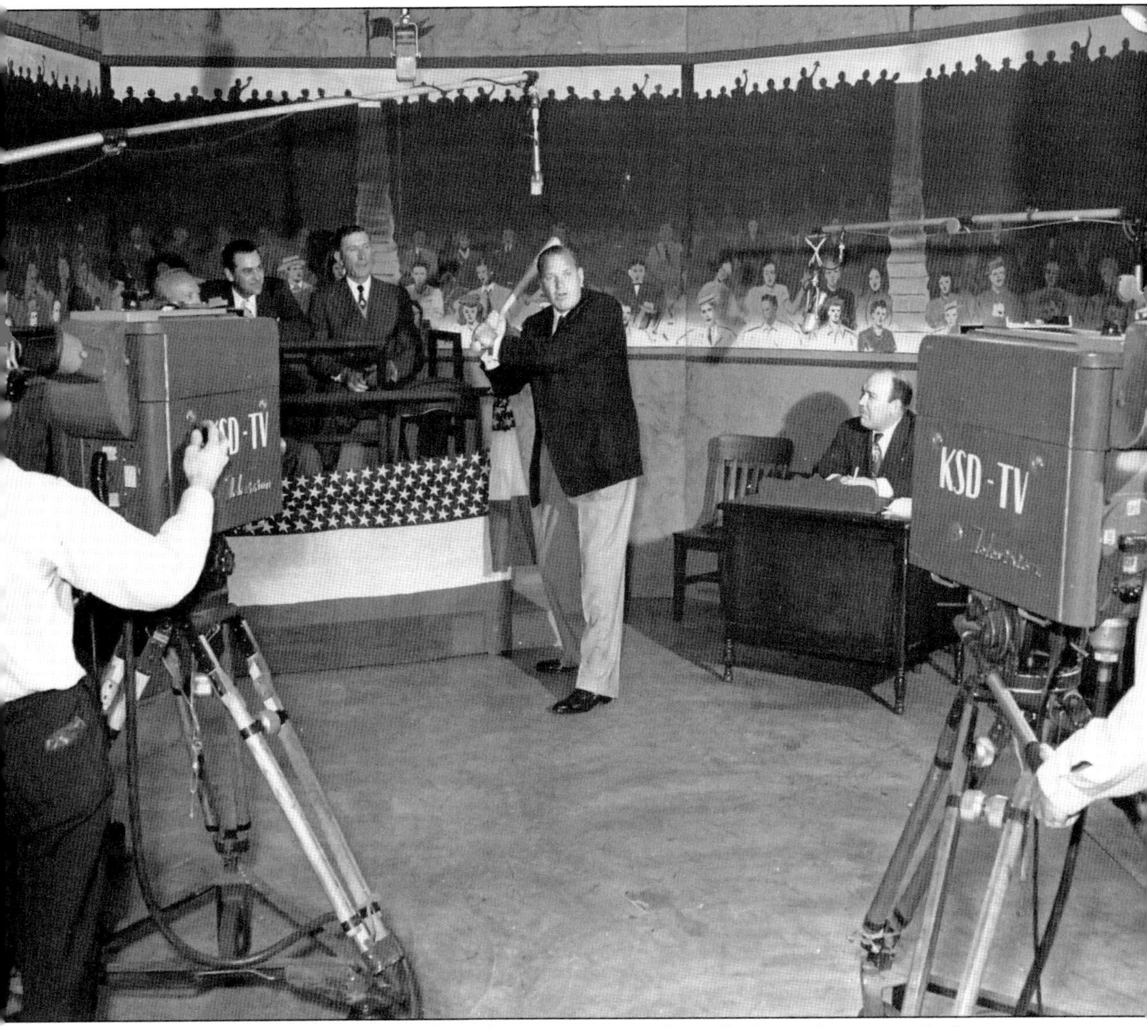

In the early 1950s, KSD-TV still had a television monopoly in St. Louis because of a licensing freeze imposed by the Federal Communications Commission. Although the station was affiliated with the NBC network, it still originated local shows, like this sports show featuring Dizzy Dean, (with a baseball bat in his hands). The station's Frank Eschen is seated to the right of Dean. (St. Louis Media Archive.)

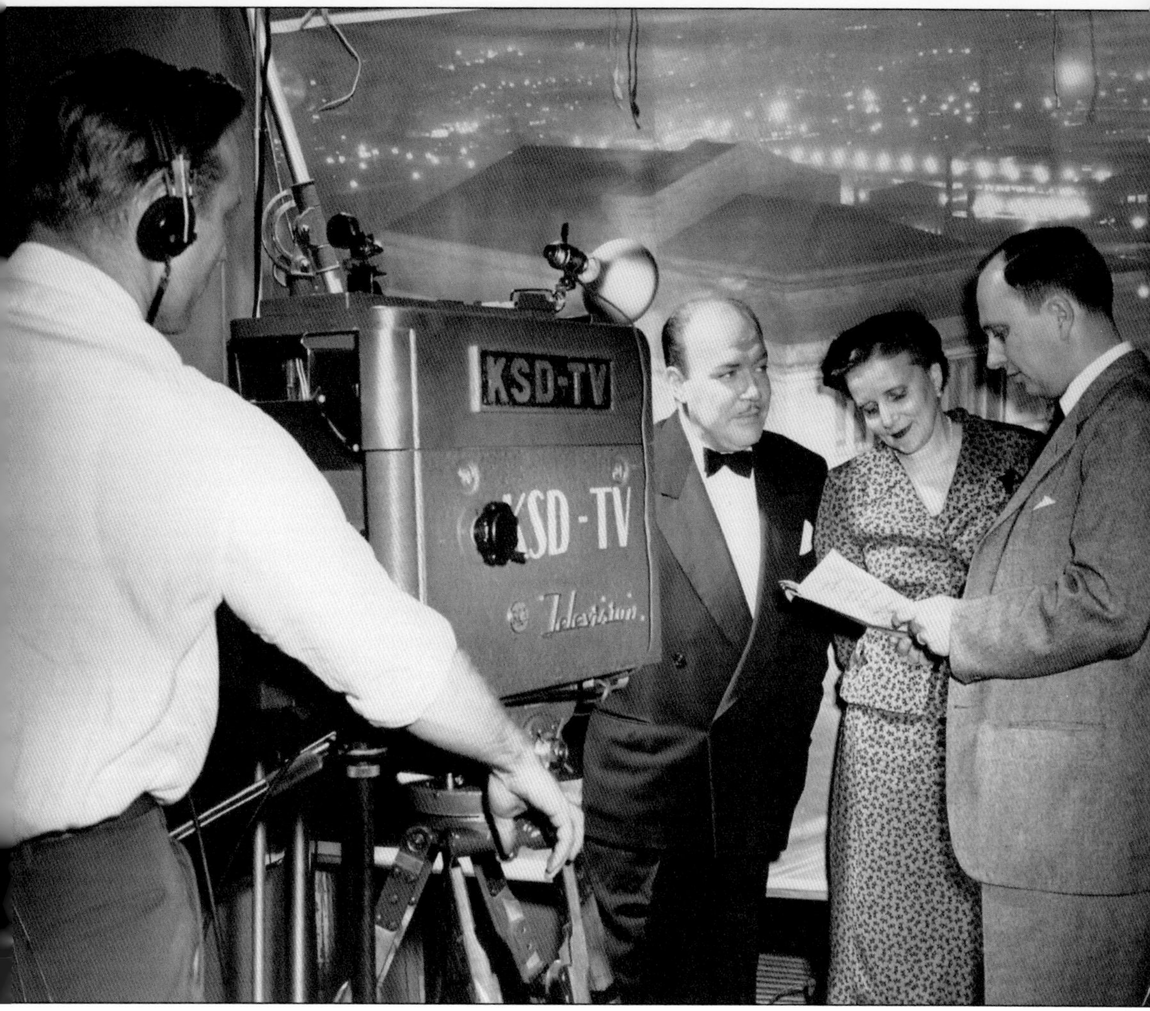

Frank Eschen (center) was the station's utility man, seemingly asked to perform every kind of announcing duty in the early days. (St. Louis Media Archive.)

Live hillbilly music could still be heard on the city's airwaves. Frankie Townsend appeared on Saint Louis University's WEW. (St. Louis Media Archive.)

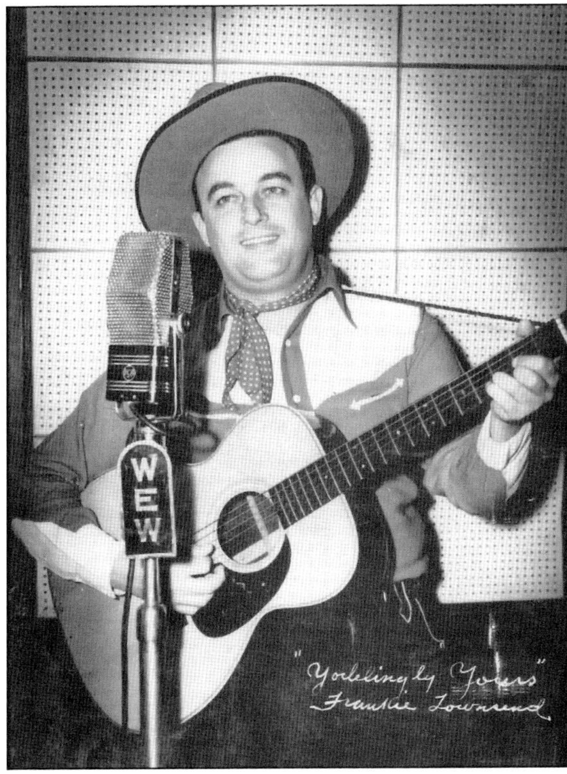

Wiley Price was St. Louis's first African American disc jockey, taking a job at WTMV in 1944. He is shown here at KSTL in 1951 with an unidentified station staffer. (St. Louis Media Archive.)

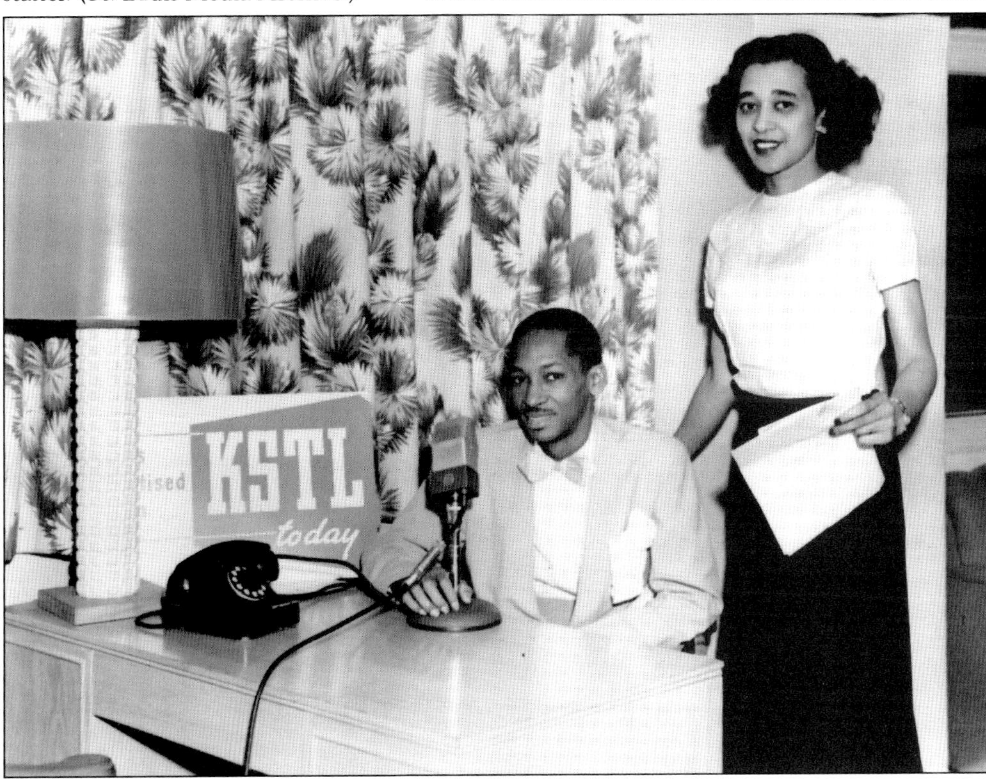

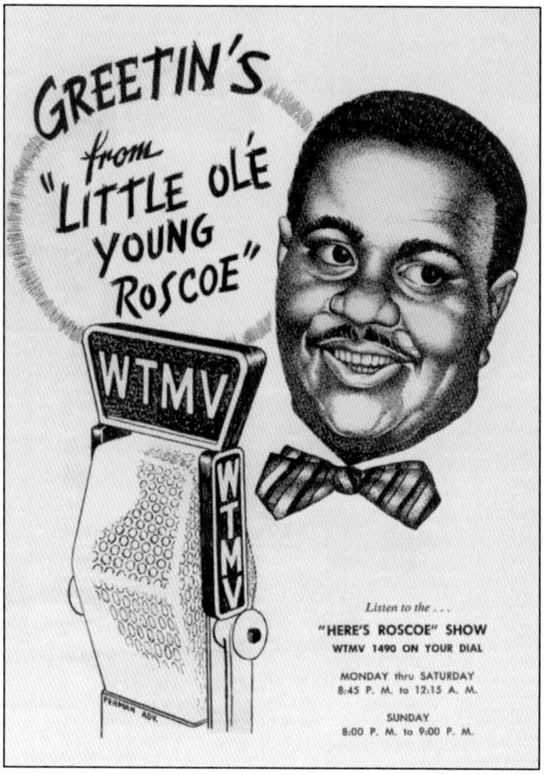

In the 1940s and 1950s, several radio stations in St. Louis broadcast what was generally called "race music." Roscoe McCrary's program on WTMV was part of a varied schedule on that station designed to appeal to a broad spectrum of listeners. (St. Louis Media Archive.)

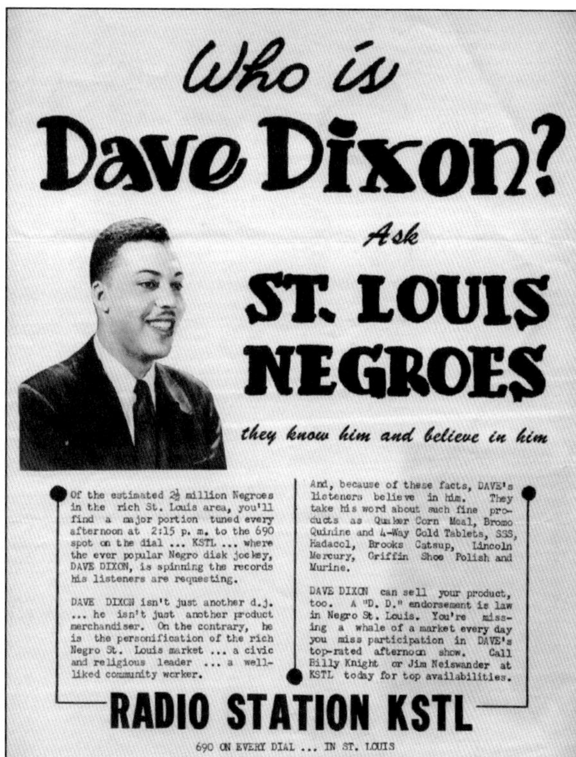

This brochure, touting the station's ability to reach "the rich Negro St. Louis market," was distributed to potential advertisers by KSTL. (St. Louis Media Archive.)

KXLW was evolving into a full-time black-oriented radio station. Spider Burks's programs of jazz and live remote broadcasts from local clubs also proved a draw for white listeners who pursued music not found on other stations. (St. Louis Media Archive.)

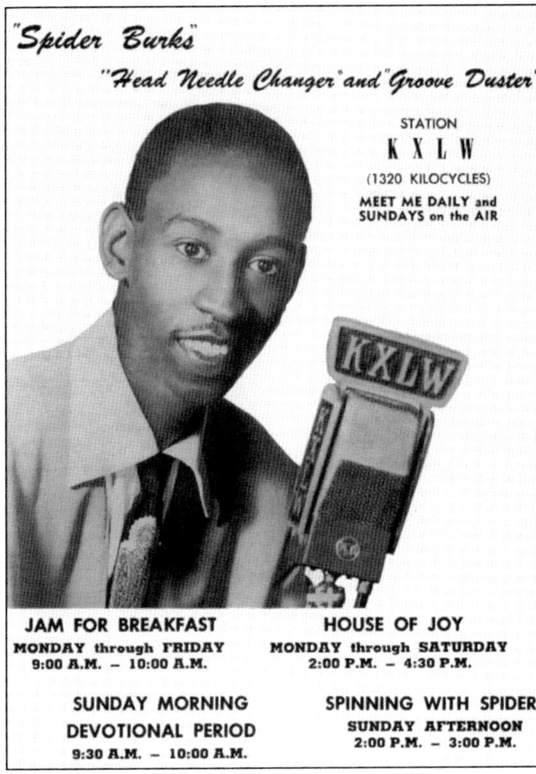

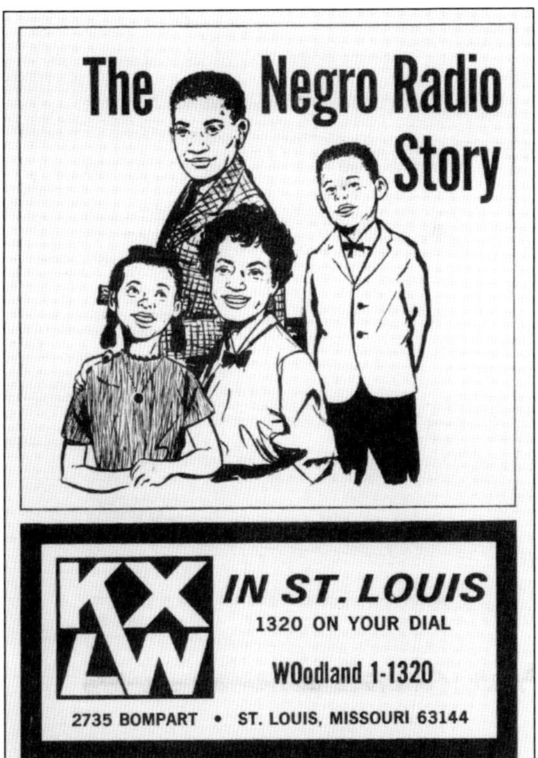

Management of KXLW published a booklet describing the qualities of its listening audience in the 1950s and telling potential advertisers that it was a wise decision to target the African American audience. (St. Louis Media Archive.)

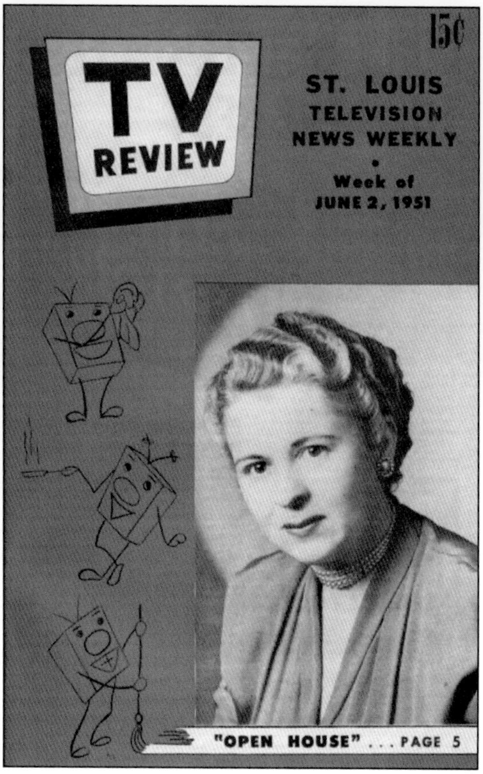

When this guide to local television programs, featuring Kay Morton on the cover, was published in 1951, there was only one television station in St. Louis. (Dr. Wayne Brasler.)

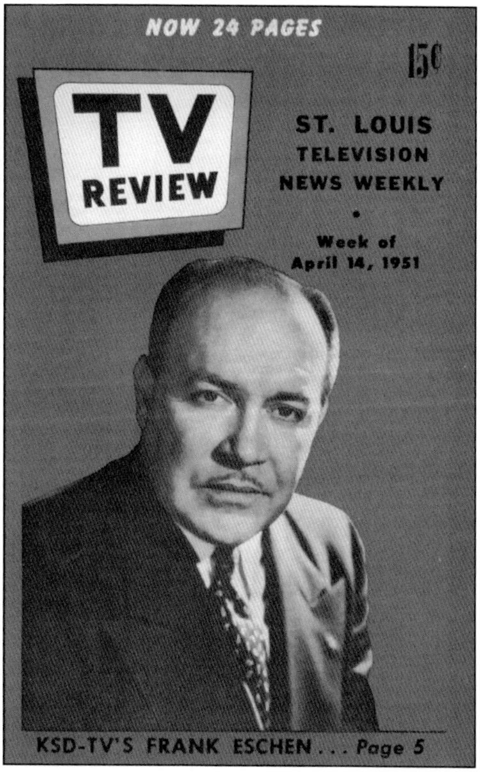

The guide came out each week and usually featured a personality from KSD-TV or NBC television on the cover. (Dr. Wayne Brasler.)

Russ Severin, the subject of this issue's cover story, hosted *To the Ladies* on KSD-TV with announcer Harry Honig. Charlotte Peters, who also performed, later took over the hosting of the program. (Dr. Wayne Brasler.)

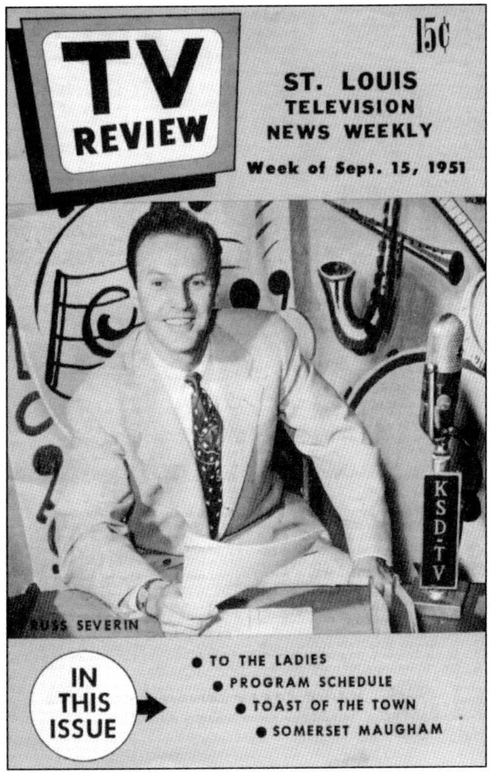

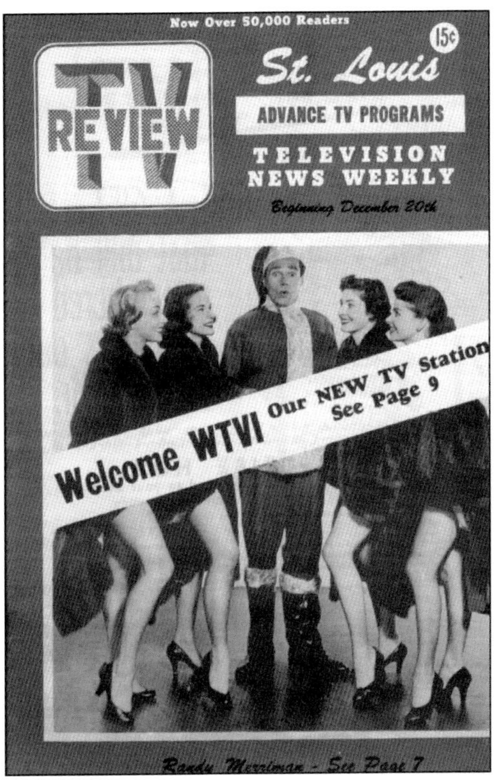

Finally, in 1953, the St. Louis market got another television station, as noted on the cover of this issue. (Dr. Wayne Brasler.)

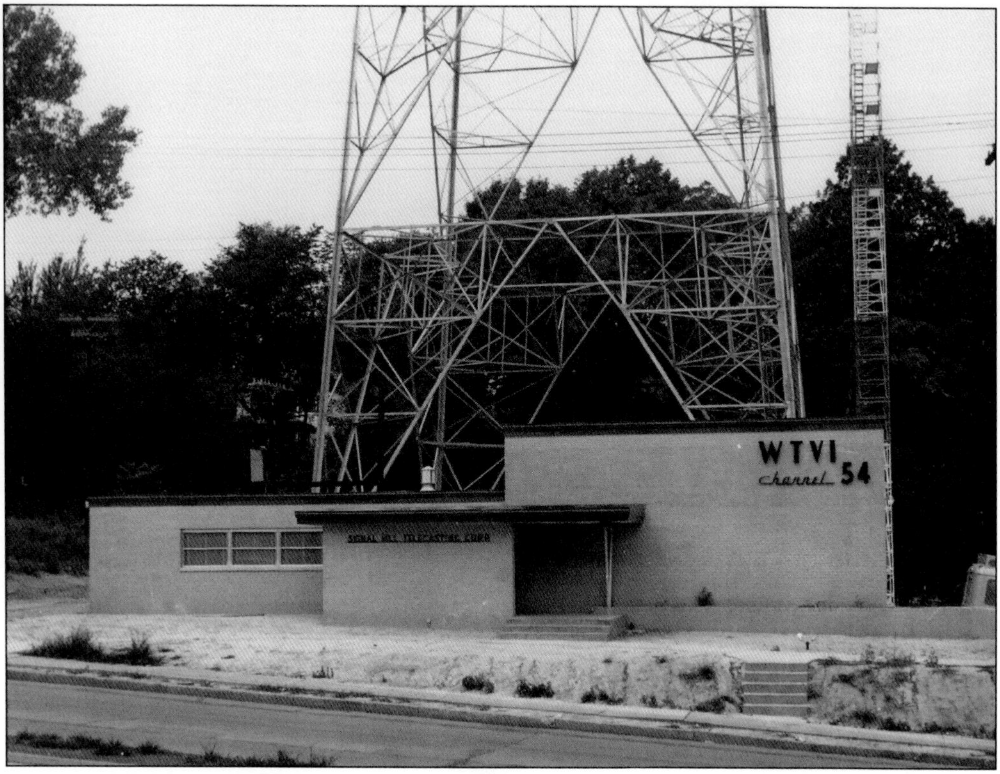

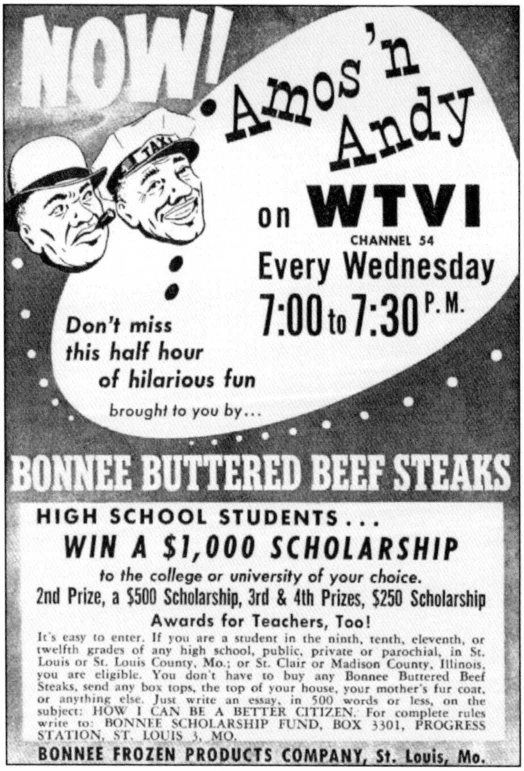

That new station, WTVI, had studios and a transmitter in Belleville on Signal Hill. Viewers needed a special tuner to receive channel 54, which was a UHF channel. (Don Rockwell.)

WTVI carried programming from the DuMont and CBS networks. Two other short-lived UHF stations signed on around the same time: KACY-TV and KSTM-TV. Later, WTVI moved its studios to St. Louis and became KTVI. The owners were able to acquire an assignment to channel 2, which effectively assured the station's successful future since a relatively small number of people watched UHF stations. (St. Louis Media Archive.)

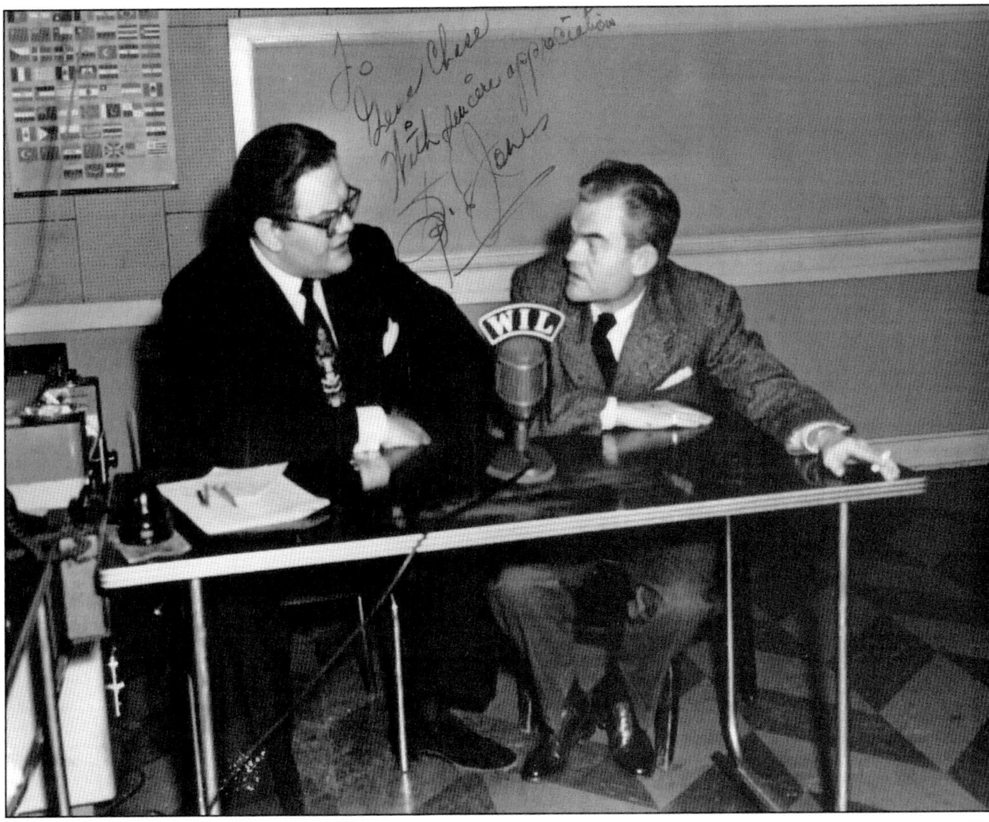

Most area radio stations were making a transition away from network programming in the early 1950s. WIL disc jockey Gene Chase (left) interviewed visiting celebrities like musical funnyman Spike Jones. (St. Louis Media Archive.)

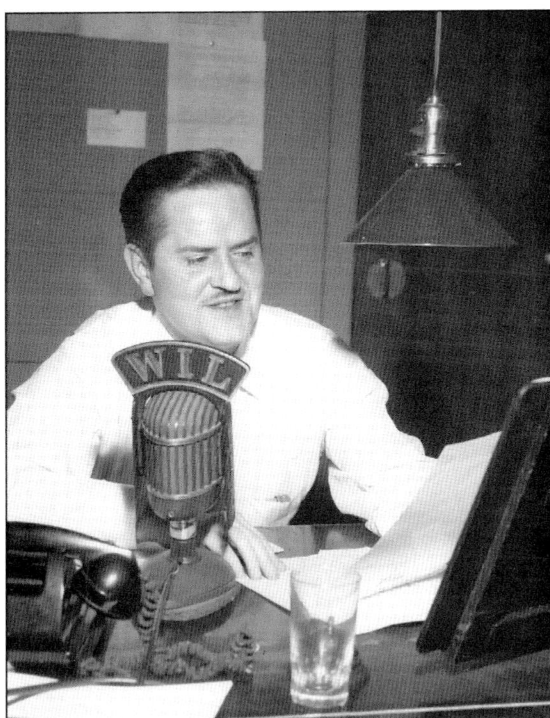

Ray Manning's record shows were designed to appeal to a wide age range, and he had a vocal teenage following, due in part to the fact that he appeared as the host at many area teen dances. (St. Louis Media Archive.)

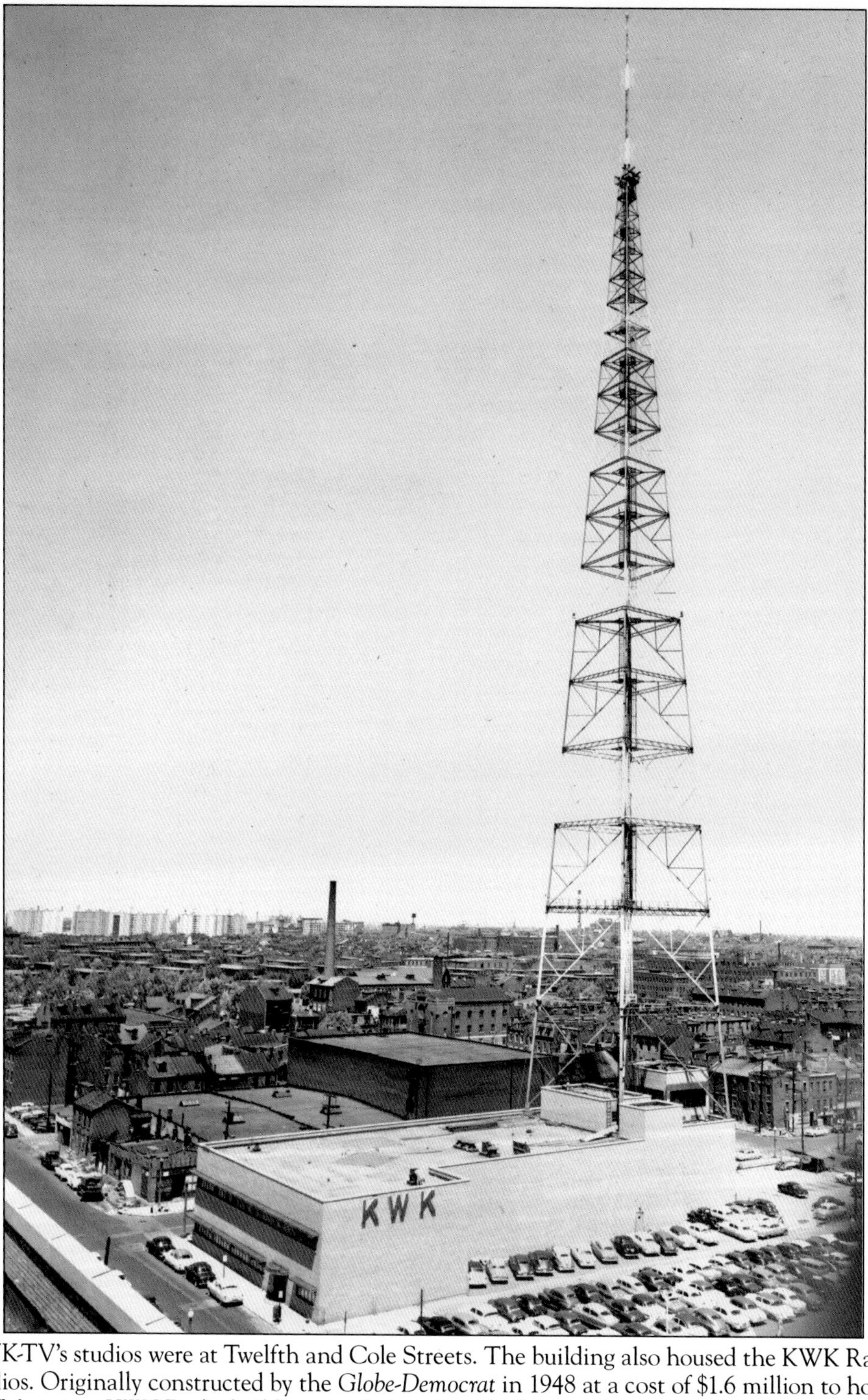

KWK-TV's studios were at Twelfth and Cole Streets. The building also housed the KWK Radio studios. Originally constructed by the *Globe-Democrat* in 1948 at a cost of $1.6 million to house its FM station, KWGD, the building was designed to also house television studios in anticipation of the newspaper receiving a license, as its competitor the *Post-Dispatch* had done. (St. Louis Mercantile Library Association.)

Early production was crude, as seen in this photograph of the program *Guided Missals*, produced in conjunction with the St. Louis Archdiocese. (St. Louis Media Archive.)

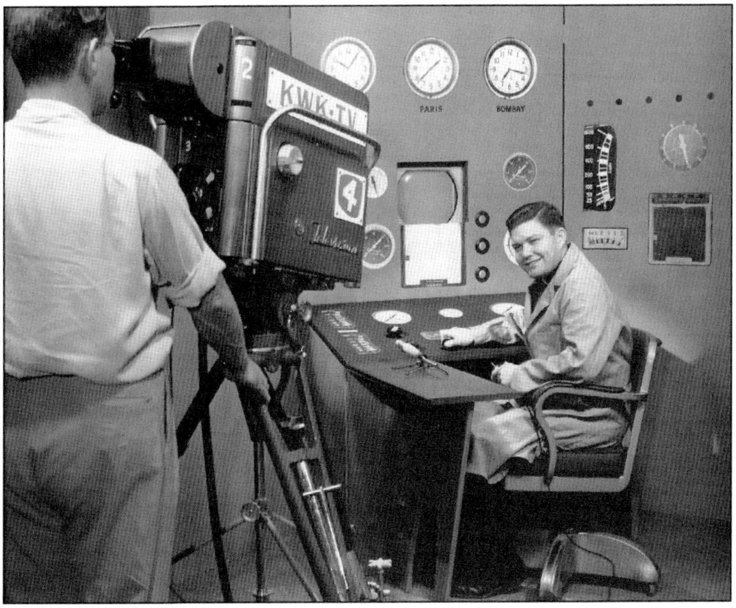

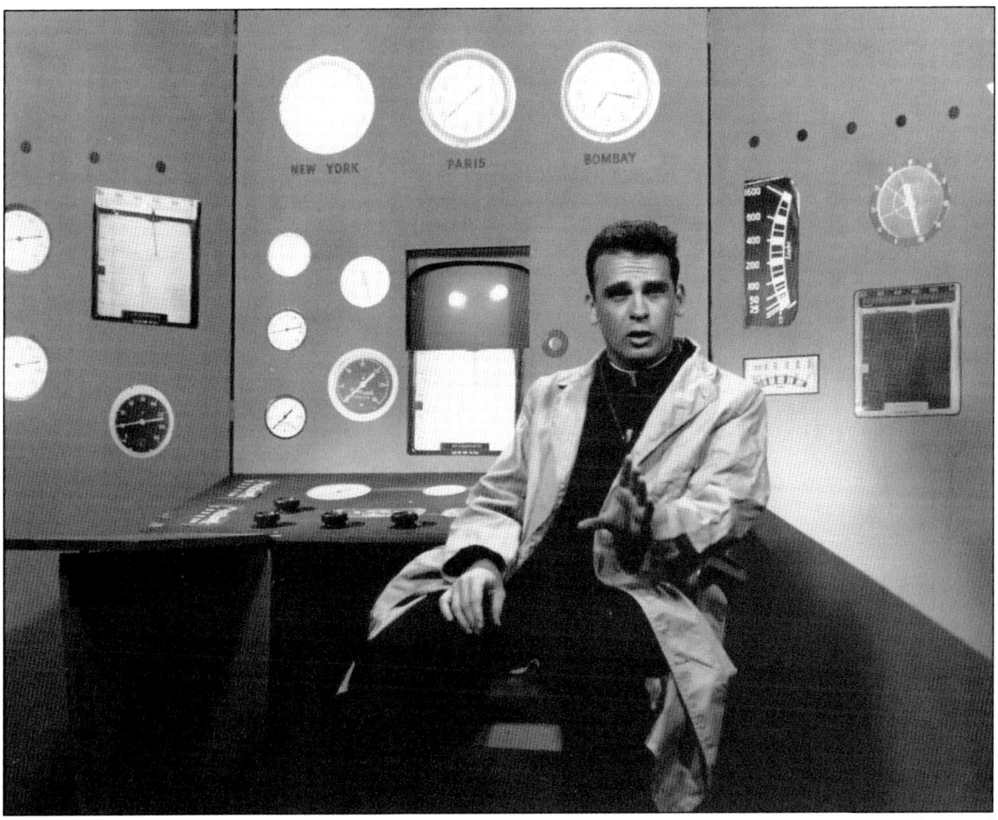

Fr. Edward O'Donnell also served as host of the show. He was later elevated to bishop and served as administrator of the St. Louis Archdiocese. (St. Louis Media Archive.)

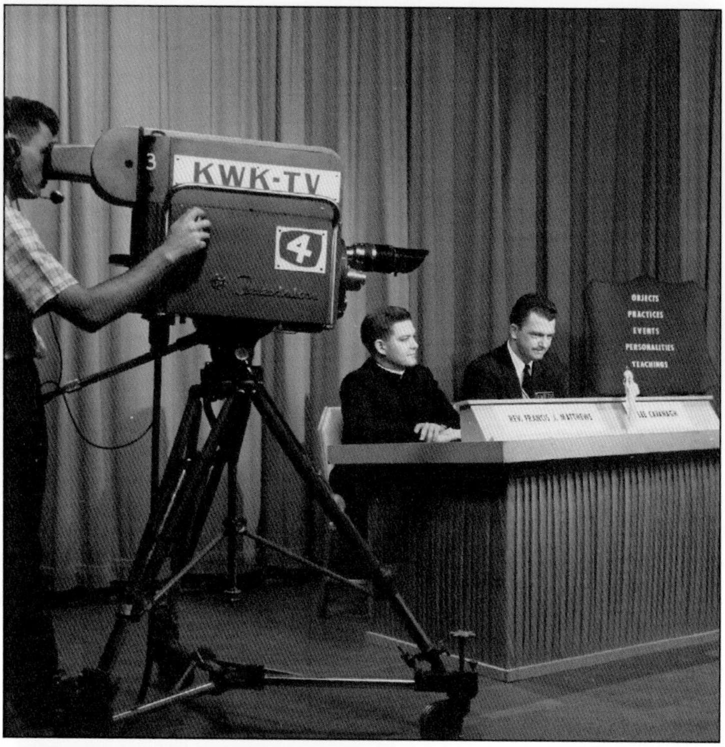

KWK-TV staff announcer Lee Cavanaugh (far right) hosted another program of religious orientation, *Quiz a Catholic*. (St. Louis Media Archive.)

Tom Dailey had been a successful radio host on KWK for many years. Like many other radio announcers, he was pressed into service on television, hosting a women's program. (St. Louis Media Archive.)

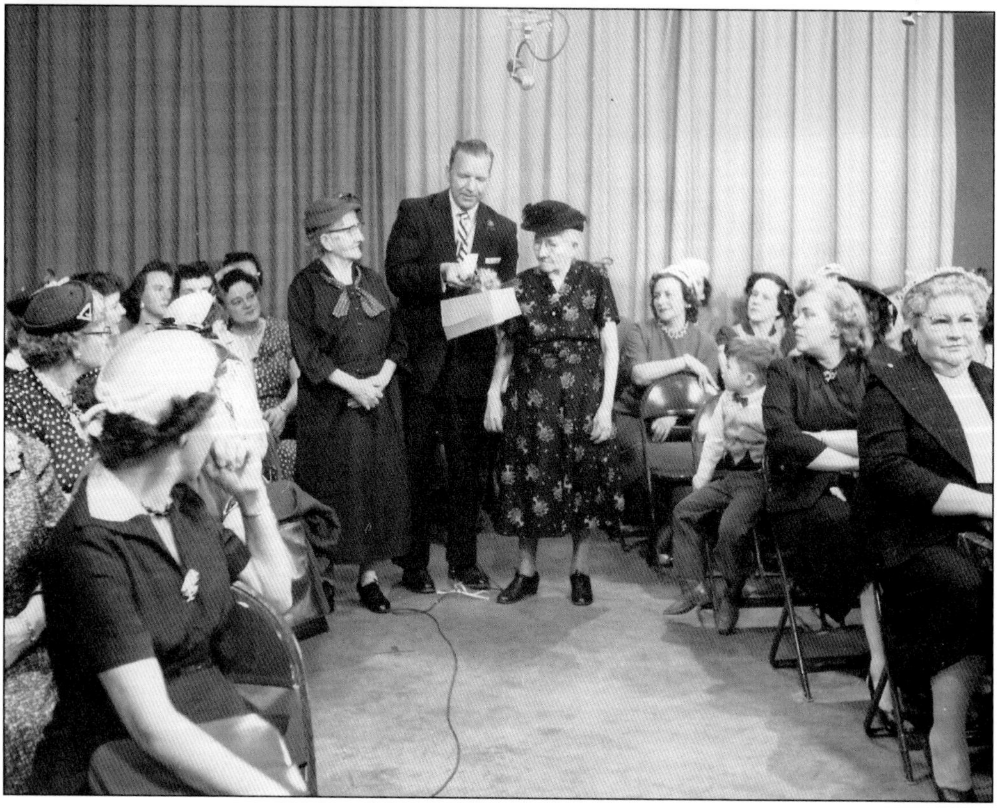

Like Belleville's WTVI, KSTM-TV was another UHF station. It was on the air less than a year. KACY-TV, on channel 14, was licensed to Festus, Missouri. It lasted five months. (St. Louis Media Archive.)

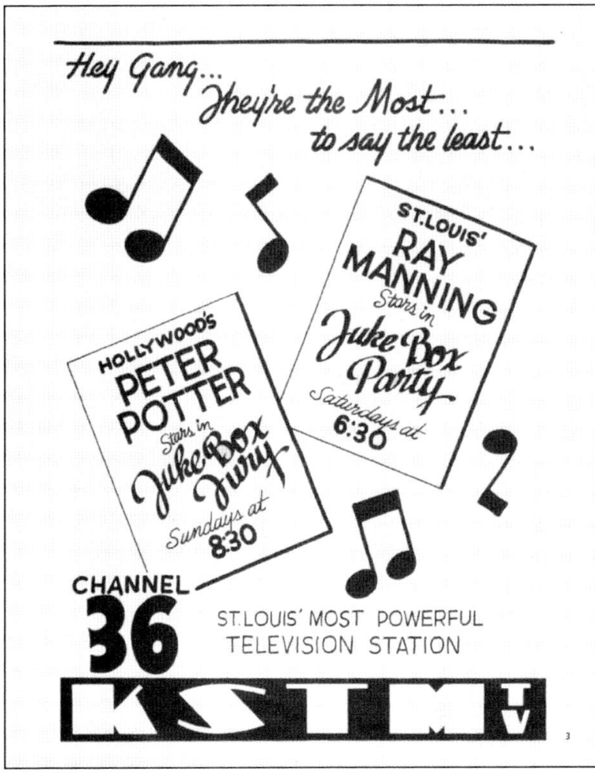

The market's educational television station, KETC-TV, signed on from studios at the edge of the Washington University campus in September 1954. (KETC-TV archives.)

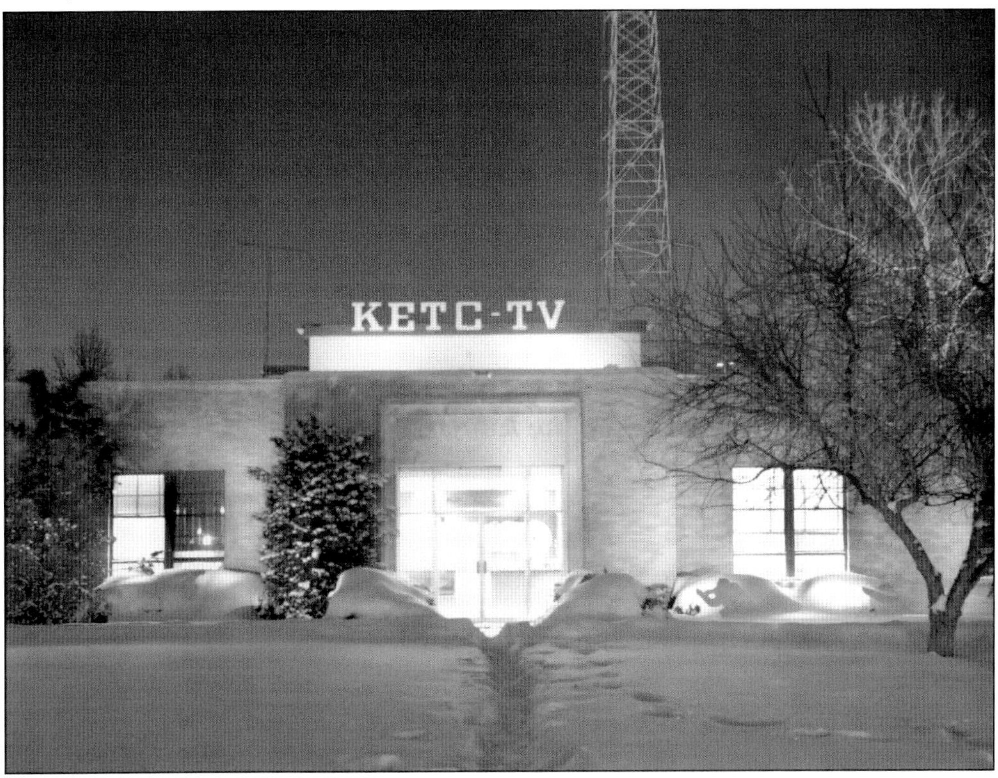

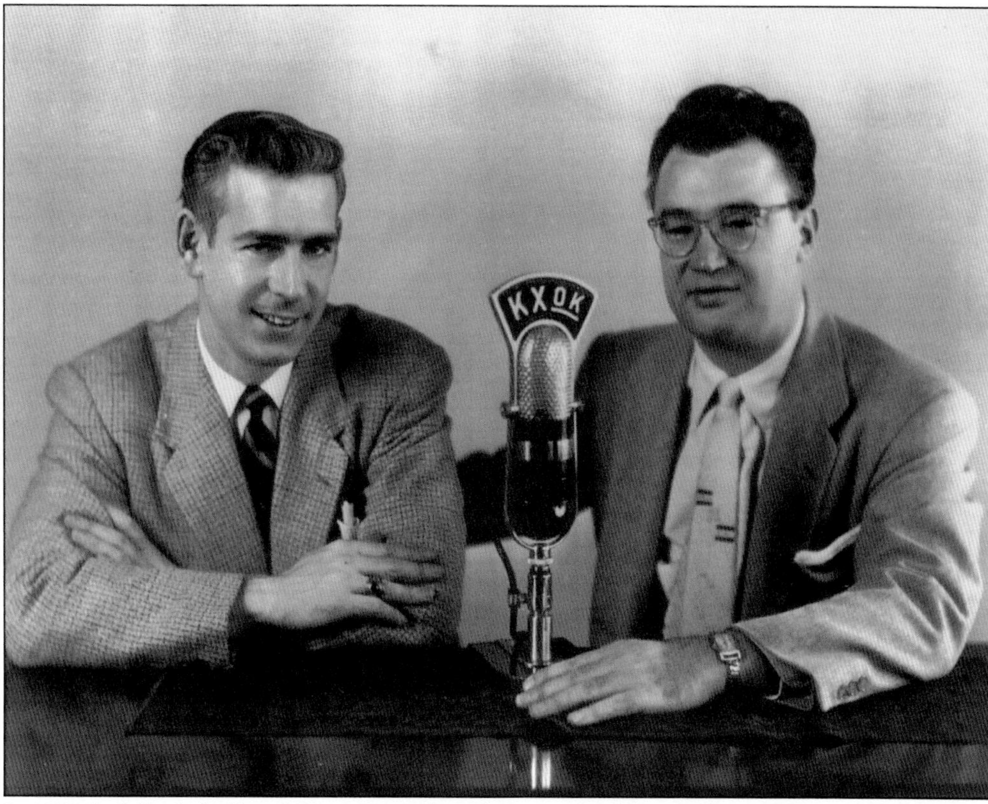

In 1954, Jack Buck (left) and Harry Caray broadcast Cardinal baseball over KXOK. The following year, KMOX picked up the broadcast rights and held them for the next 50 years. (St. Louis Media Archive.)

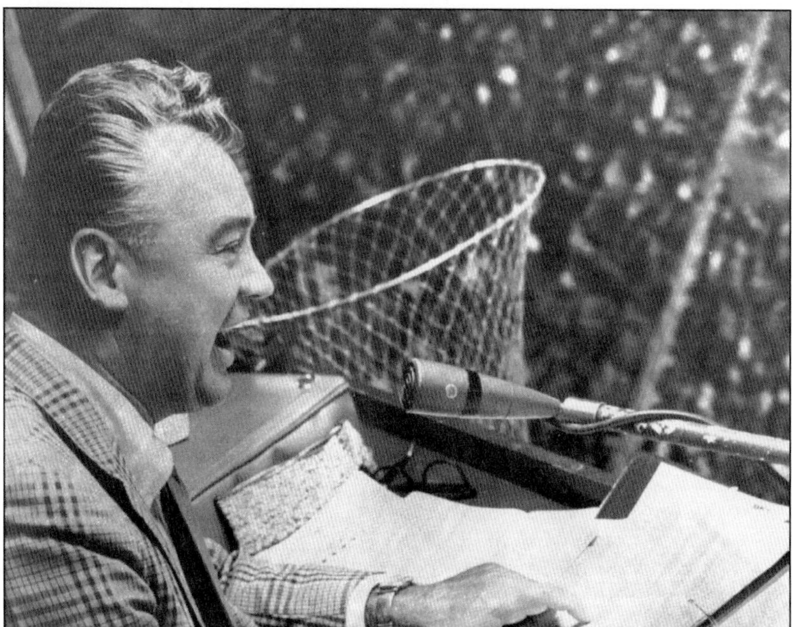

Caray, shown here in the broadcast booth at Sportsman's Park, often used his trusty net to snag foul balls. (St. Louis Media Archive.)

Four

More Television, More Radio

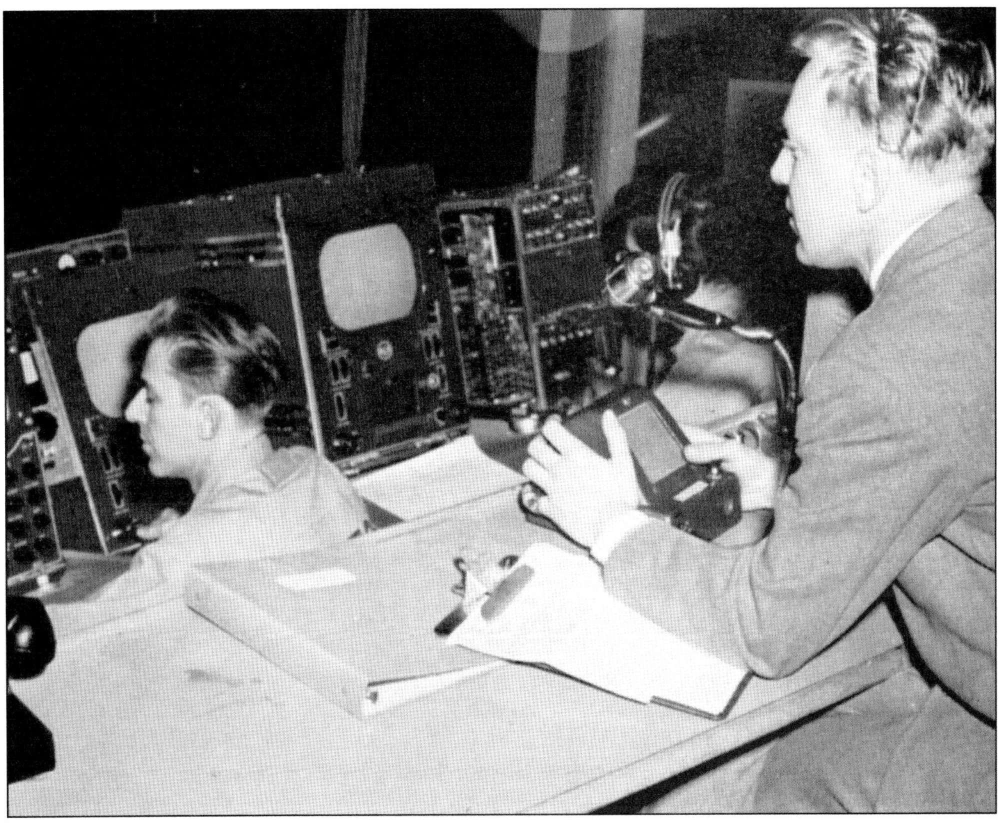

New television and radio stations were licensed to St. Louis and the surrounding area, providing the public with more program variety. At the same time, "educational television" was gaining a small following. KETC's control room, shown here, was comparable to the other St. Louis stations even though it was a non-commercial operation relying on donations and underwriting. (KETC-TV archives.)

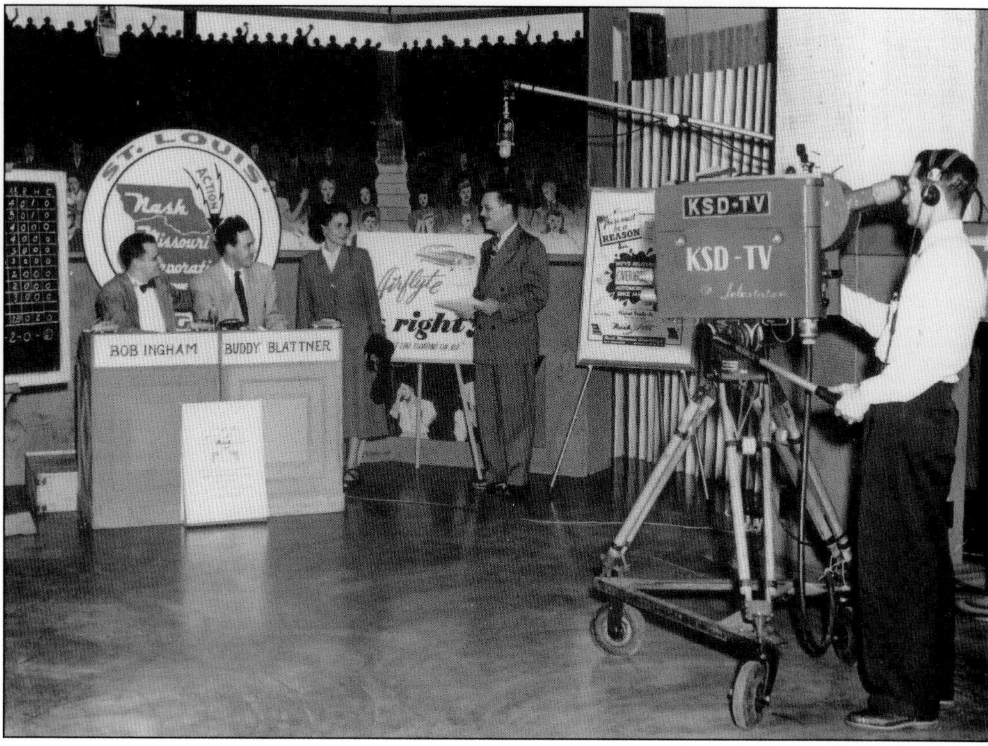

During this KSD-TV sports report, commercials for Nash automobiles were done by a live announcer with the help of poster boards shown on studio easels. KSD radio and television announcer Sterling Harkins is seen standing under the microphone. (St. Louis Media Archive.)

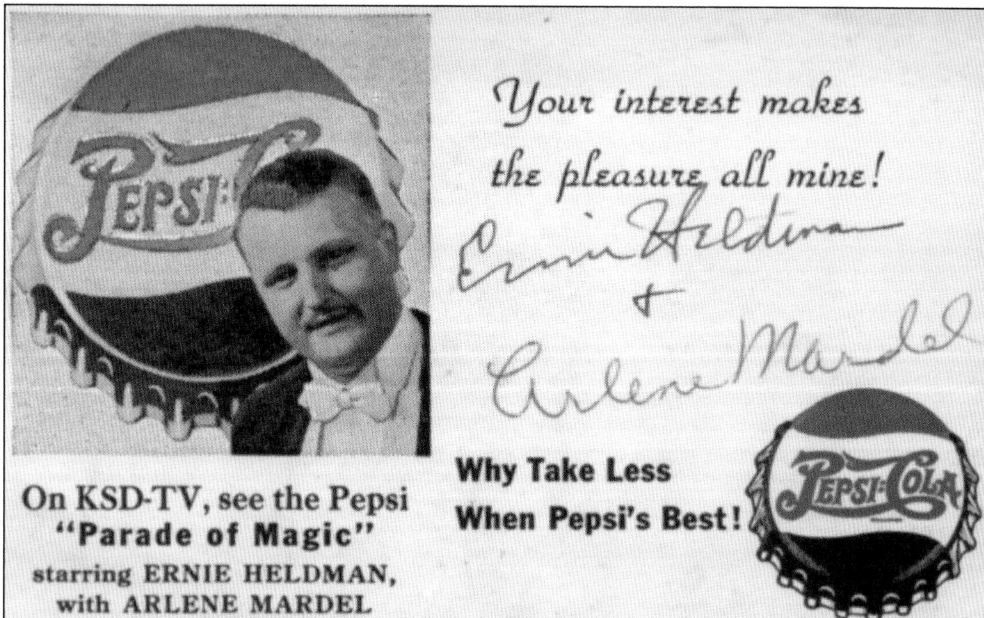

St. Louis nightclub magician Ernie Heldman had a weekly show on KSD-TV; Arlene Mardel was his assistant. (St. Louis Media Archive.)

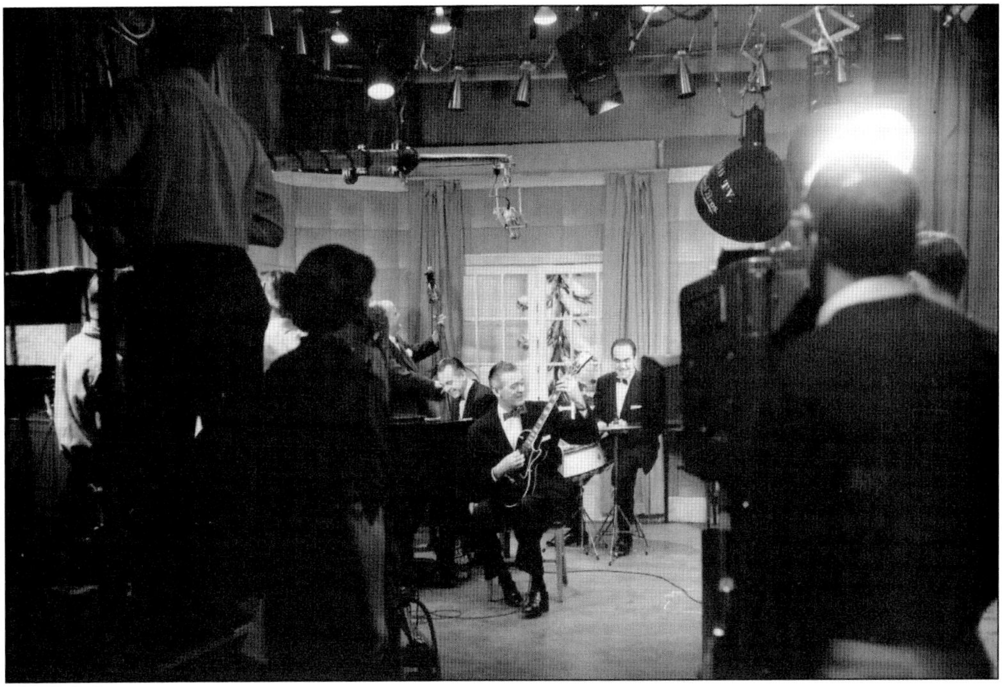

Music man Russ David, seen at the piano, divided his time between the KSD Radio microphones and the hot lights in the studio at KSD-TV. (Sue Dorn.)

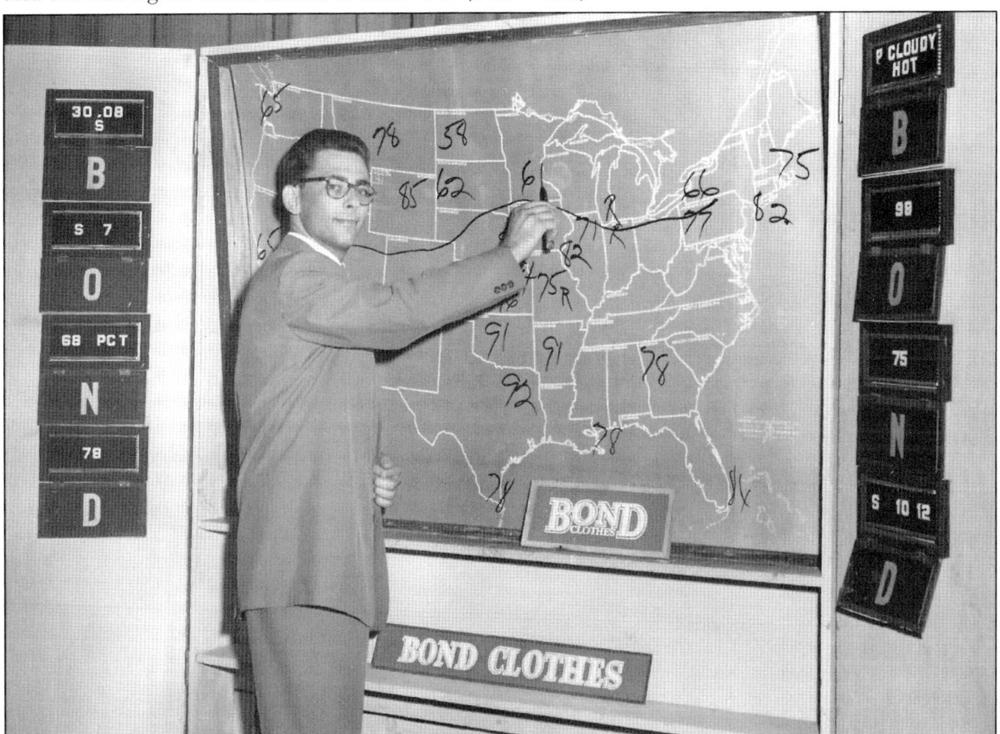

By 1956, Howard DeMere's personable weather reports had become a fixture at KSD-TV. He also held down a nightly music-show slot on KSD Radio. (Howard DeMere.)

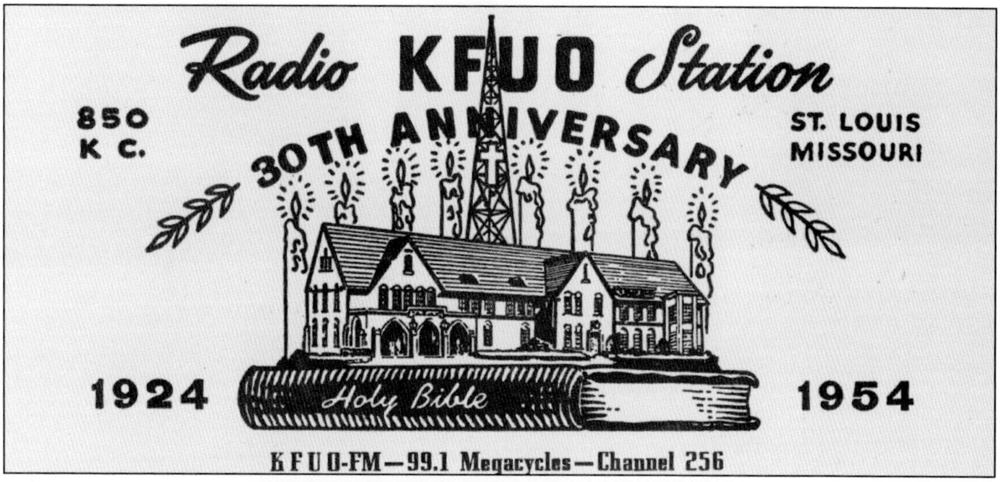

When KFUO, owned by Lutheran Church Missouri Synod, celebrated its 30th year on the air in 1954, it also promoted its sister FM station. KFUO-FM was one of the first FM stations to sign on in St. Louis. (St. Louis Media Archive.)

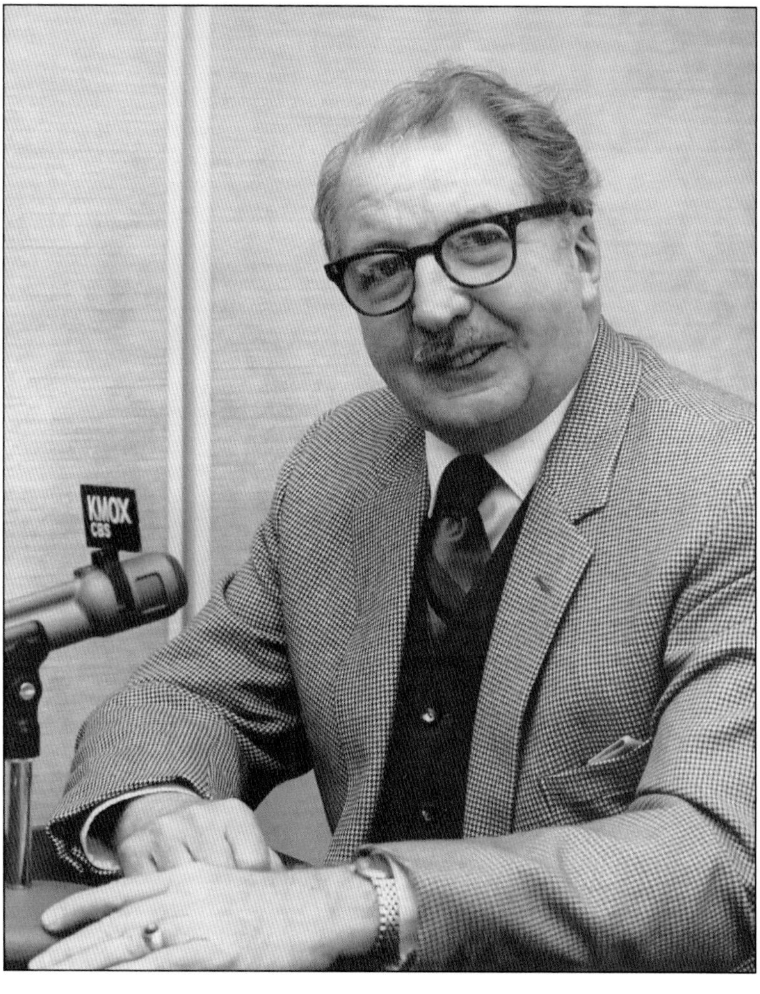

Rex Davis came to KMOX from Cincinnati in 1946. His extended career at the "Voice of St. Louis" made him one of the most-respected news broadcasters in the market. (St. Louis Media Archive.)

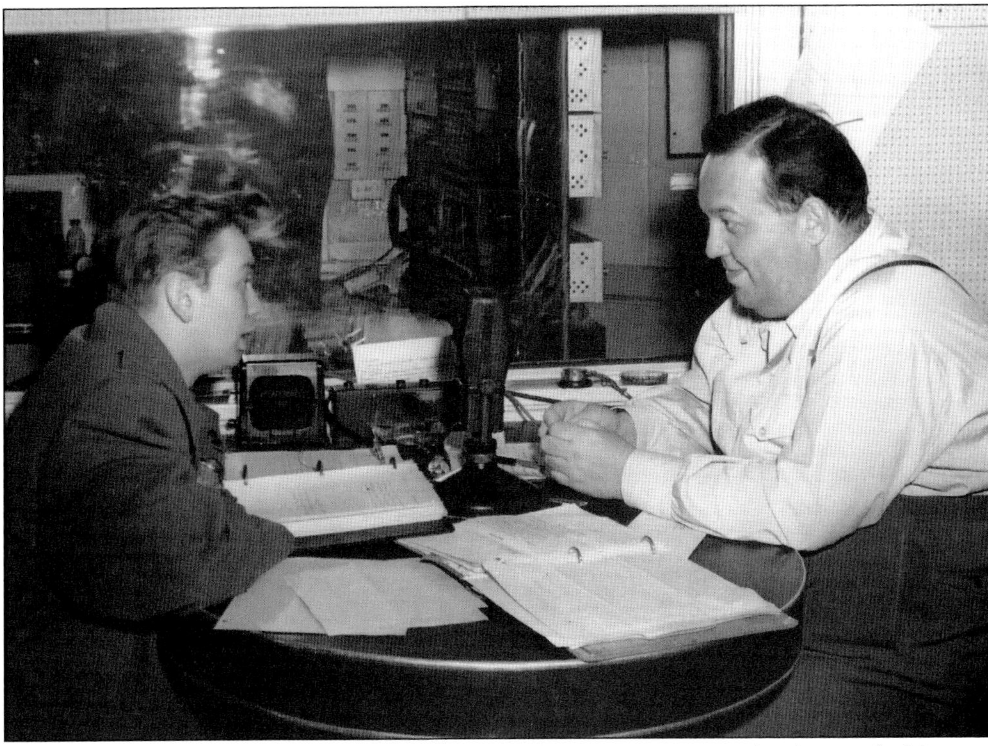

Disc jockey/announcer Ed Wilson was a personality on St. Louis radio for nearly 30 years. He is seen on the right interviewing up-and-coming singer Mel Torme on KWK. (St. Louis Media Archive.)

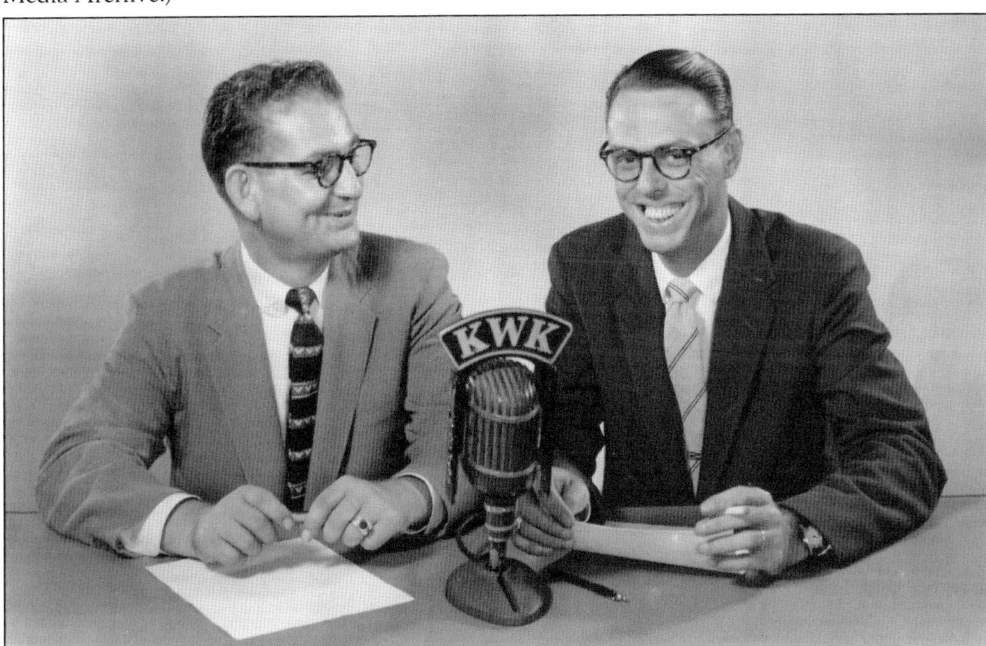

The nighttime *Jack and Jerry* show on KWK featured Jack Donnell (left) and Jerry Brown, who often left the studio to spotlight the city's nightlife. (St. Louis Media Archive.)

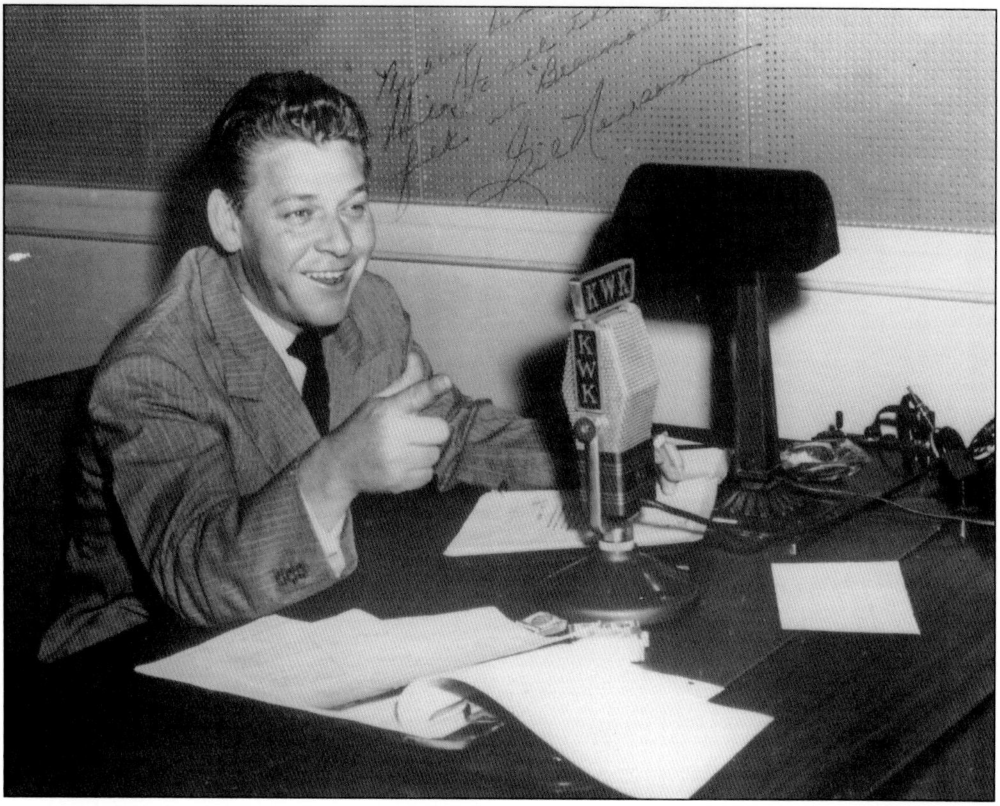

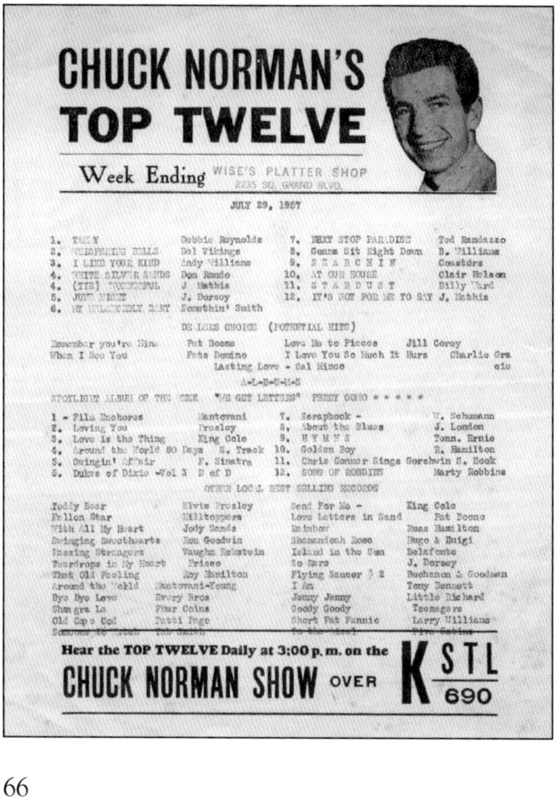

CHUCK NORMAN'S TOP TWELVE

Week Ending WISE'S PLATTER SHOP
2235 SO. GRAND BLVD.

JULY 29, 1957

1.	TAMMY	Debbie Reynolds	7.	NEXT STOP PARADISE	Ted Randazzo
2.	WHISPERING BELLS	Del Vikings	8.	Gonna Sit Right Down	B. Williams
3.	I LIKE YOUR KIND	Andy Williams	9.	S E A R C H I N	Coasters
4.	WHITE SILVER SANDS	Don Rondo	10.	AT OUR HOUSE	Clair Nelson
4.	(TIE) WONDERFUL	J Mathis	11.	S T A R D U S T	Billy Ward
5.	JUNE NIGHT	J. Dorsey	12.	IT'S NOT FOR ME TO SAY	J. Mathis
6.	MY MELANCHOLY BABY	Somethin' Smith			

DE LOES CHOICE (POTENTIAL HITS)

Remember you're Mine	Pat Boone	Love Me to Pieces	Jill Corey
When I See You	Fats Domino	I Love You So Much It Hurs	Charlie Gracie

Lasting Love - Sal Mineo

A-L-B-U-M-S

SPOTLIGHT ALBUM OF THE WEEK "WE GET LETTERS" PERRY COMO * * * * *

1 -	Film Enchores	Mantovani	7.	Scrapbook -	W. Schumann
2.	Loving You	Presley	8.	About the Blues	J. London
3.	Love is the Thing	King Cole	9.	H Y M N S	Tenn. Ernie
4.	Around the World 80 Days	S. Track	10.	Golden Boy	R. Hamilton
5.	Swingin' Affair	F. Sinatra	11.	Chris Connor Sings Gershwin S. Book	
6.	Dukes of Dixie -Vol 3	D of D	12.	SONG OF ROBBINS	Marty Robbins

OTHER LOCAL BEST SELLING RECORDS

Teddy Bear	Elvis Presley	Send For Me -	King Cole
Fallen Star	Hilltoppers	Love Letters in Sand	Pat Boone
With All My Heart	Jody Sands	Rainbow	Russ Hamilton
Swinging Sweethearts	Ron Goodwin	Shenandoah Rose	Hugo & Luigi
Passing Strangers	Vaughn Eckstein	Island in the Sun	Belafonte
Teardrops in My Heart	Prisco	So Rare	J. Dorsey
That Old Feeling	Roy Hamilton	Flying Saucer # 2	Buchanan & Goodman
Around the World	Mantovani-Young	I Am	Tony Bennett
Bye Bye Love	Every Bros	Jenny Jenny	Little Richard
Shangra La	Four Coins	Goody Goody	Teenagers
Old Cape Cod	Patti Page	Short Fat Fannie	Larry Williams

Hear the TOP TWELVE Daily at 3:00 p. m. on the

CHUCK NORMAN SHOW OVER **KSTL 690**

Gil Newsome had an extended run as a disc jockey on a couple of St. Louis stations. On KWK, he had a youthful audience. Later, on KSD, his target audience was adult, which was actually the same audience who had grown up listening to him. (St. Louis Media Archive.)

Chuck Norman began his career as a teenage disc jockey. He later hosted a television program on KTVI and ended his broadcast career as the owner of radio station WGNU. (St. Louis Media Archive.)

He was King Richard on KWK and Dick Richards on KSHE, but his given name was Rich King. He ended his very successful radio career in Florida. (St. Louis Media Archive.)

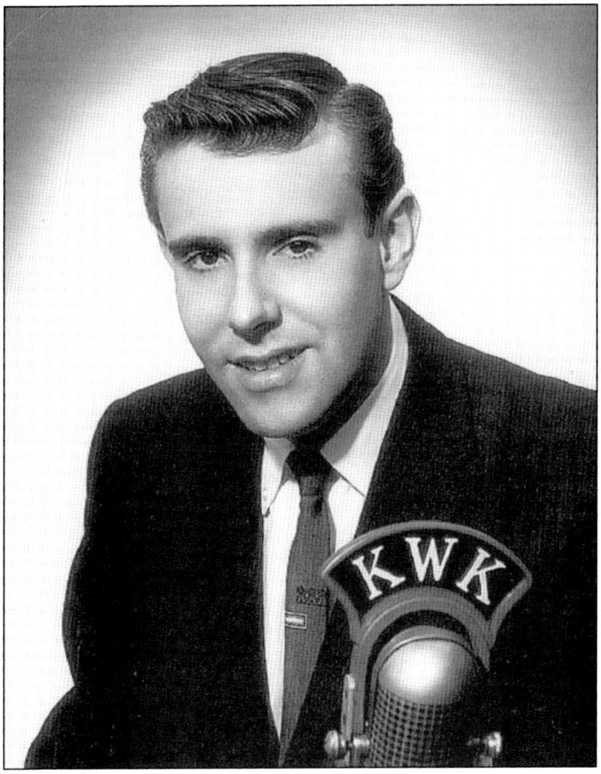

After working for 10 years as a disc jockey at East St. Louis's WTMV, Roscoe McCrary (seen on the right interviewing John Buckner) moved across the river for a similar position at KXLW. (St. Louis Media Archive.)

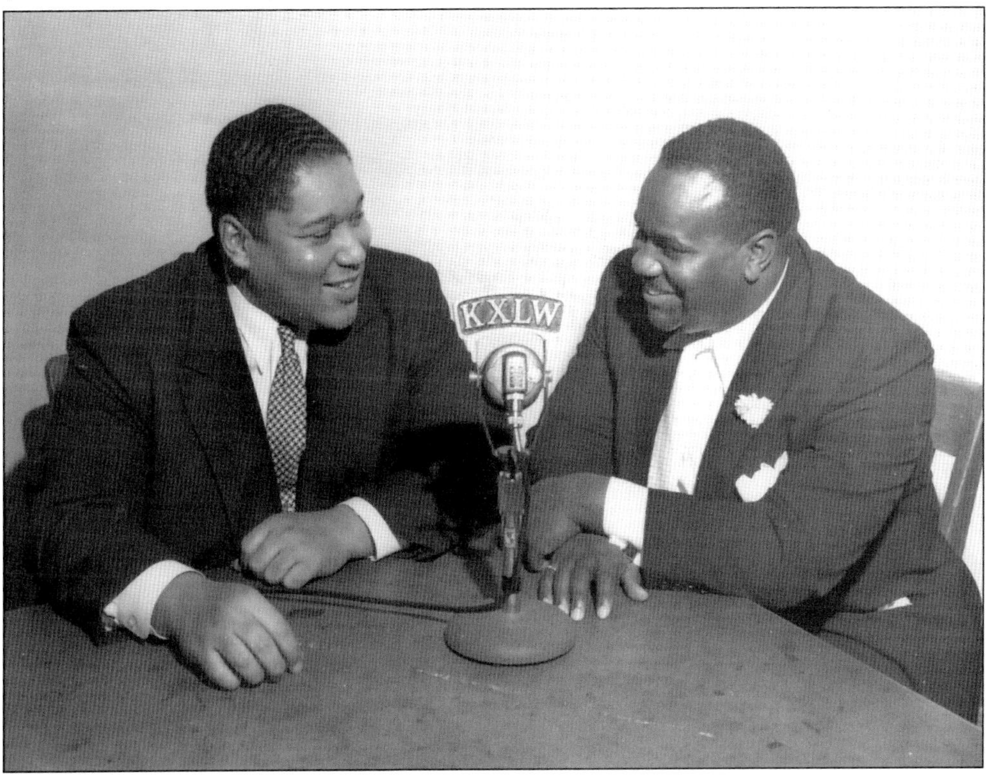

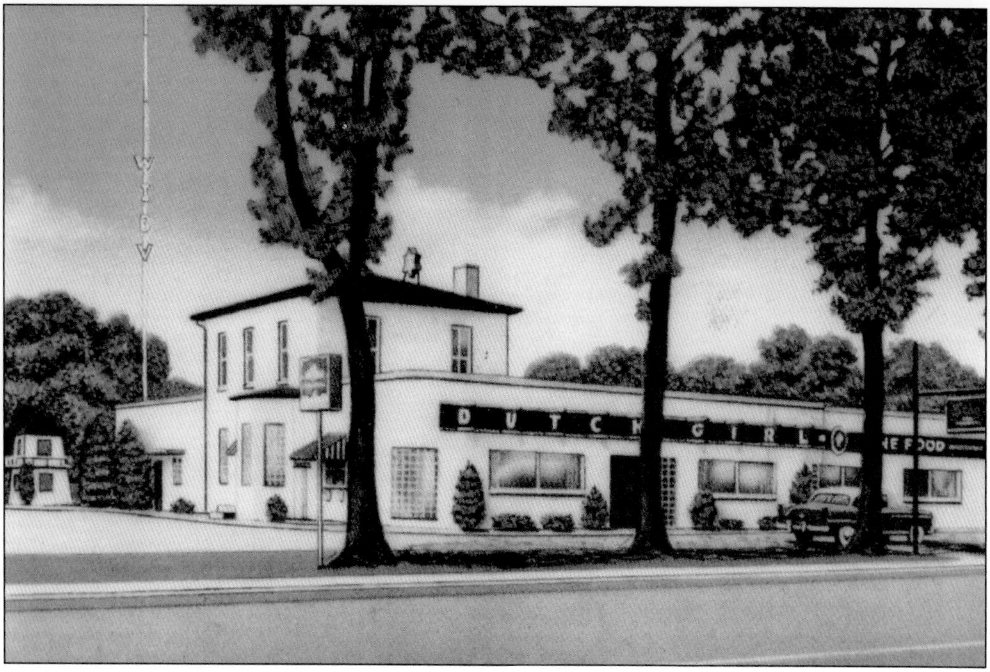

Fischer's Dutch Girl Restaurant on Belleville's Main Street was the first site of the WIBV Radio studios. Later, the station moved its studios and transmission facilities south of town, but there were still several interview programs that originated from the main dining room of the restaurant. (Jack LeChien.)

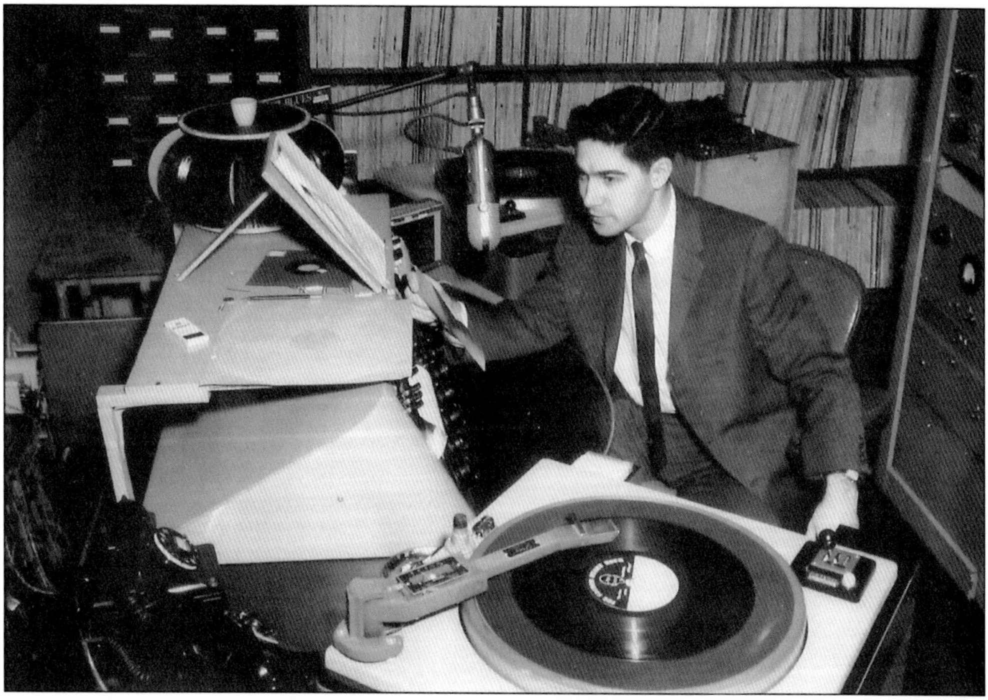

A young Norm Greenberg worked as a WIBV disc jockey, eventually rising to the general manager's job. (Jack LeChien.)

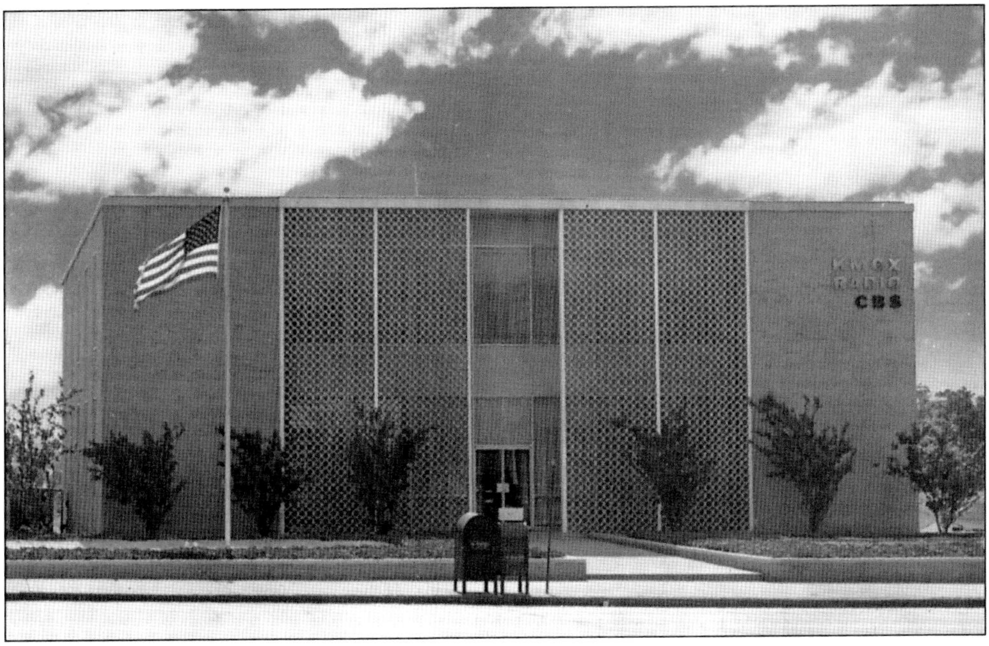

By 1959, KMOX had downsized its operation considerably. There was no longer a need for major network radio productions. The new studios were built at 1144 Hampton Avenue. (St. Louis Media Archive.)

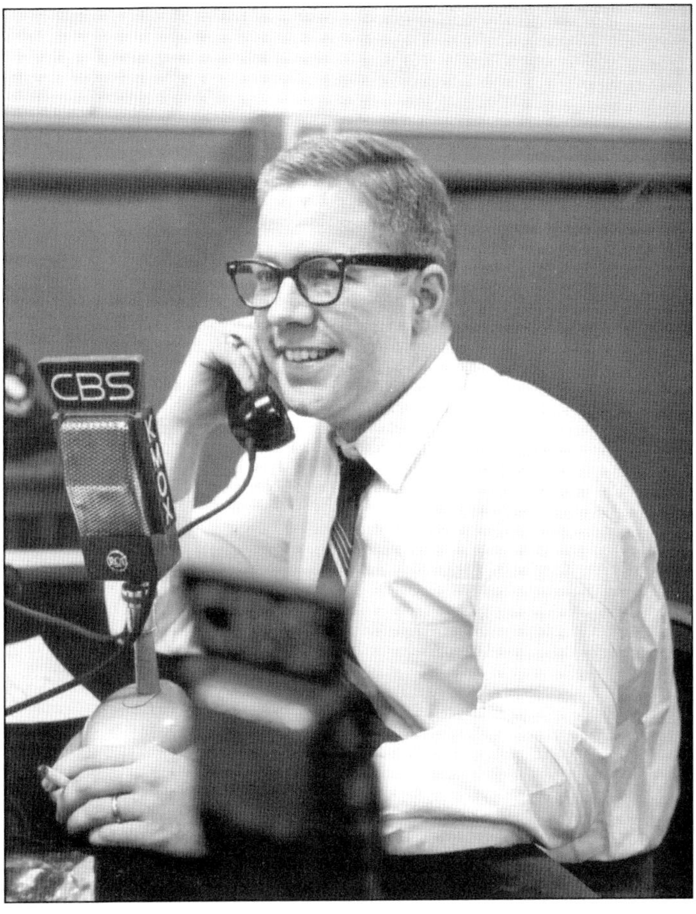

Jim Butler, the popular longtime KMOX announcer, was dubbed the "Night Mayor of St. Louis" because of his popular late-evening show. (St. Louis Media Archive.)

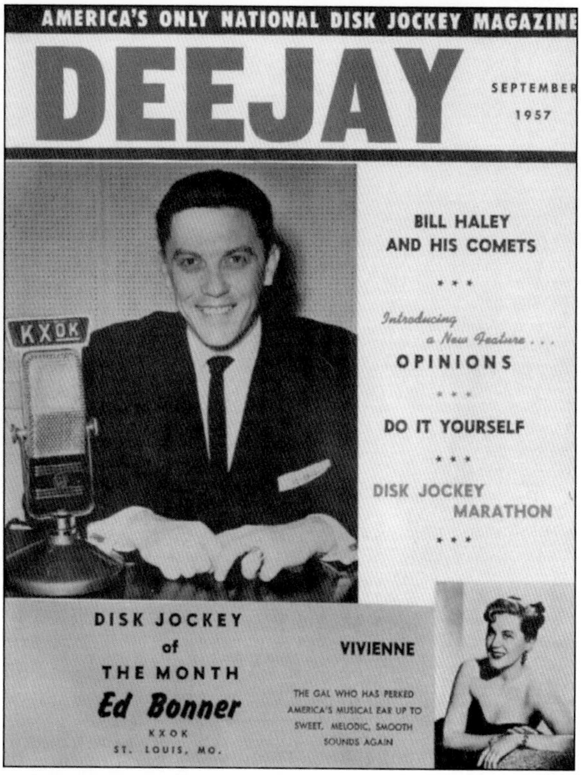

By the late 1950s, the disc jockey was a major part of nearly everyone's lives. Personality radio was the rule, and St. Louis's Ed Bonner was featured on the cover of a national trade magazine. (St. Louis Media Archive.)

Stars and would-be stars knew the value of personal appearances on the air with top DJs. Rosemary Clooney and an unidentified associate are seen here visiting with KXOK's Bruce Hayward (far right). (St. Louis Media Archive.)

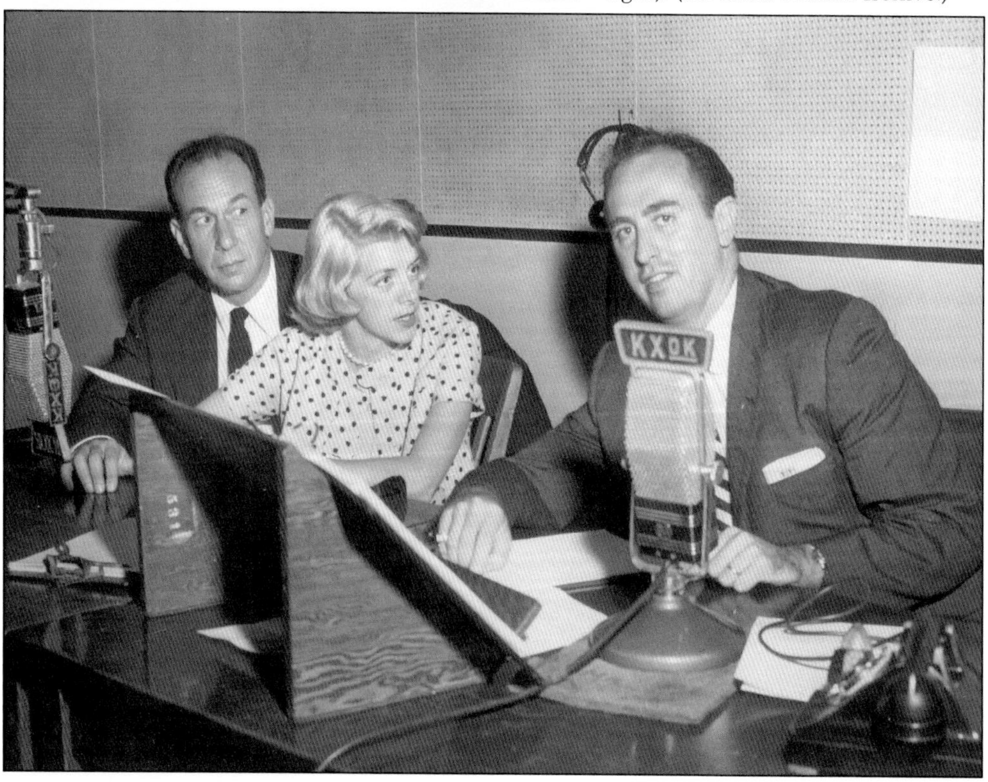

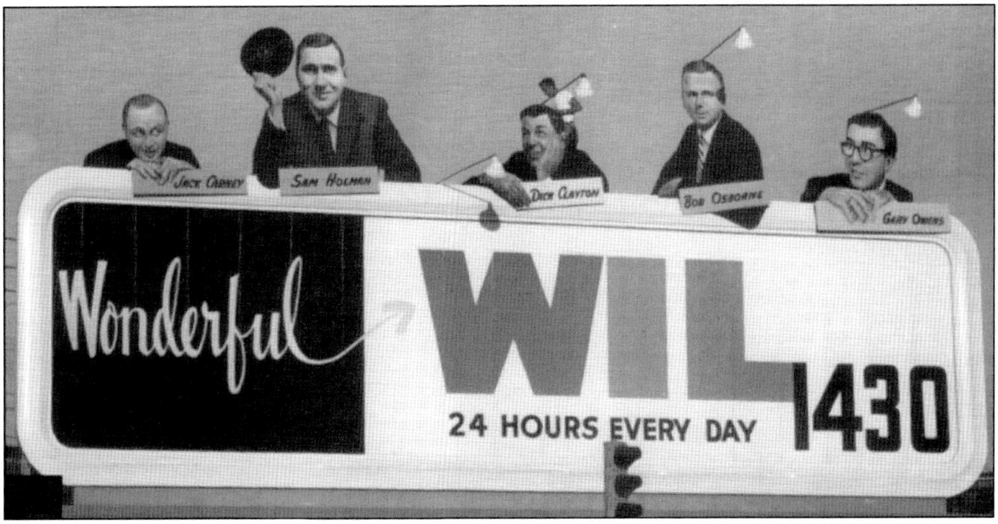

The 1958 DJ lineup on WIL included, from left to right, Jack Carney, Sam Holman, Dick Clayton, Bob Osborne, and Gary Owens. Within a couple years, they had all been hired away by other radio stations. (St. Louis Media Archive.)

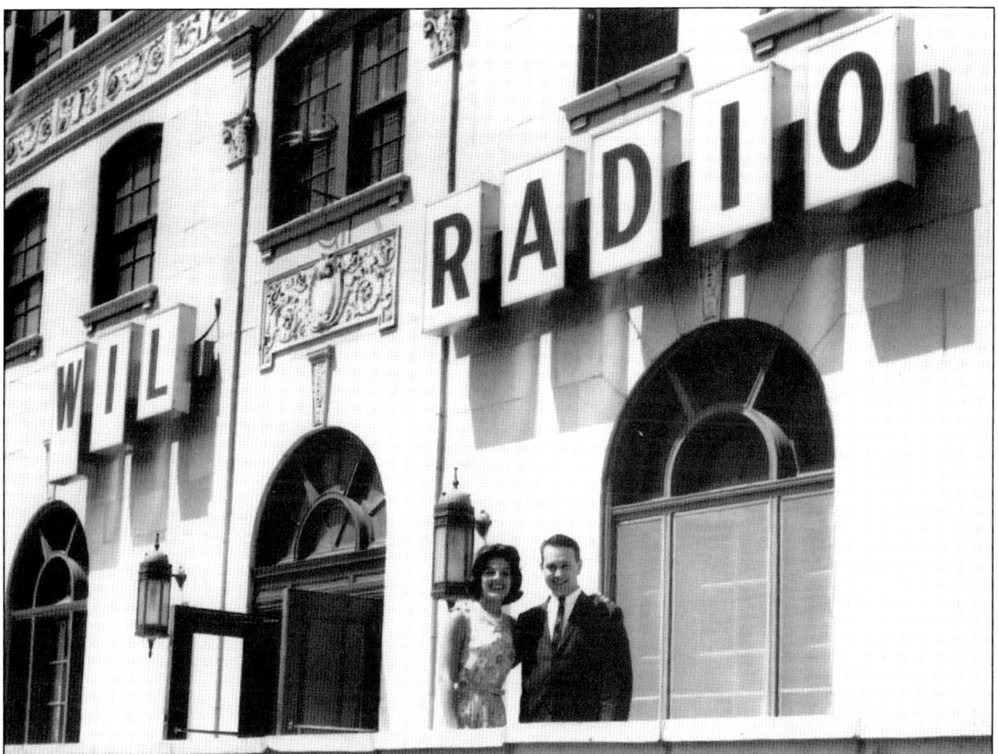

The WIL studios were housed in the basement of the Coronado Hotel on Lindell Boulevard. A station executive is seen in front of the building with recording star Anita Bryant. (St. Louis Media Archive.)

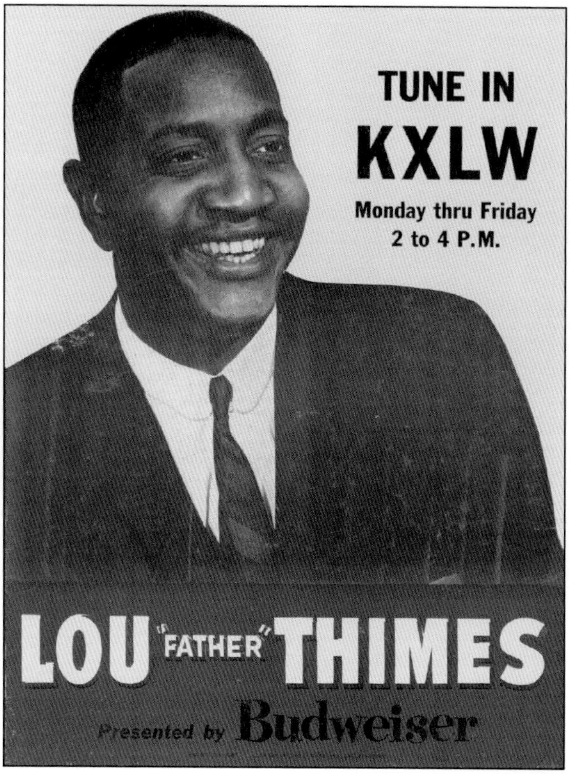

By now, the slightly derogatory term "race radio" was gone, and national advertisers knew the value of targeting all audiences. This poster promoting one of KXLW's most popular personalities illustrates how the beer brand cross-promoted the radio show in local taverns. (Dwayne Marburger.)

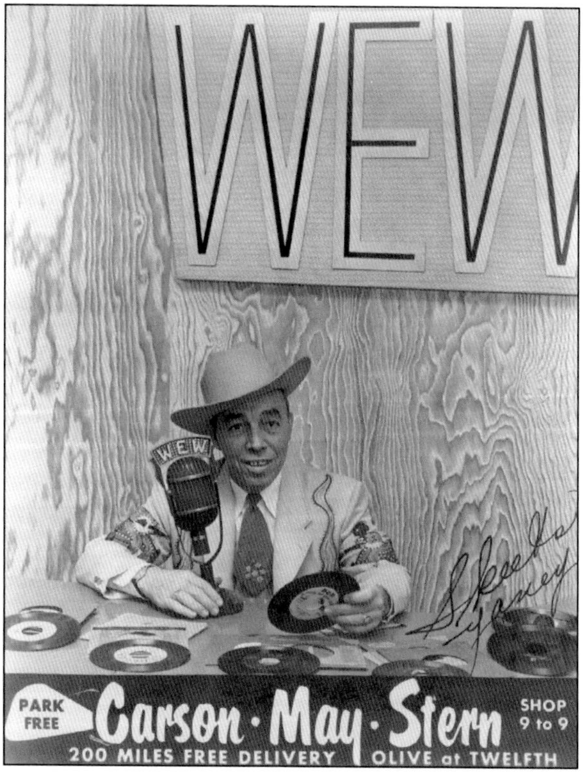

Once a full-fledged hillbilly musician/celebrity, Skeets Yaney was able to continue his radio work as a country and western disc jockey when live music performances were phased out of radio. (St. Louis Media Archive.)

The KXOK studios moved out of downtown after the station was sold by the *Star-Times*, landing at a site on North Kingshighway dubbed "Radio Park." The building became a mecca of sorts for kids who wanted to drop in to watch their favorite disc jockeys at work. Newsmen Bob Shea (left) and Bill Murphy pose next to the news car in the circular driveway. (St. Louis Media Archive.)

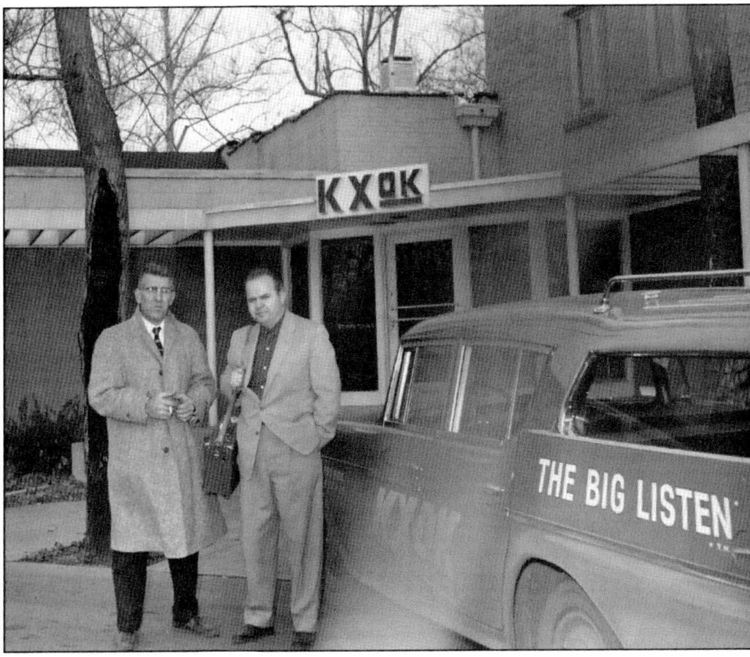

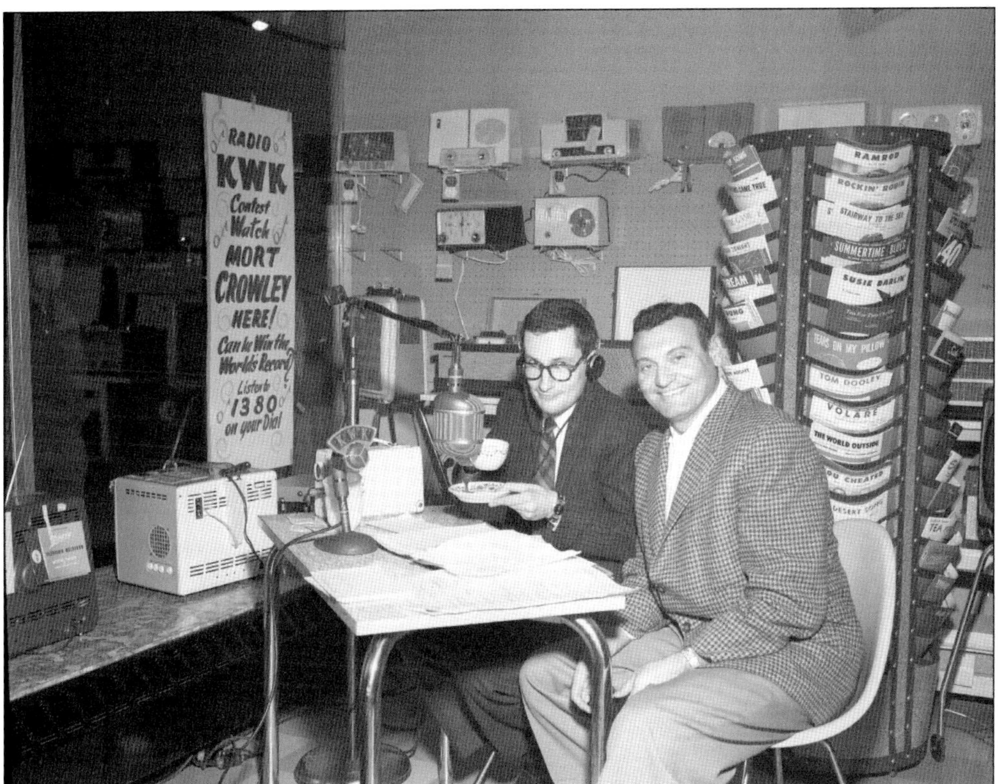

KWK also went the personality route with DJs like Mort Crowley, shown here on the left at a remote broadcast with singer Frankie Laine. (St. Louis Media Archive.)

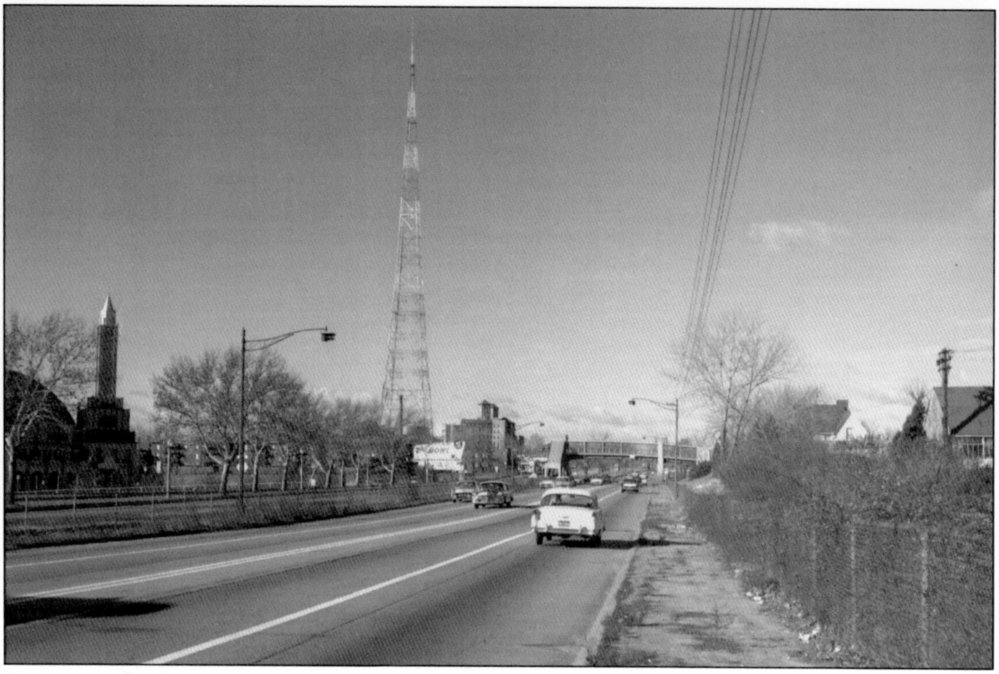

Drivers on the Daniel Boone Expressway (Highway 40) in the late 1950s had this view of the new 575-foot KTVI-TV tower at the Hampton Avenue interchange. One of the two matching towers on the entrances to the St. Louis Arena is seen at the far left. (Joe Sonderman.)

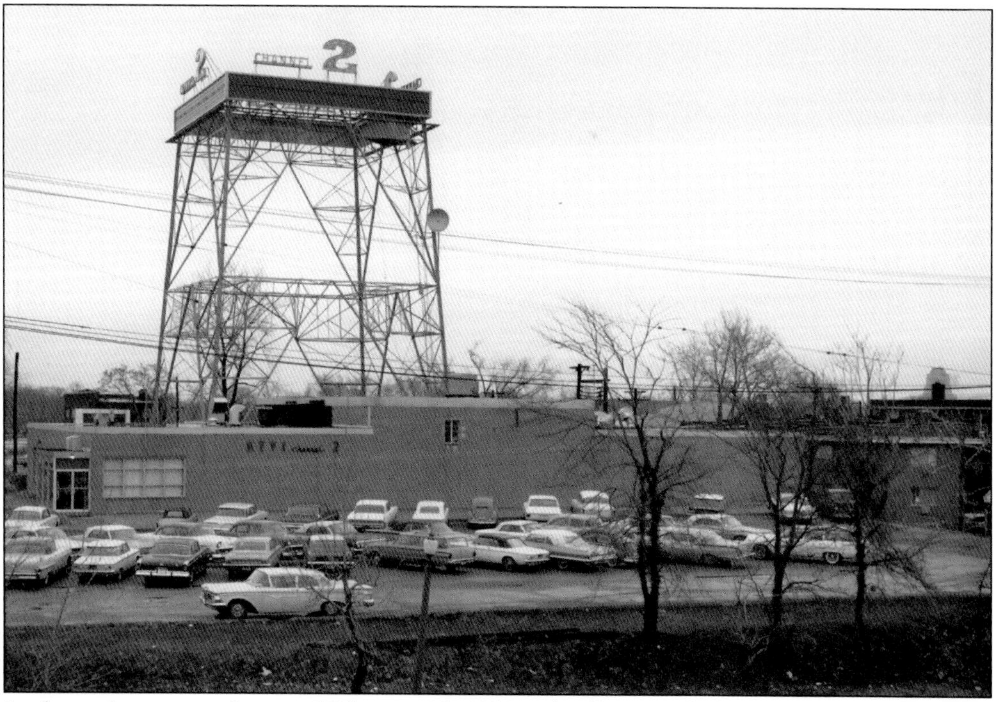

In the early morning hours of February 10, 1959, a deadly tornado hit St. Louis, toppling the KTVI tower. The base remained in place next to the studio building for over 20 years. (KTVI-TV archives.)

A couple of St. Louis radio stations stood out because they were not playing "popular" music. KCFM, one of very few stations on the local FM dial in 1960, promoted a "beautiful music" format. (St. Louis Media Archive.)

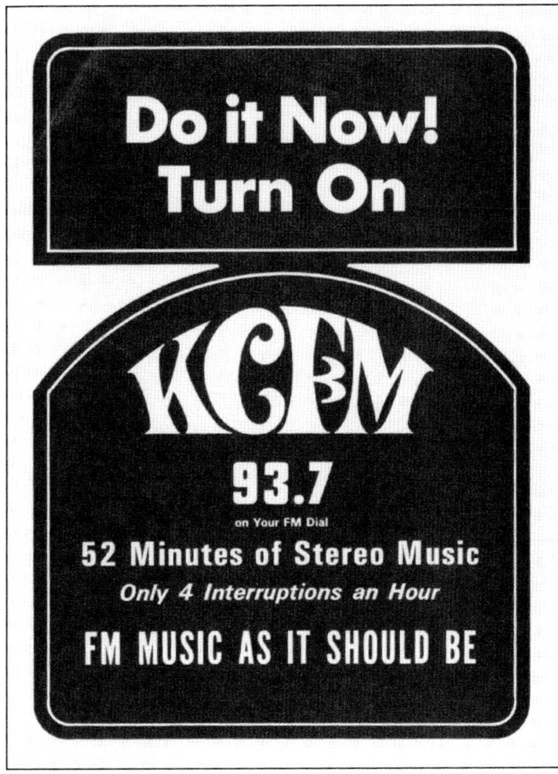

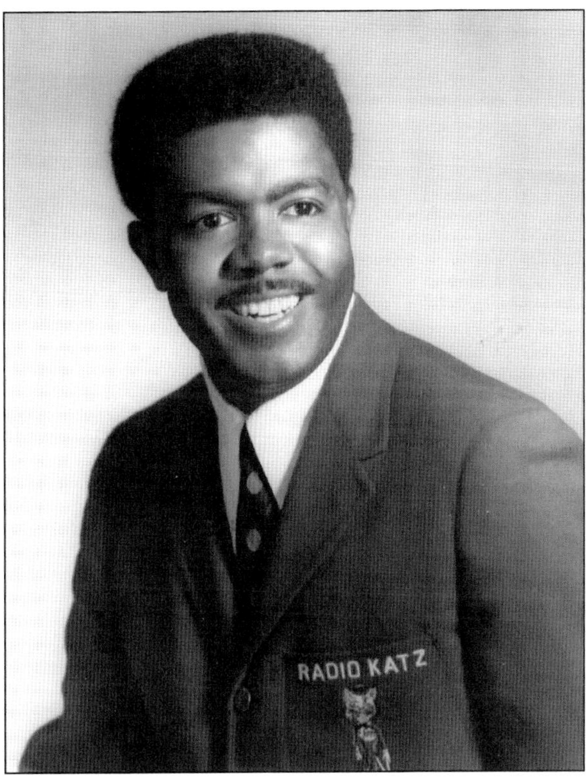

Doug Eason was a personality on KATZ. Well liked, Eason was given the nickname "the Leprechaun" by co-workers. Later, he became the station's manager. (St. Louis Media Archive.)

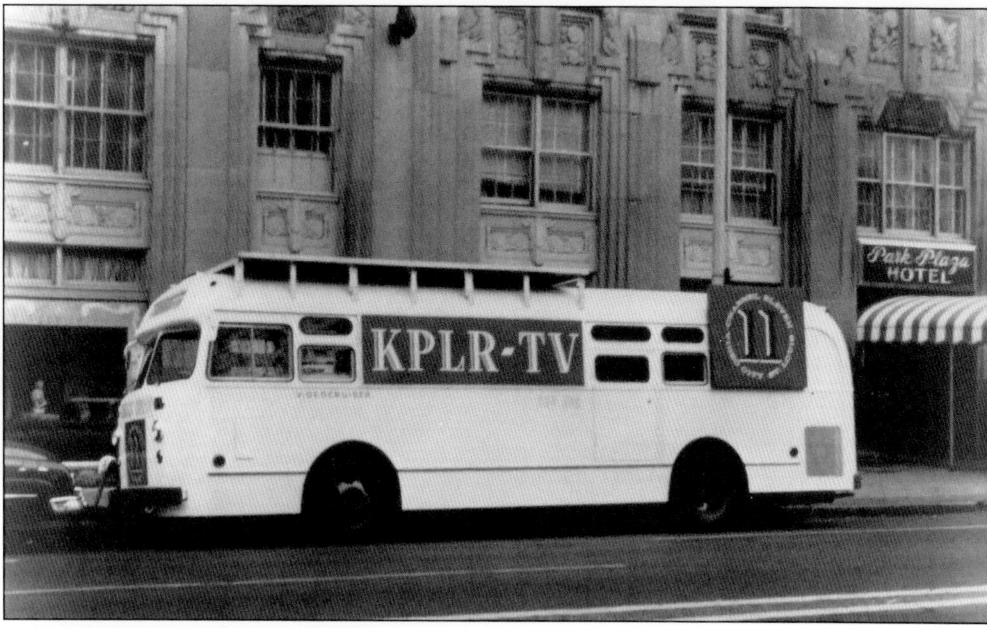

In 1960, KPLR-TV fielded a mobile production unit improving the station's capability of producing on-site broadcasts. It was also used by the station's commercial production division to provide location shots. (KPLR-TV archives.)

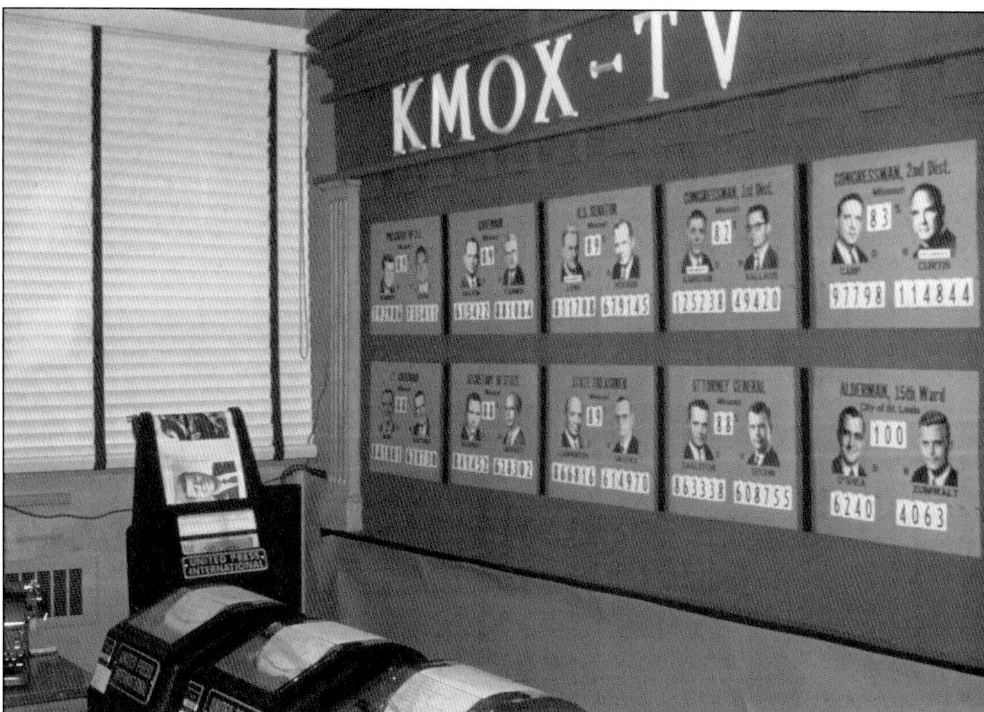

The technical gimmicks seen today had not yet invaded television in 1960. For the elections that year, KMOX-TV constructed this set to show vote totals. (Spencer Allen family archives.)

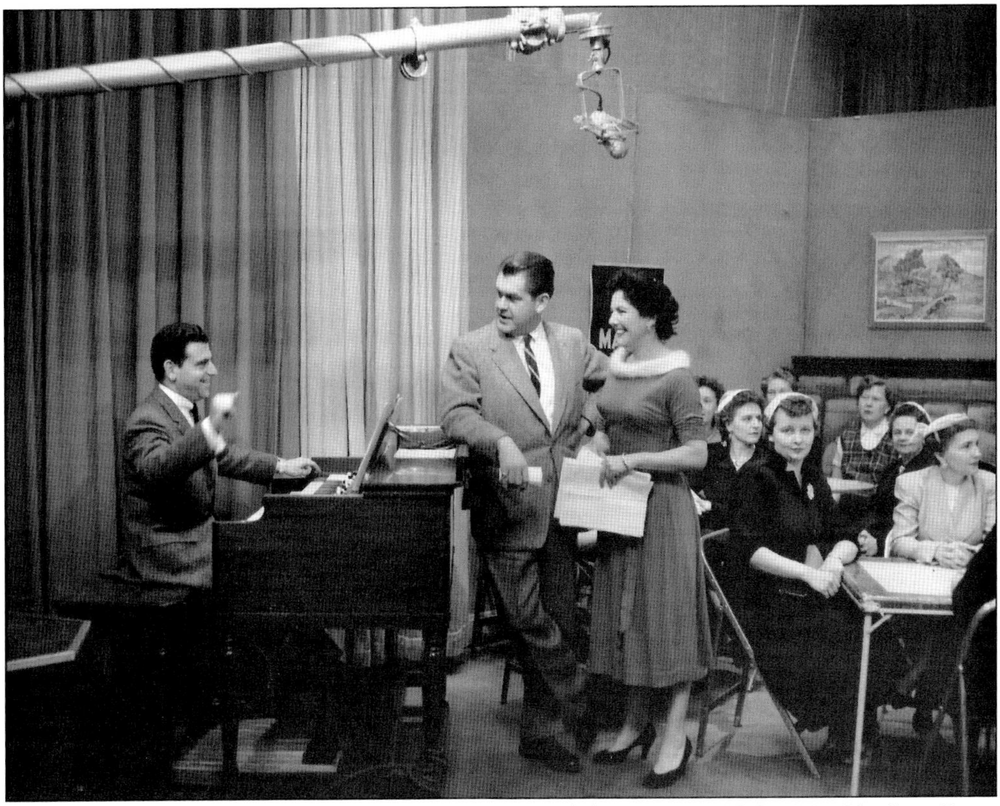

One of the most popular women's television shows of the time was KSD-TV's *Charlotte Peters Show*. Stan Kann is shown at the organ and John Roedel is the announcer. Roedel later joked that it was a full-time job trying to rein in the creative Ms. Peters (to the right of Roedel). (St. Louis Media Archive.)

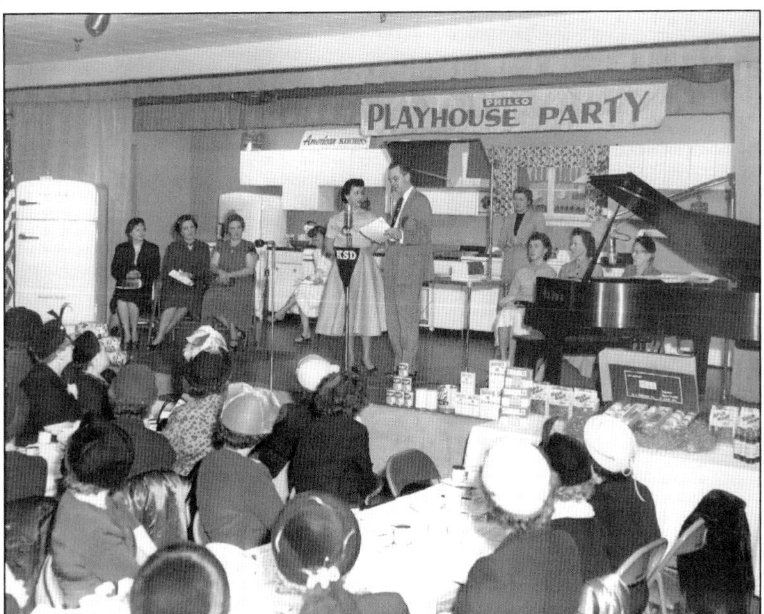

KSD's Russ David had the top women's radio show, the *Playhouse Party*, which was broadcast live each weekday. Audience participation was a large part of each day's show. (Sue Dorn.)

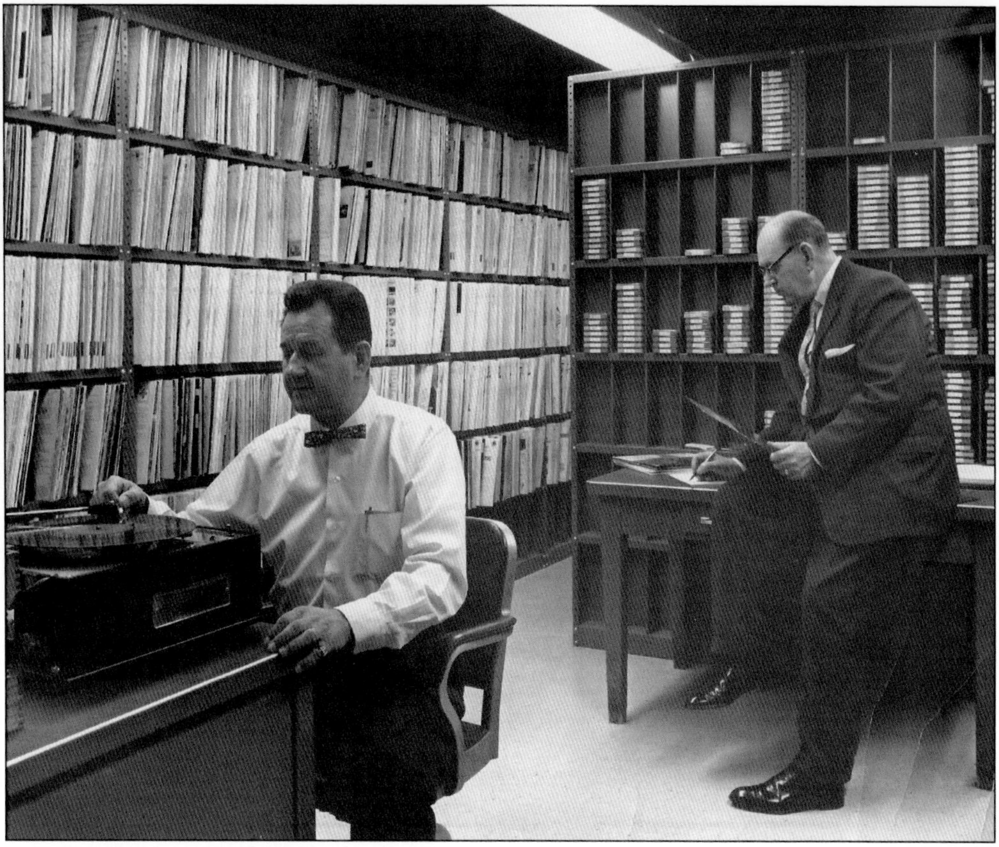

For many years, all the songs played on the radio were chosen and scheduled by someone other than the announcers. Every radio station had a record library, where staffers cataloged and cross-referenced every recording. Shown in KSD's library are Charlie Novak (left) and John Piskulic. (St. Louis Media Archive.)

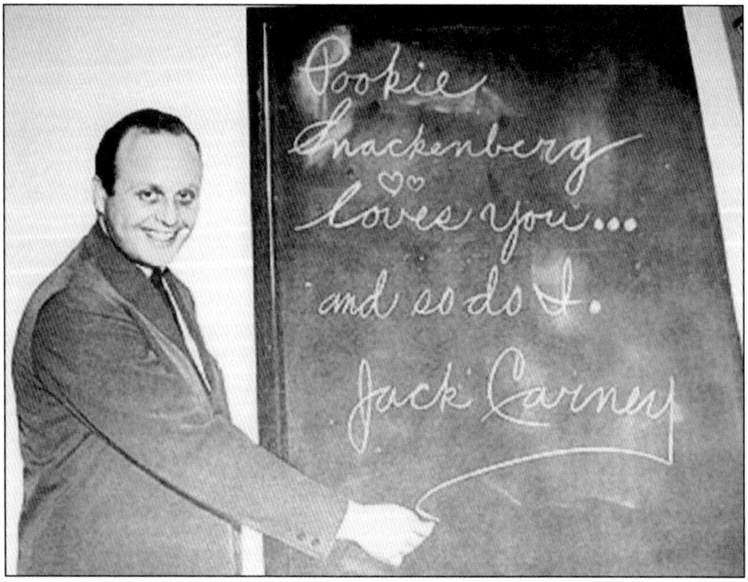

Jack Carney, who was WIL's morning DJ, once conducted a promotion involving the fictional character Pooky Snackenberg. He left WIL after a of couple years but returned and gained national prominence as a top-rated program host on KMOX. (St. Louis Media Archive.)

Five

Entering the 1960s

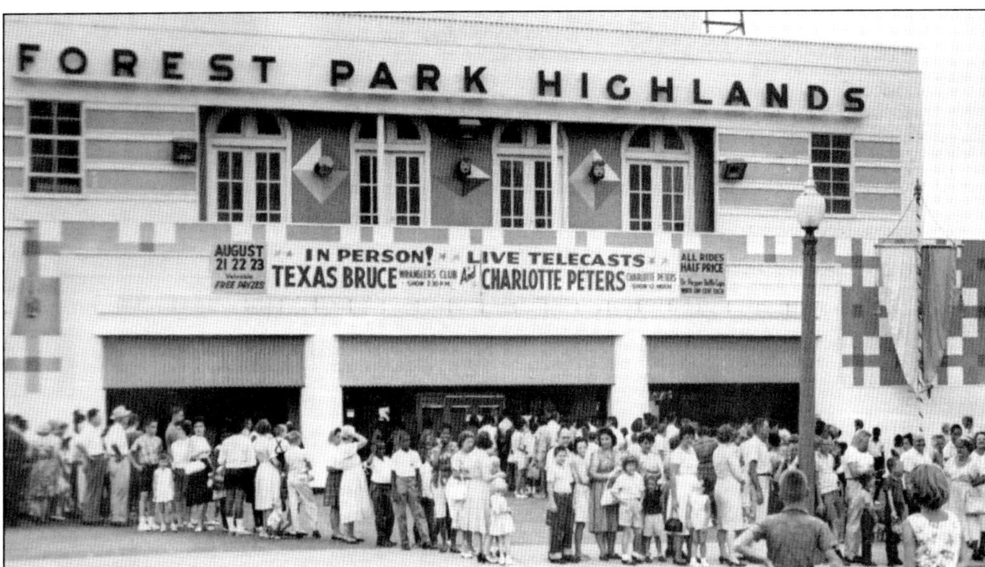

No one could have predicted how tumultuous the 1960s would be in the United States, especially if radio and television were being used as a barometer. Broadcasting seemed to be on an upward swing at the beginning of the decade. It would become the decade of the local media personality: radio stations promoted their disc jockeys, and television stations offered their on-air staff members for personal appearances like this one at Forest Park Highlands. (St. Louis Media Archive.)

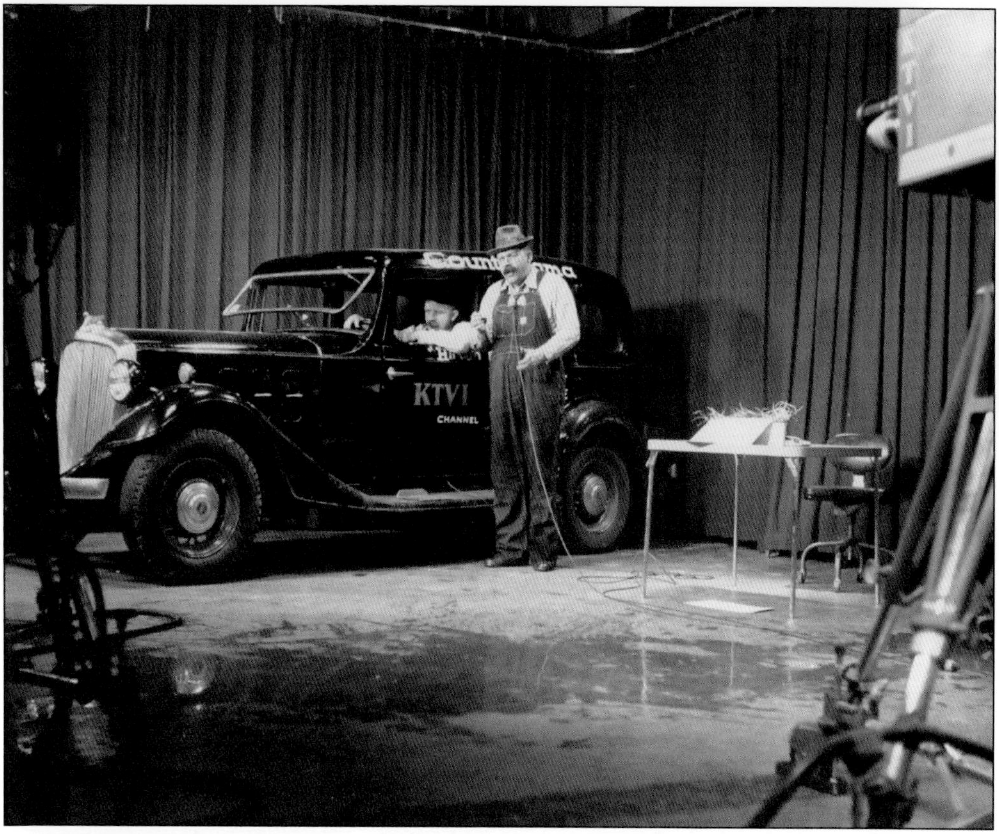

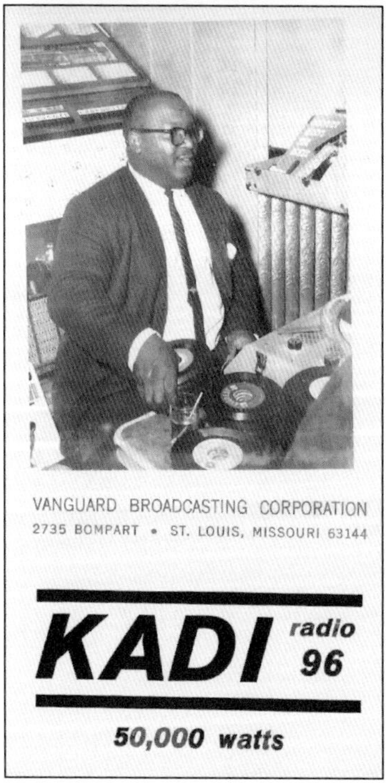

Jack Murdock was one of the market's most prolific television character actors. He is seen standing in character on KTVI's *Jack Murdock Show*. (St. Louis Media Archive.)

Leo Chears, "the man in the red vest," was heard on KADI-FM in the mid-1960s. He later gained a loyal following as the market's top jazz disc jockey. (St. Louis Media Archive.)

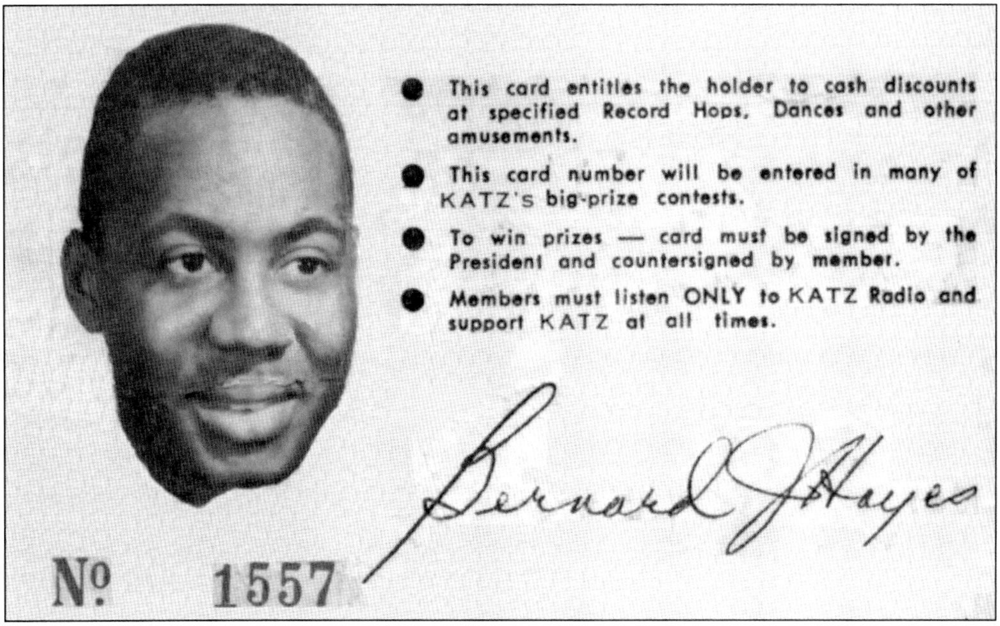

Fans of Bernie Hayes on KATZ were encouraged to write in for this special card, which would give them discounts on purchases. (St. Louis Media Archive.)

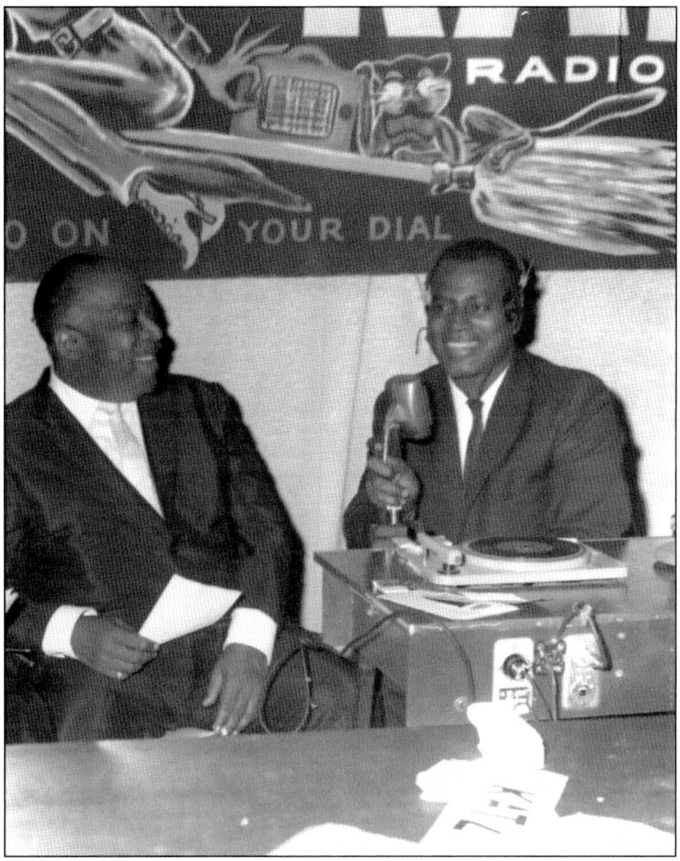

Top musicians made a sincere effort to connect with their fans by personally visiting top radio personalities in the nation's larger radio markets. Count Basie (on the left) is seen chatting at an on-air remote with KATZ personality Robert BQ. (St. Louis Media Archive.)

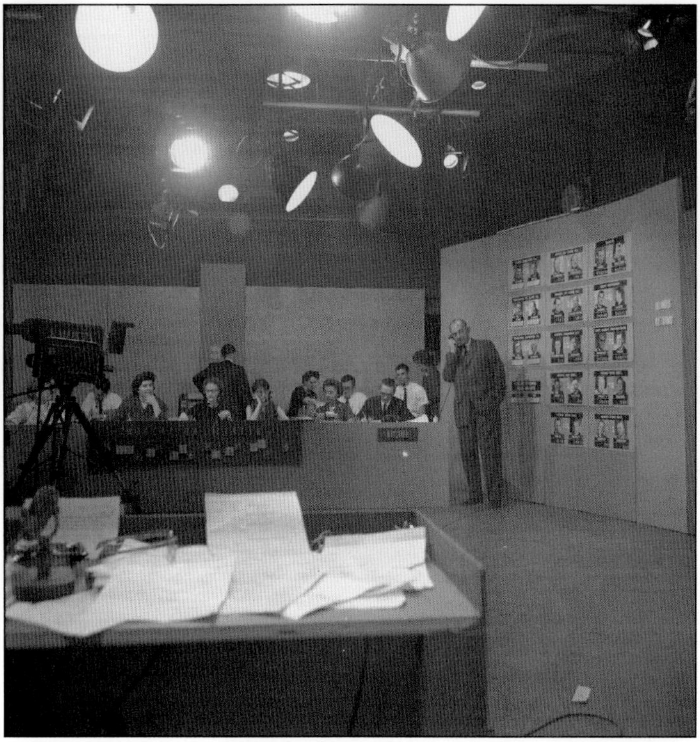

Spencer Allen is shown taking a call on the set prior to airtime during KMOX-TV's 1962 election coverage. The studio was the former KWK-TV facility at Twelfth and Cole Streets. (KMOX-TV Collection, Missouri History Museum.)

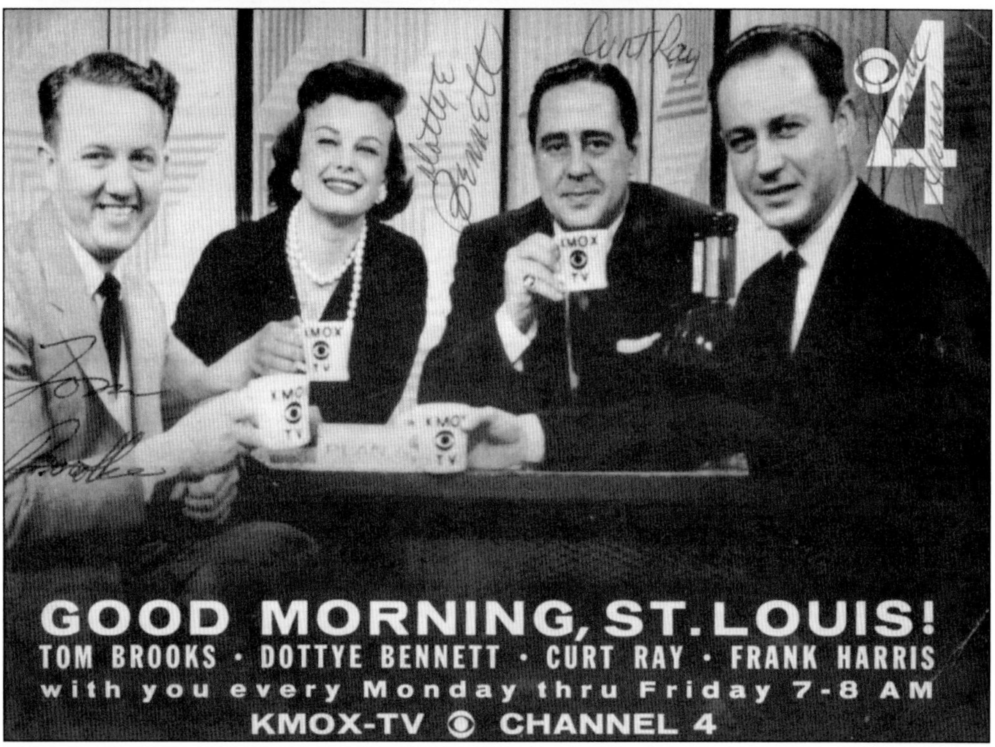

Viewers who wrote in requesting autographed photographs of personalities on the KMOX-TV morning show received this card. (St. Louis Media Archive.)

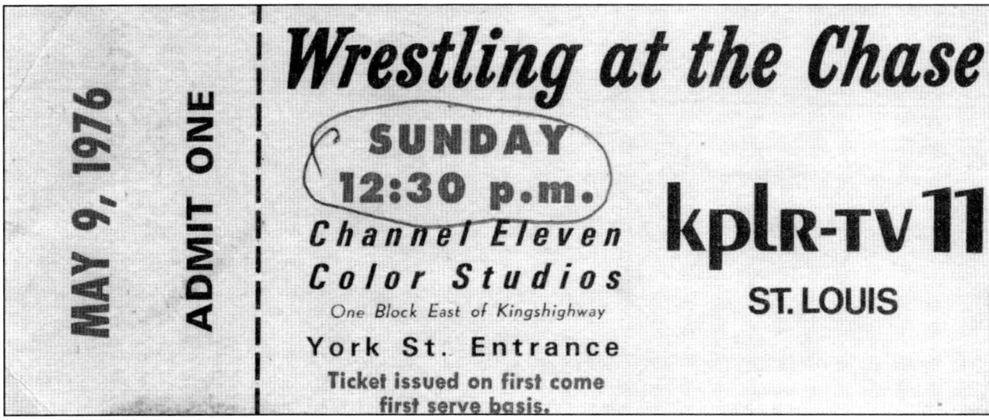

Through its entire run on KPLR-TV, *Wrestling at the Chase* had a large cult following. Joe Garagiola was one of the hosts of the weekly program. (St. Louis Media Archive.)

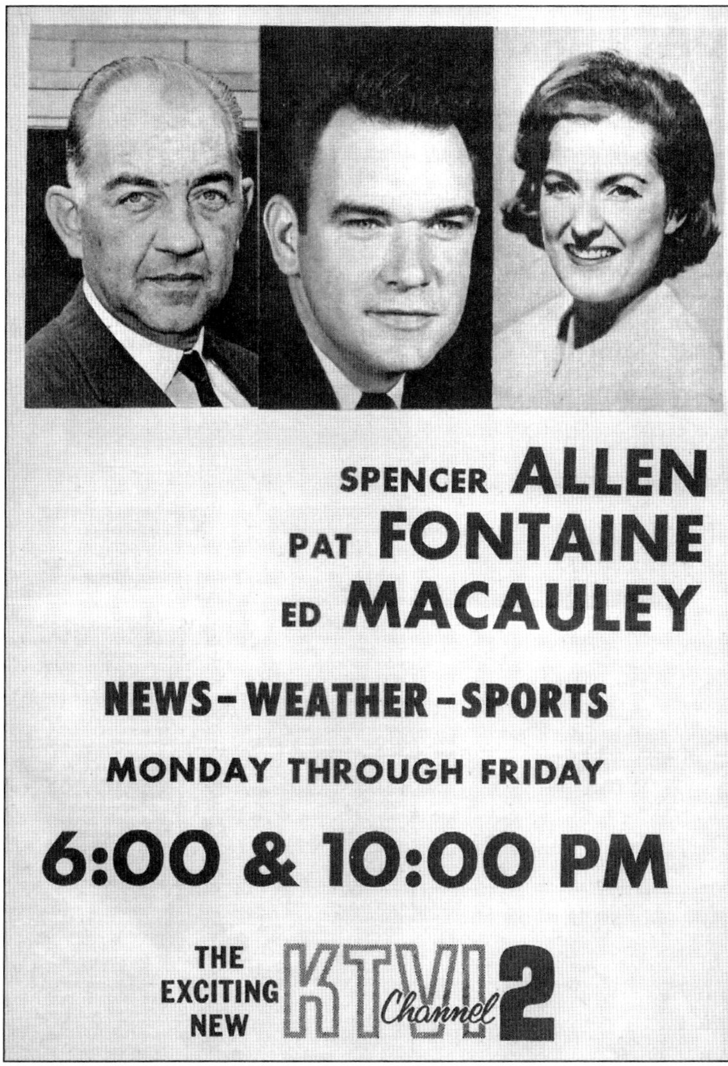

In what was seen by some as a major talent shuffle, newsman Spencer Allen (left) was hired away from KMOX-TV. KTVI also brought back Pat Fontaine, a veteran of KSD-TV, for its broadcast team. (St. Louis Media Archive.)

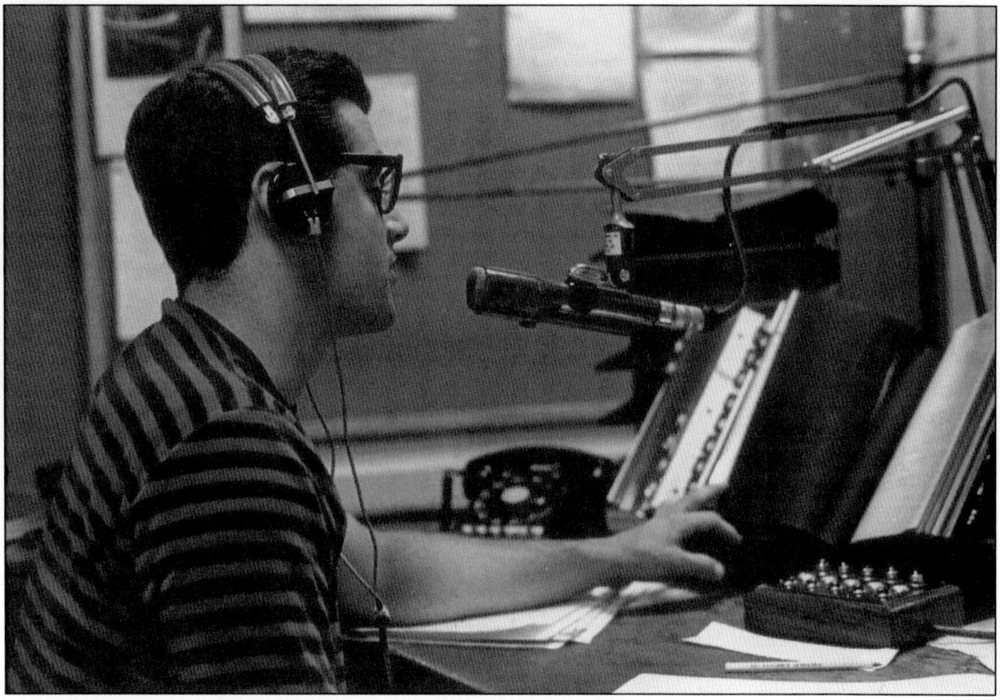

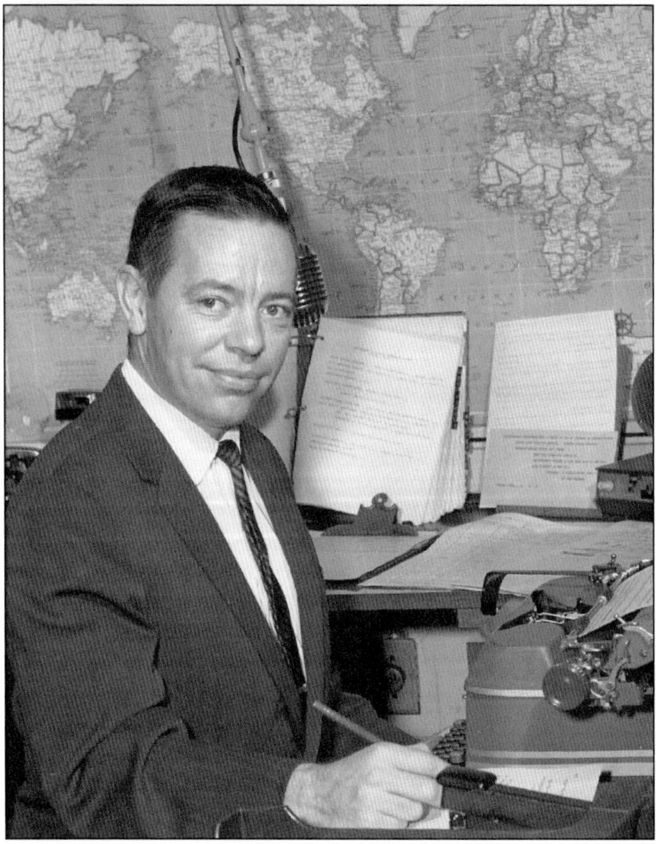

Disc jockey Ray Otis worked at KXOK from 1962 to 1970. He is remembered for his long stint as the station's morning announcer. (St. Louis Media Archive.)

Robert R. Lynn began working as a newsman at KXOK in 1959 and stayed for 20 years before moving to KMOX. He was also heard as a voice-over talent on many commercials. (St. Louis Media Archive.)

Don Pietromonaco was KXOK's memorable "Johnny Rabbitt," heard weeknights in the '60s. St. Louis teenagers had a visible love affair with this man, who ruled the city's nighttime airwaves. Pietromonaco, as Rabbitt, is remembered by hundreds of people today for his creativity and humor. (St. Louis Media Archive.)

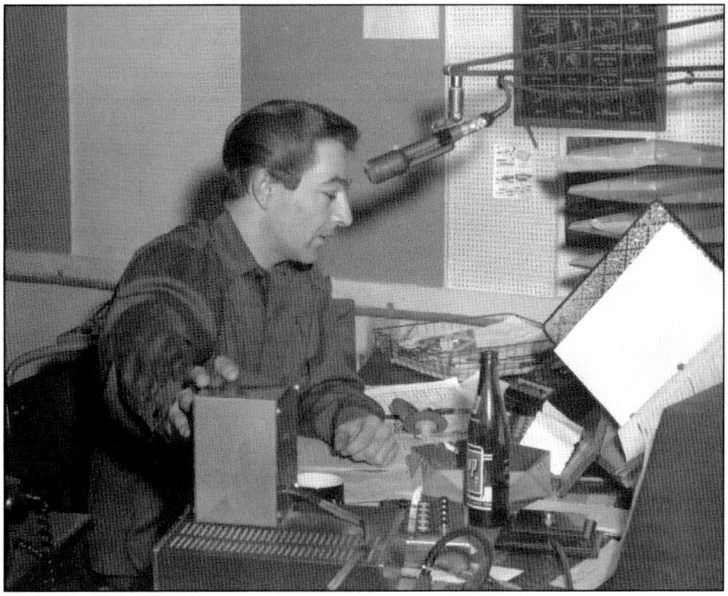

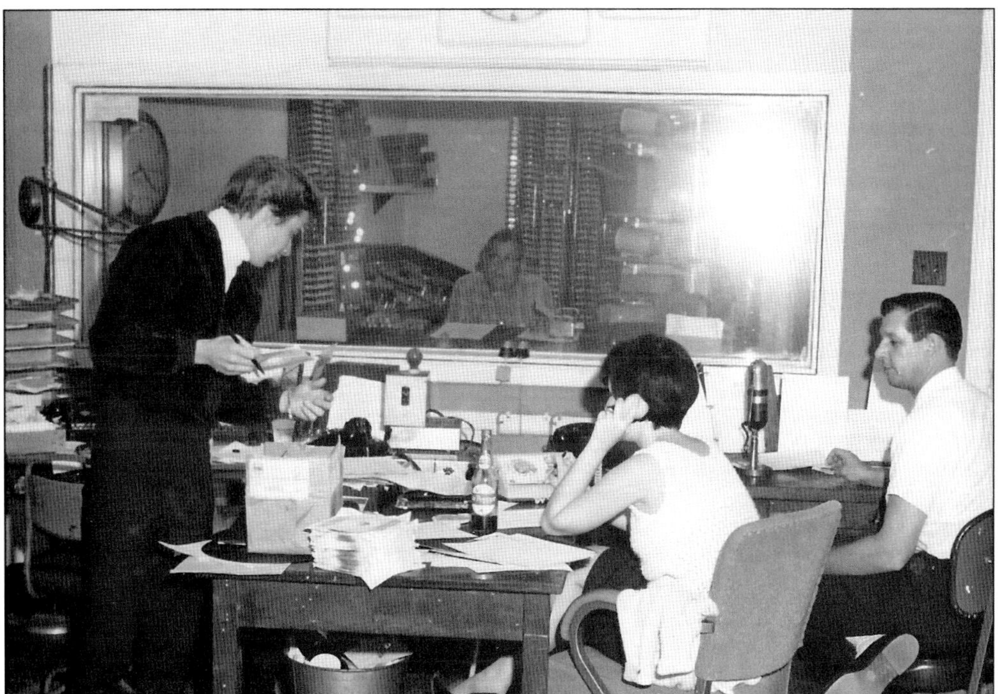

In this studio shot of the *Johnny Rabbitt Show*, newsman Dan Allison is seen on the right, and Linda Rauchelbach, who was KXOK's "Kay," was responsible for answering phones. Recording artist Bobby Sherman is standing. (St. Louis Media Archive.)

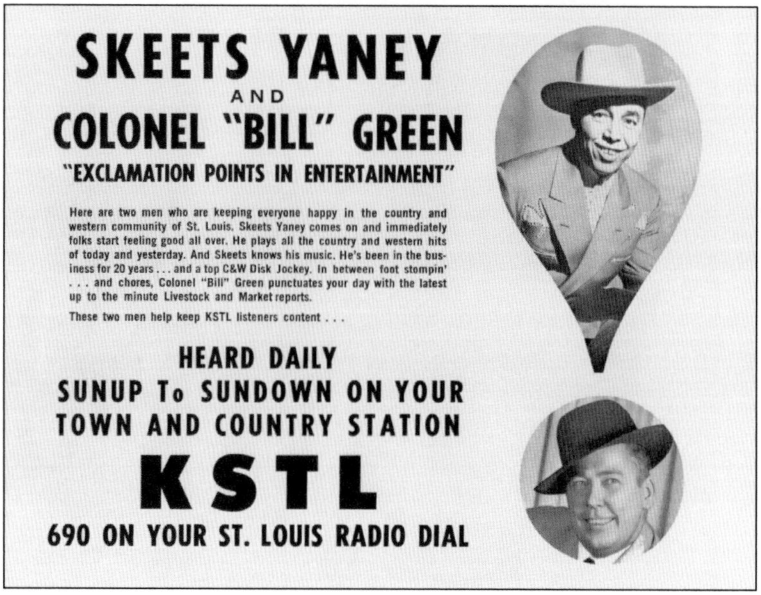

The slogan, "Your town and country station," succinctly describes KSTL's approach to programming in the 1960s. (St. Louis Media Archive.)

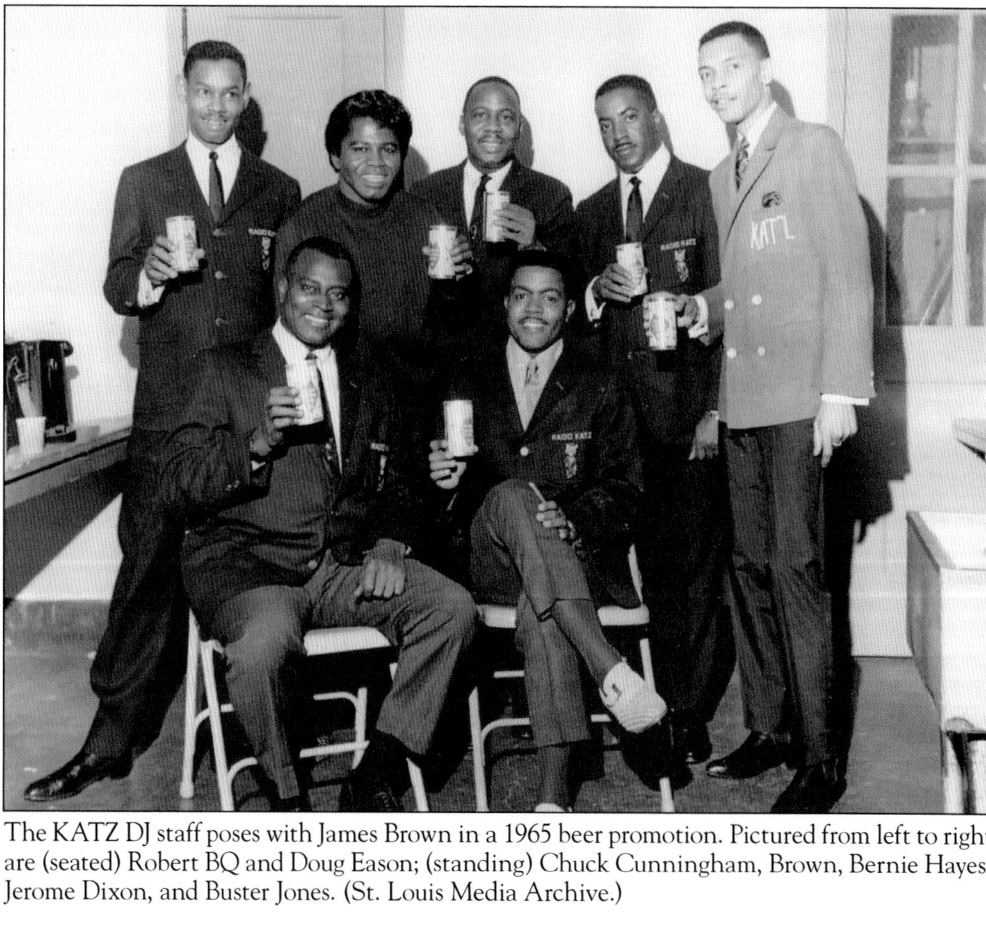

The KATZ DJ staff poses with James Brown in a 1965 beer promotion. Pictured from left to right are (seated) Robert BQ and Doug Eason; (standing) Chuck Cunningham, Brown, Bernie Hayes, Jerome Dixon, and Buster Jones. (St. Louis Media Archive.)

In 1967, KMOX ran this advertisement in *Prom*, a local magazine for teens. The station made an effort to divorce itself from the belief that only old people listened to it, stressing the appeal of baseball to local teenagers. (St. Louis Media Archive.)

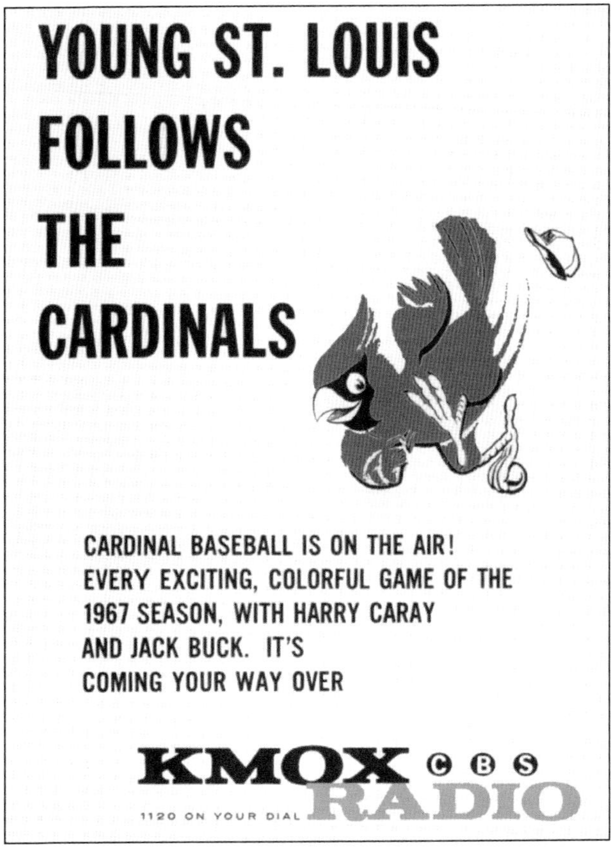

Joseph Pulitzer's KSD switched its emphasis away from NBC, whose network programming had been almost completely phased out by the 1960s. Instead, listeners got strong local personalities on the station, like Grant Horton (right), who is seen with traffic reporter Don Miller. (St. Louis Media Archive.)

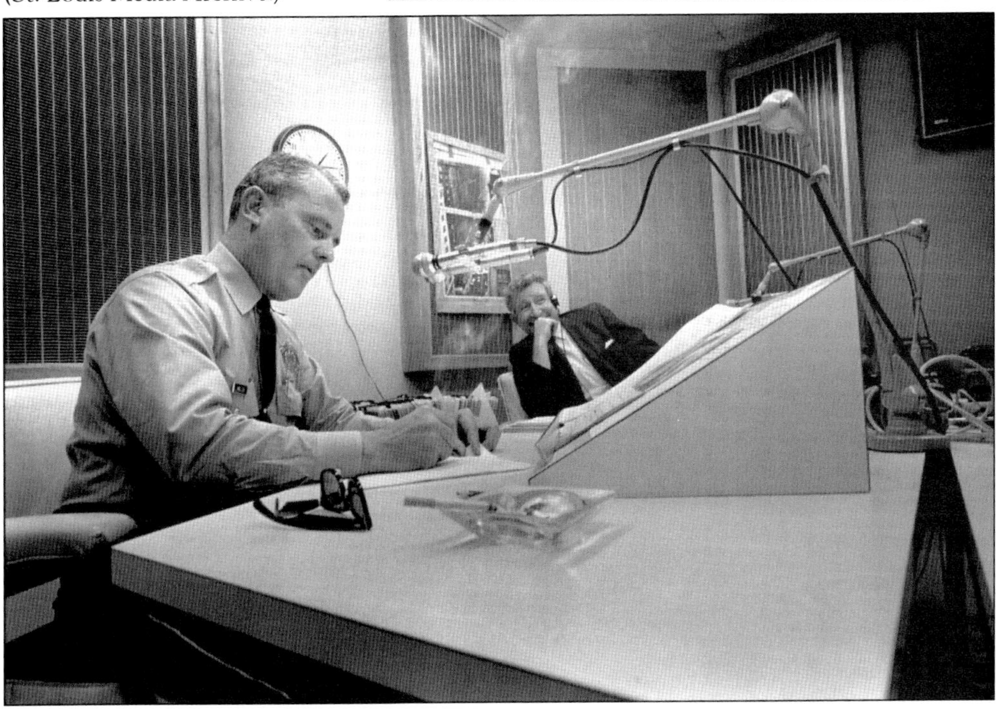

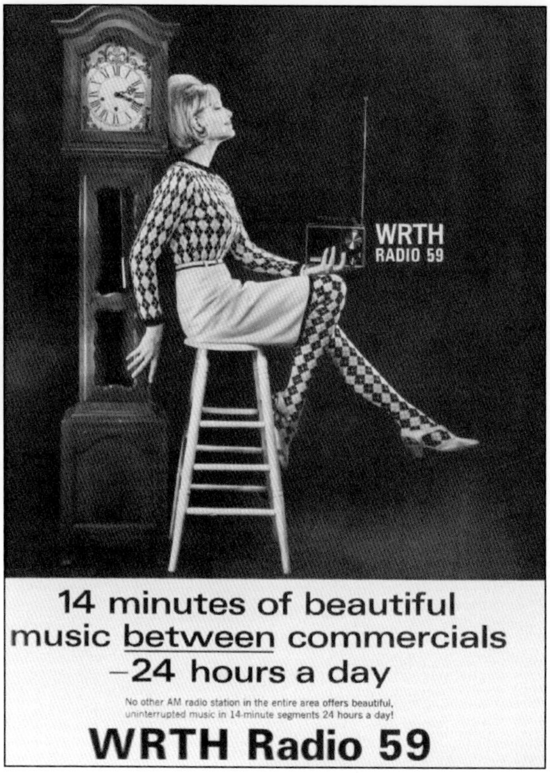

Another local AM station, WRTH, which was licensed to Wood River, Illinois, opted to place programming emphasis on the music and minimize personality involvement. (St. Louis Media Archive.)

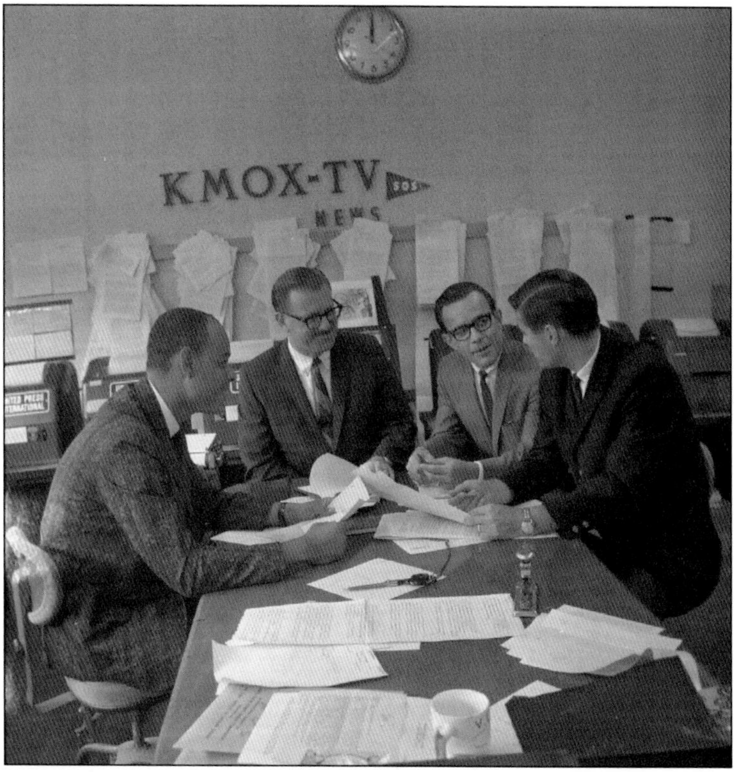

In television, the 1960s represented a major expansion of local news efforts. Stations like KMOX-TV assembled a team of professionals including, from left to right, Harry Porterfield, Max Roby, Jim Kincaid, and Les Carmichael. (KMOX-TV Collection, Missouri History Museum.)

Six

KIDS' TELEVISION IN ST. LOUIS

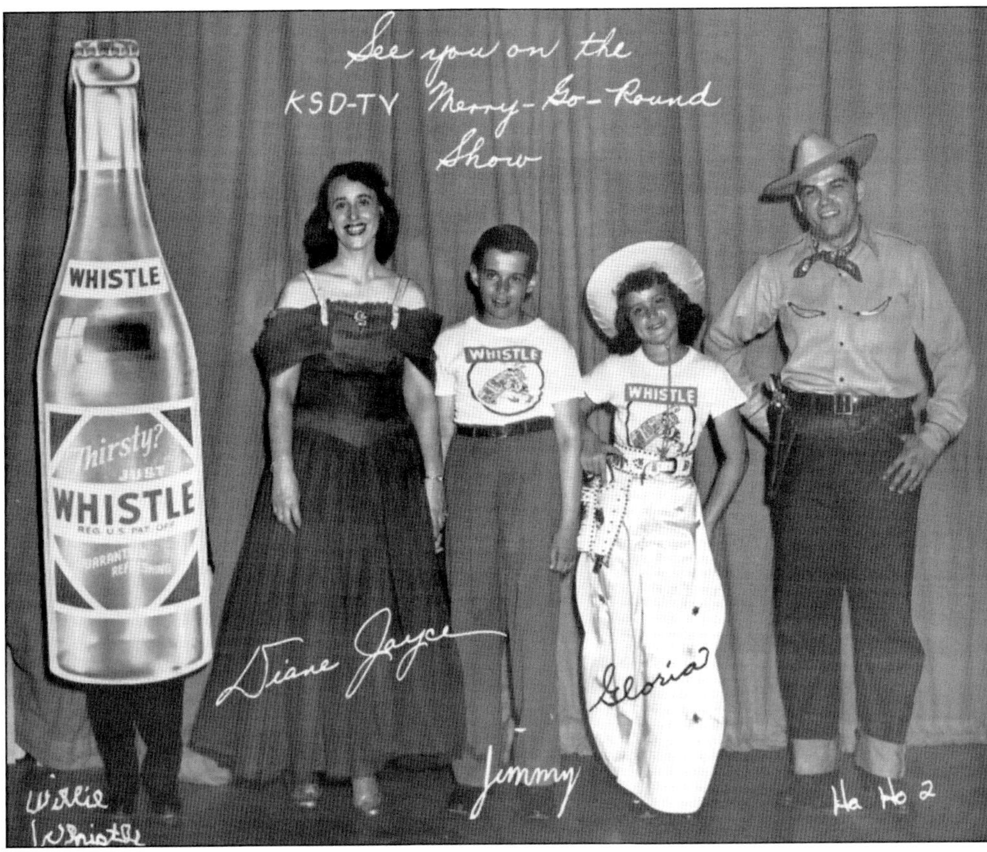

Children's programs had long been a staple of electronic media. Radio programs originating at the networks and the local stations often directly involved members of their young audience. As television developed, the same principle was used. One of the early children's television programs in the 1950s in St. Louis was hosted by Diane Joyce, who had been doing the same job on the radio using the air name Janet Dailey. Her co-host, "Ha-Ho," was Harry Honig. (Dr. Wayne Brasler.)

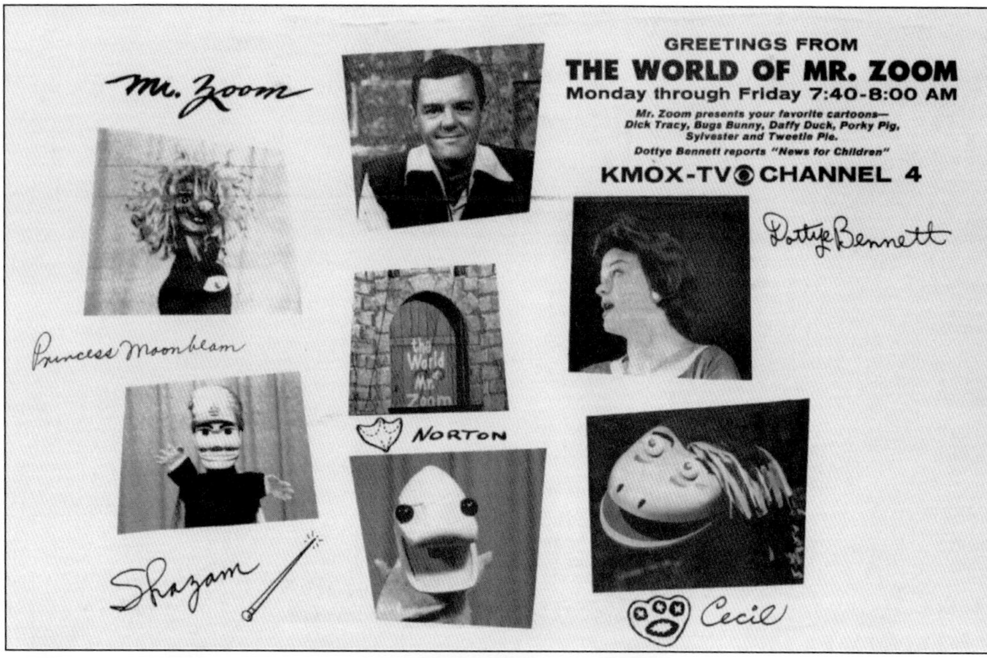

The *Mr. Zoom* show on KMOX-TV in the 1960s was a mix of favorite kids' cartoons and puppets, along with news for kids presented by Dottye Bennett. (St. Louis Media Archive.)

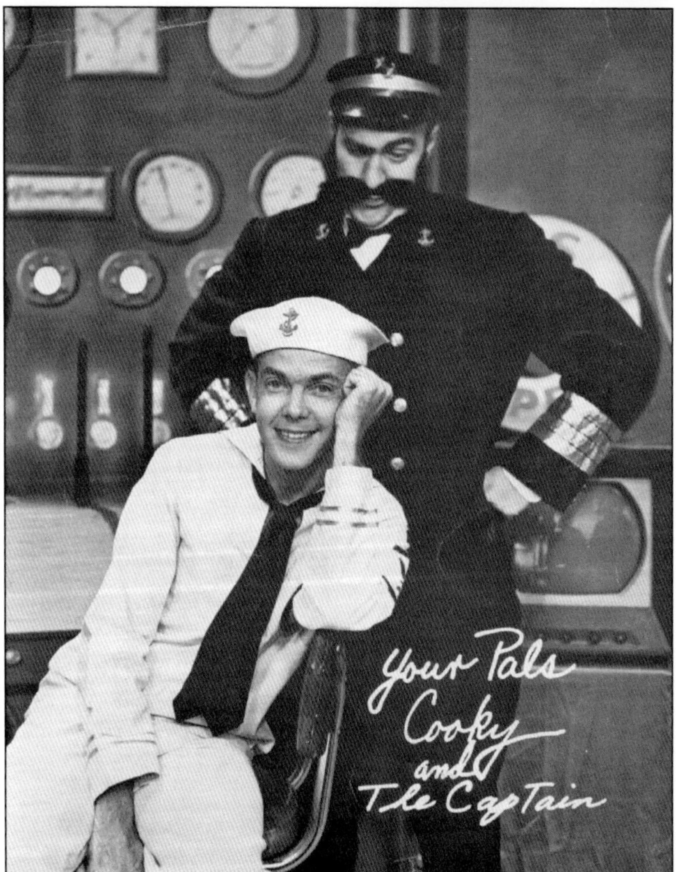

The favorite KMOX-TV kids' show was *Cooky and the Captain*, featuring the Captain (Dave Allen) and Cooky (Jim Bolen). (St. Louis Media Archive.)

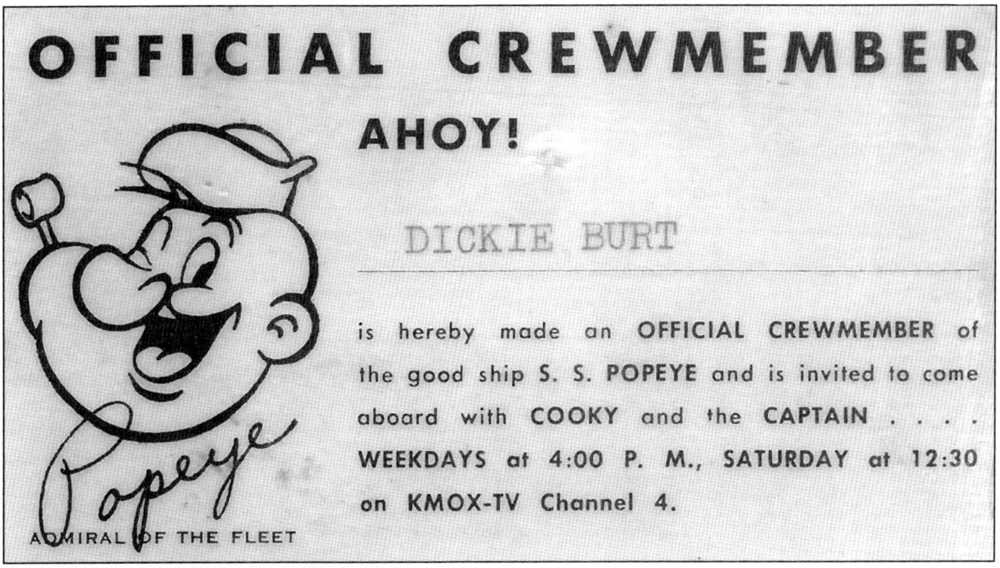
OFFICIAL CREWMEMBER

AHOY!

DICKIE BURT

is hereby made an OFFICIAL CREWMEMBER of the good ship S. S. POPEYE and is invited to come aboard with COOKY and the CAPTAIN . . . . WEEKDAYS at 4:00 P. M., SATURDAY at 12:30 on KMOX-TV Channel 4.

Popeye

ADMIRAL OF THE FLEET

Popeye cartoons and a live studio audience of kids were the highlights of *Cooky and the Captain*. It was on the air from 1958 to 1967. (St. Louis Media Archive.)

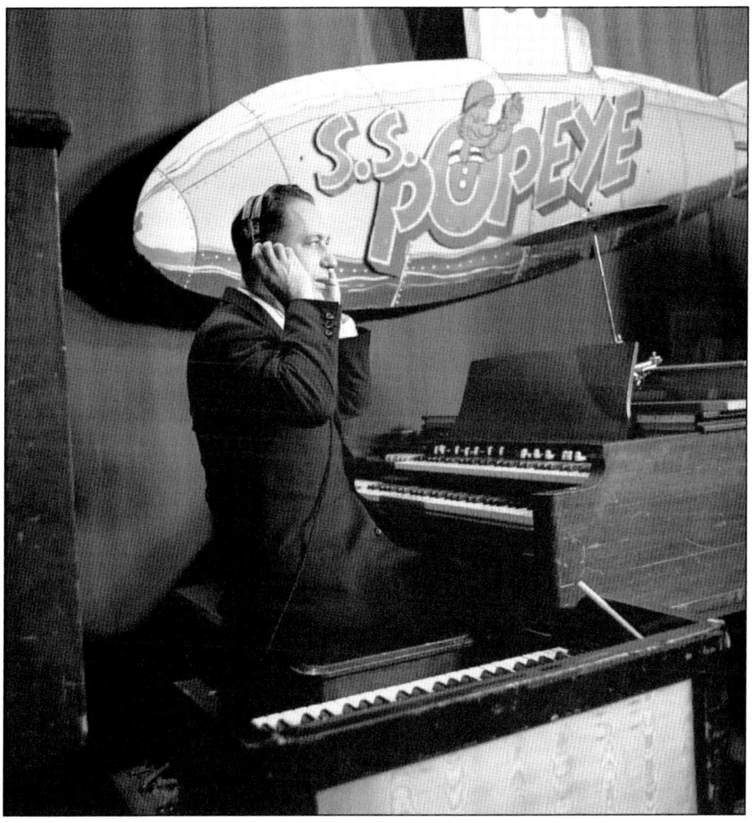

Since most kids' shows on television were produced during an age before videotape was readily available, the programs were done live. Music for the shows was often provided by an in-studio organist like KMOX-TV's Frank Harris, who was heard but not seen. (KMOX-TV Collection, Missouri History Museum.)

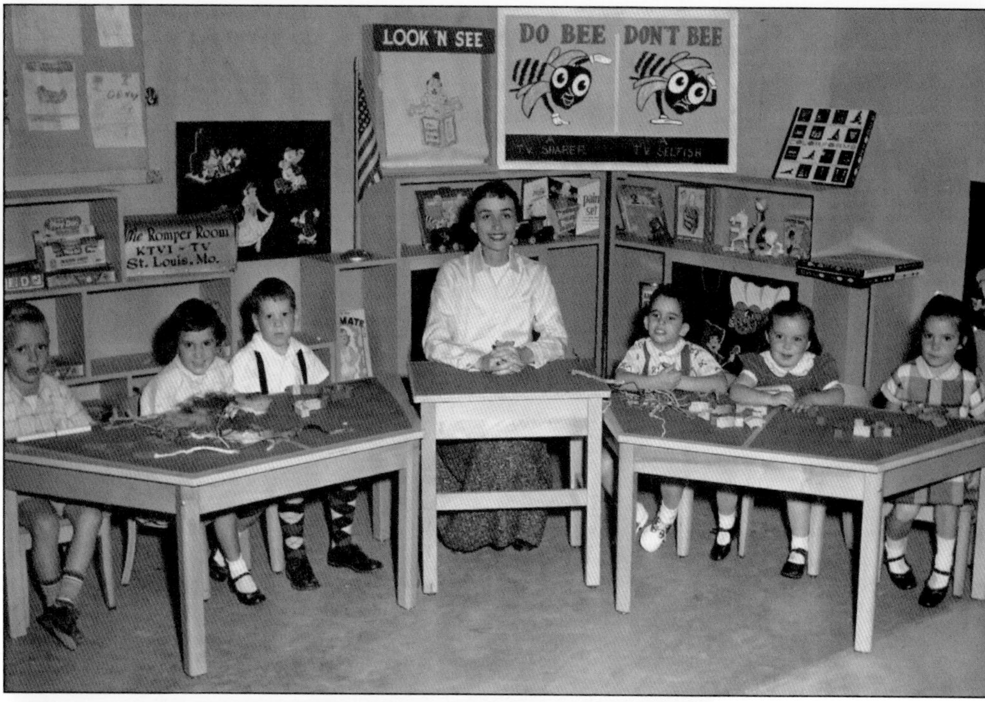

Romper Room was a children's program seen in many cities, each of which had its own local production. In St. Louis, broadcasts were seen on KTVI. (St. Louis Media Archive.)

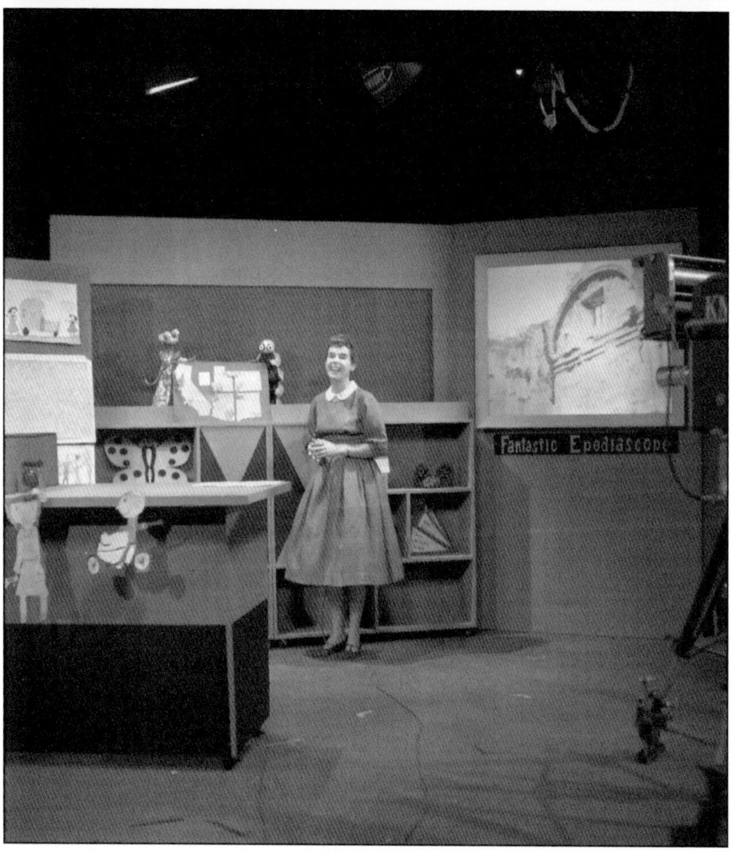

The puppets of KMOX-TV's *Fignewton Frog* are seen in this photograph with their hostess Dora. The program originated as a production of KETC-TV. (KMOX-TV Collection, Missouri History Museum.)

Of course, Santa Claus was the ultimate draw for young television viewers. This appearance was on KSD-TV. (St. Louis Media Archive.)

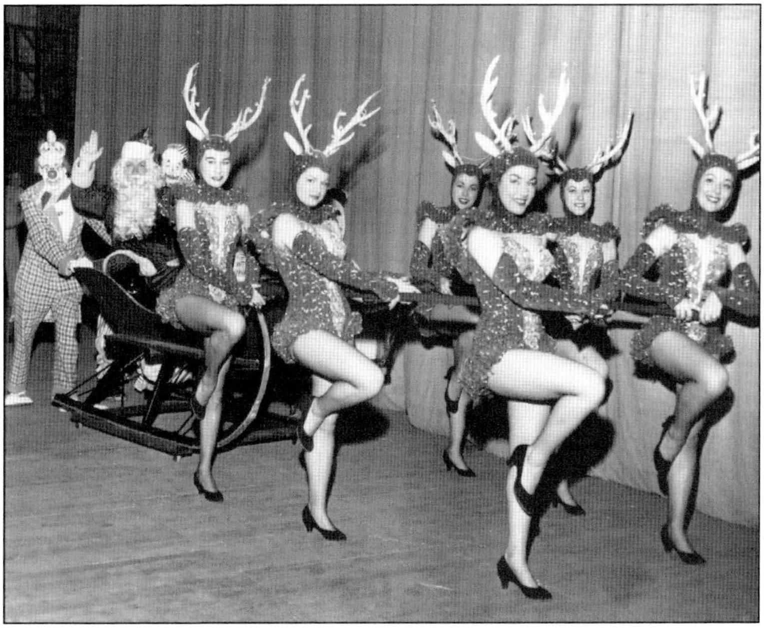

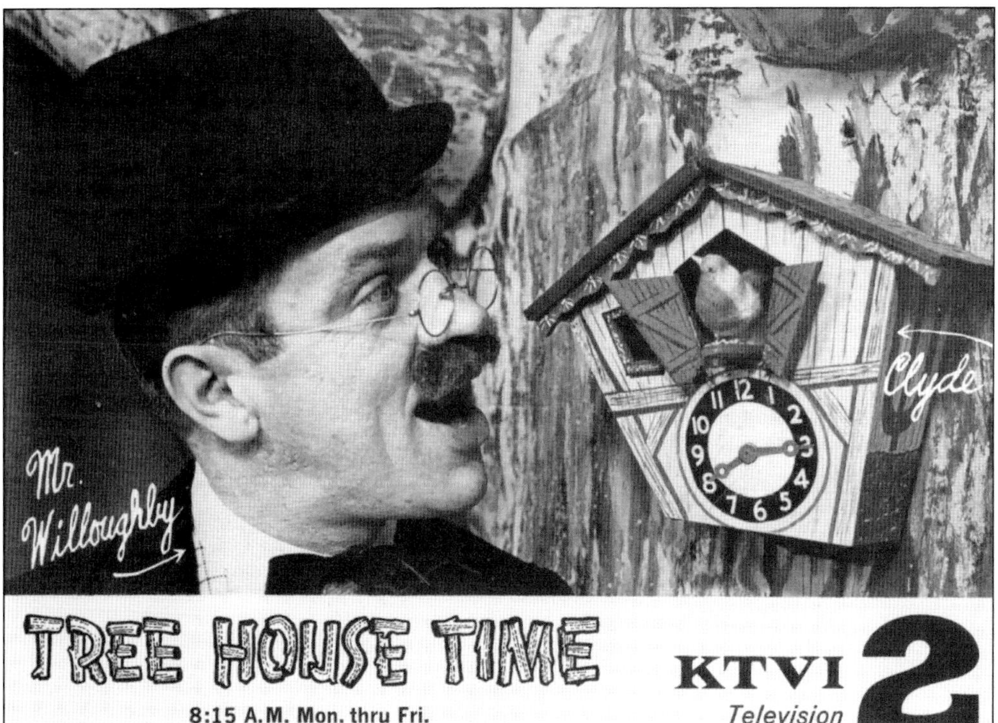

Jack Miller was the host of several St. Louis kids' shows. He was seen as Mr. Patches starting in 1961 and, later, as Mr. Willoughby on KTVI. (St. Louis Media Archive.)

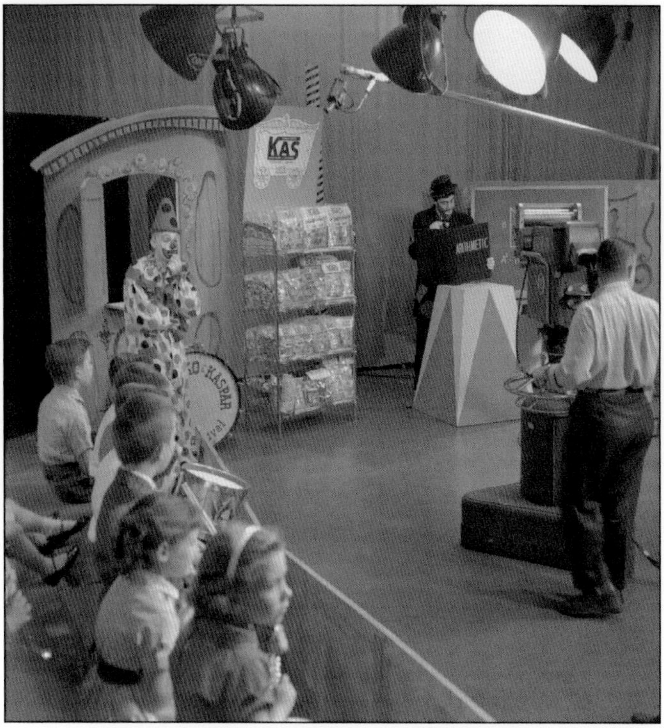

From this studio shot, it appears the *Koko and Kaspar* show on KMOX-TV did not have much of a budget for set construction. (KMOX-TV Collection, Missouri History Museum.)

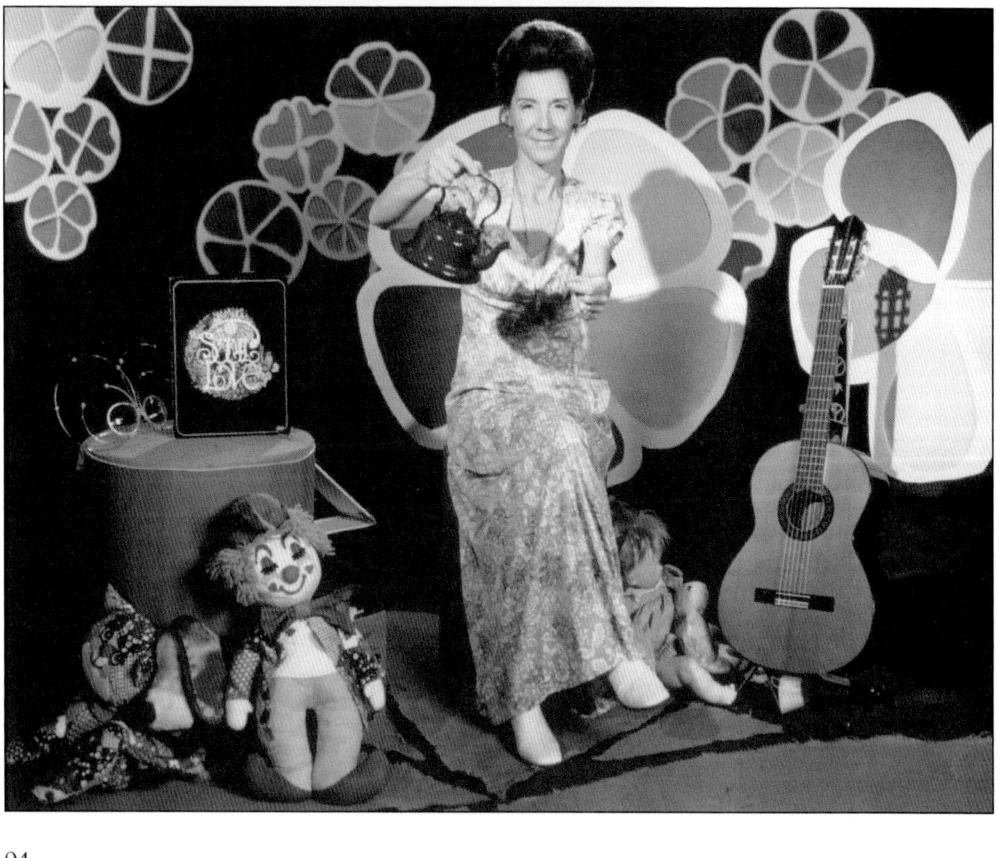

The Magic Teapot was seen on educational station KETC. Hostess Jane Jenkins is seen in a 1973 photograph while telling stories to a group of kids in the studio. (KETC-TV archives.)

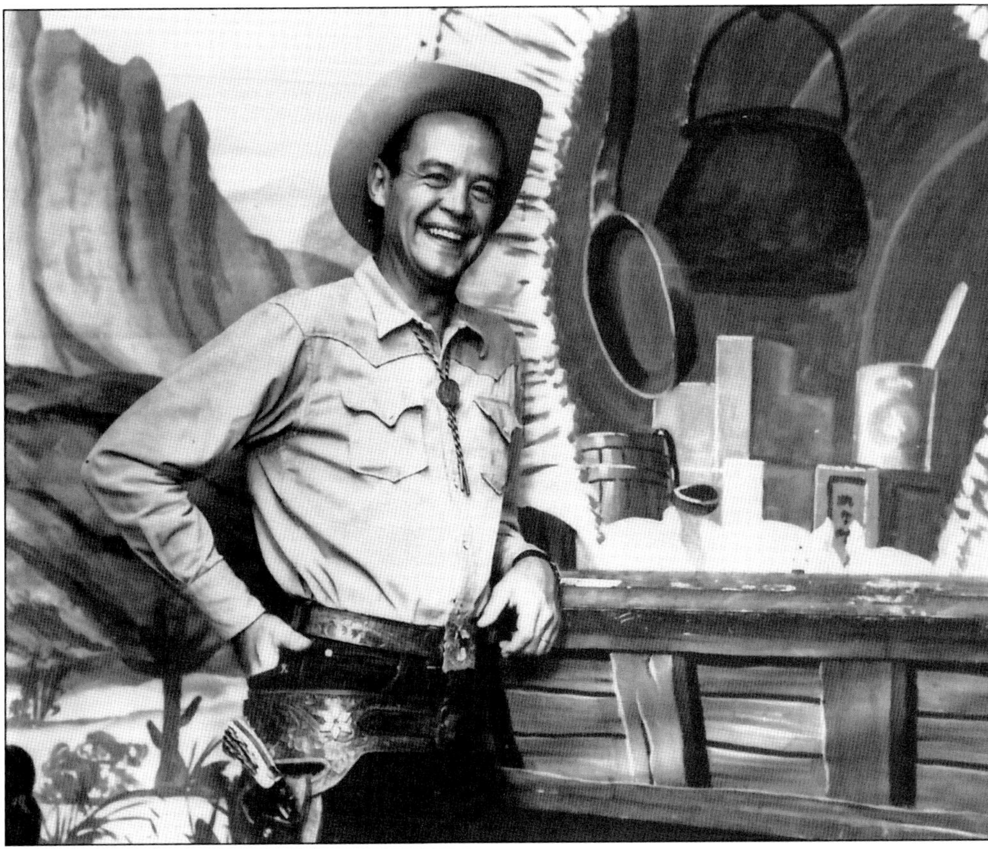

Harry Gibbs remains one of the best-remembered children's hosts in St. Louis television, where he hosted KSD-TV's *Wranglers' Cartoon Club.* (St. Louis Media Archive.)

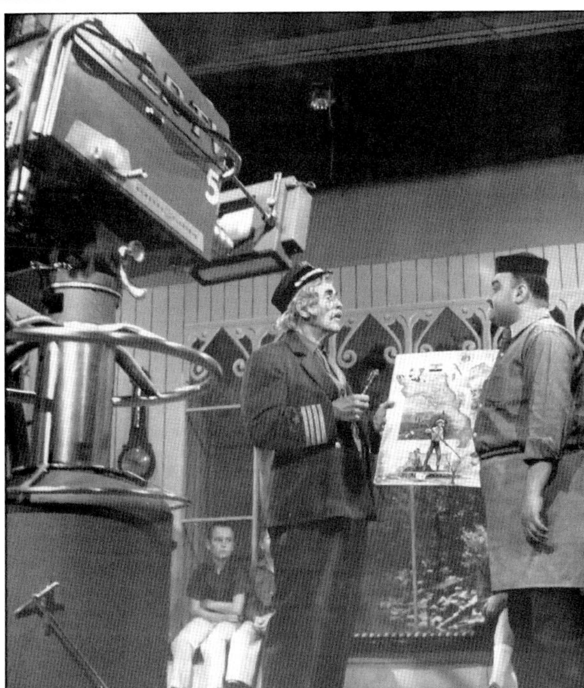

St. Louis radio vet Harry Fender had a large, loyal following in the 1960s for his *Captain 11's Showboat* program on KPLR. The largely male audience later grew into a generation that could recite, from memory, long stretches of dialogue from the Three Stooges shorts. (St. Louis Media Archive.)

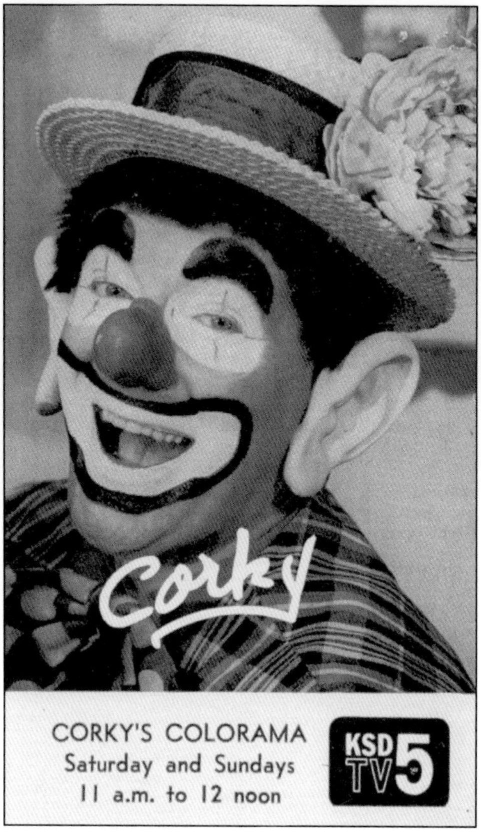

For many St. Louisans, there will never be another clown like Corky. He was portrayed by Clif St. James, who also served at various times as KSD-TV's weatherman and news anchor, as well as a personality on KSD Radio. Originally named Zippy, the clown became Corky in the mid-1950s. In 1966, it became the first local program to be broadcast in color, and the show's name became *Corky's Colorama*. (St. Louis Media Archive.)

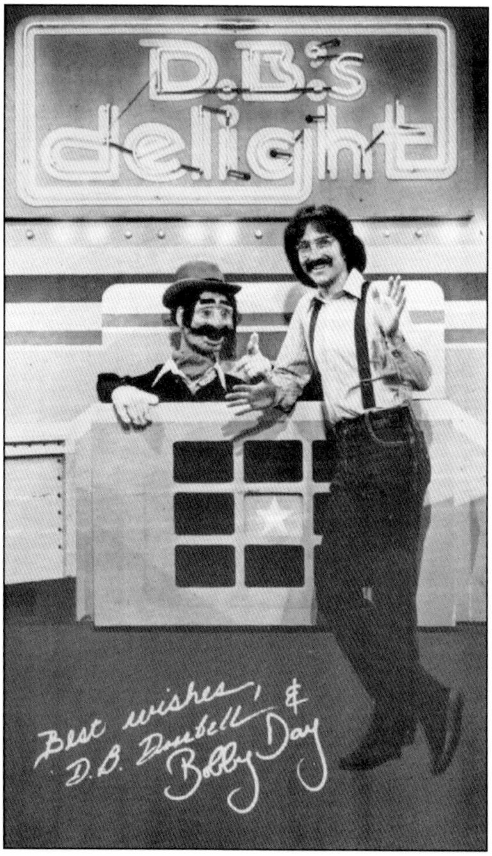

Radio personality Bobby Day was the host of *D.B.'s Delight* on KMOX-TV. The puppet D.B. Doorbell was an integral part of the children's quiz show. (Bobby Day.)

Seven

MEDIA FRAGMENTATION

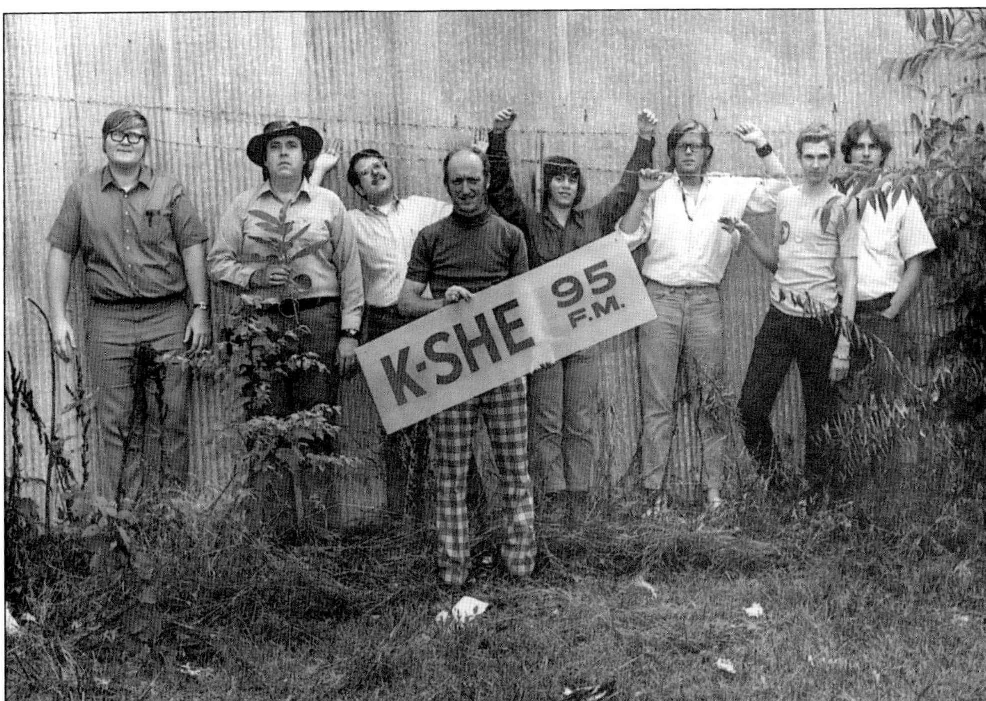

In the late 1960s, society was breaking into small groups following the "do your own thing" mantra. FM radio's popularity divided the radio audience into smaller segments with listeners seeking specific types of music. Cable television would soon offer viewers the same expanded choices. By 1970, KSHE had become St. Louis's "hard rock" station. Staffers from the station posing here are, from left to right, Sir Ed, Prince Knight, Gary Bennett, manager Shelly Grafman, Steve Rosen, John Williams, Don Corey, and Dick Merkle. (St. Louis Media Archive.)

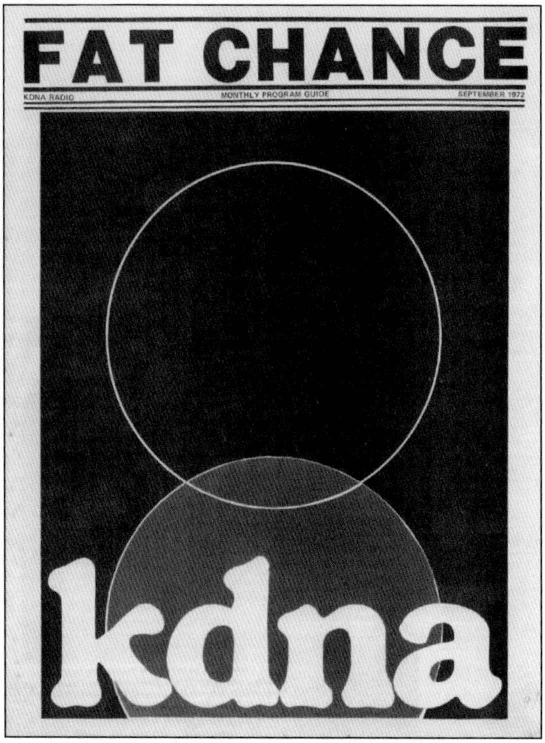

Community radio made a name for itself in the late 1960s in St. Louis. KDNA's studios were in an old house on Olive Street near Boyle Avenue. KDNA always seemed to be experiencing financial difficulties as well as soliciting donations from loyal listeners. It was on the air from February 1969 to June 1973. (St. Louis Media Archive.)

KACO-FM signed on in June 1969 but never made much of an impression on listeners. Joan Colegrove, the office manager, was the only station employee. KACO was off the air in less than a year. (St. Louis Media Archive.)

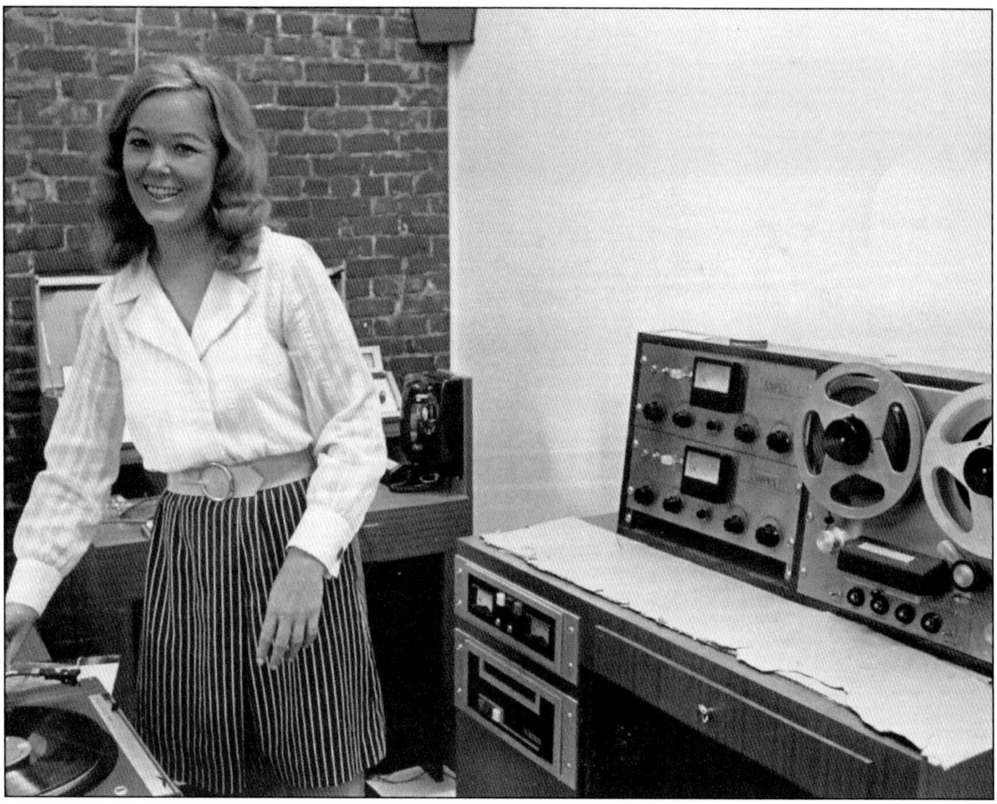

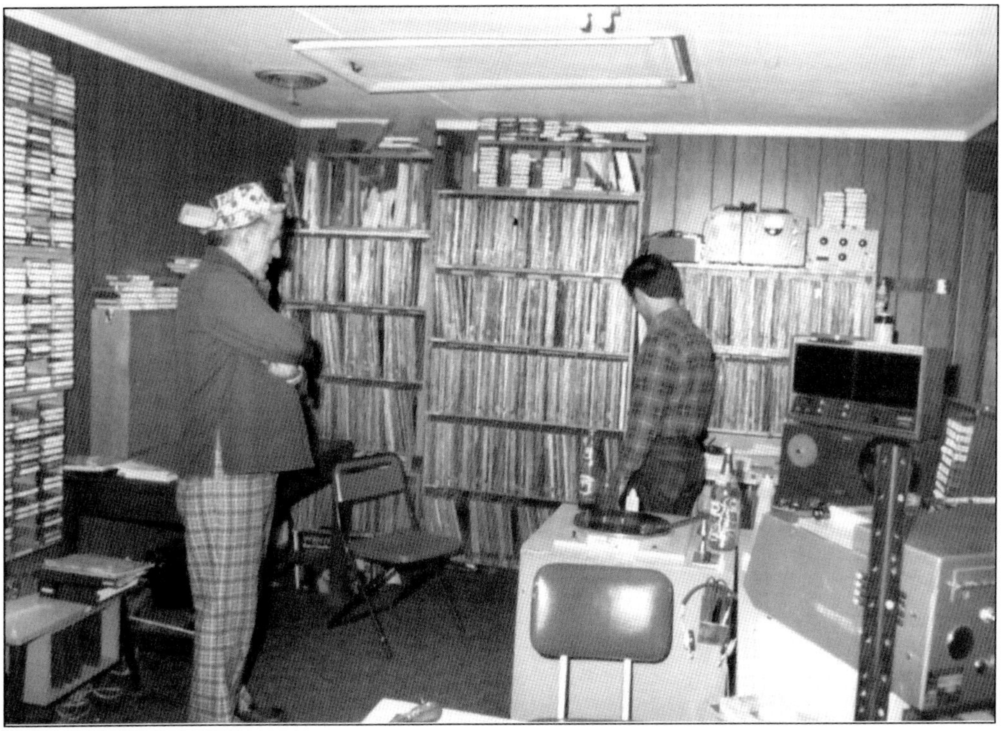

Joe Lepp (on the left) built his radio station, WCBW-FM, in the basement of his Columbia, Illinois, home in 1964. It was later moved to his attached garage, shown here. (St. Louis Media Archive.)

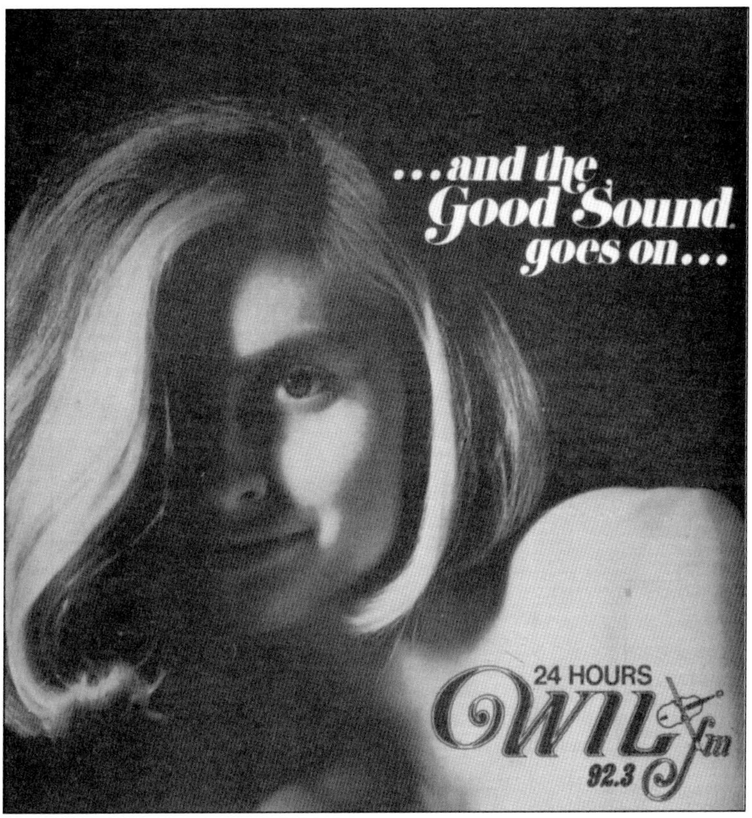

While WRTH continued to play beautiful music on the AM band, it faced more competition for its listeners as FM stations, such as WIL-FM, adopted similar music formats. (St. Louis Media Archive.)

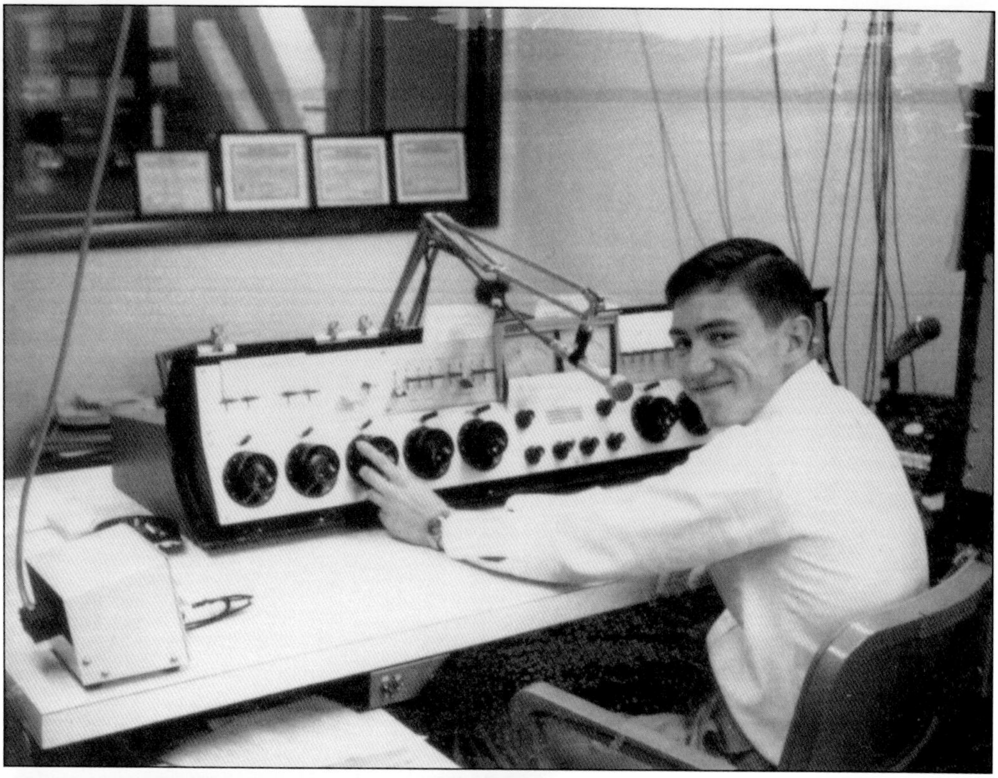

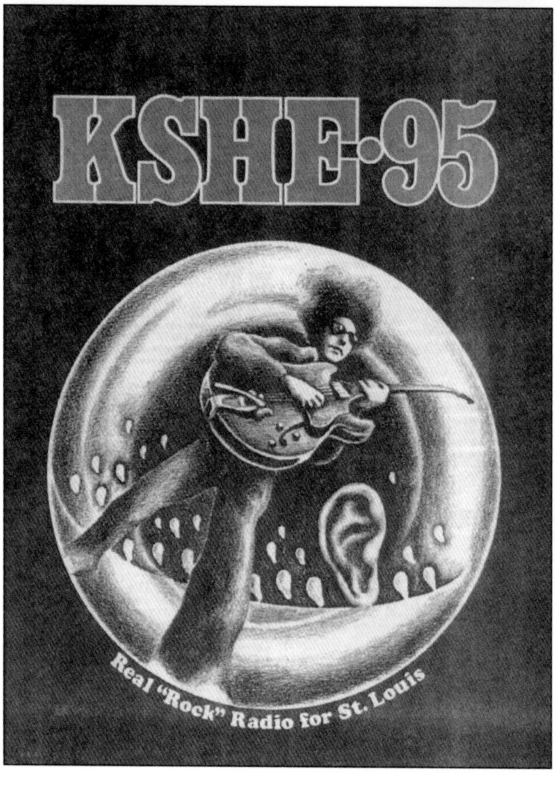

KSHE-FM, licensed to Crestwood, began its life playing light classical music under the slogan "the lady of FM." The operation was a financial failure for owner Ed Ceries. New owners nudged the format through pop music into rock music. John Roberts is shown at the control board. (St. Louis Media Archive.)

This advertisement depicts the station's format, which could be variously described as underground radio or hard rock. (St. Louis Media Archive.)

By 1970, KSHE's format had evolved to album rock, known in the industry as AOR (album-oriented rock), which placed emphasis on the musical selections on the albums that were being ignored by pop-music radio stations. (St. Louis Media Archive.)

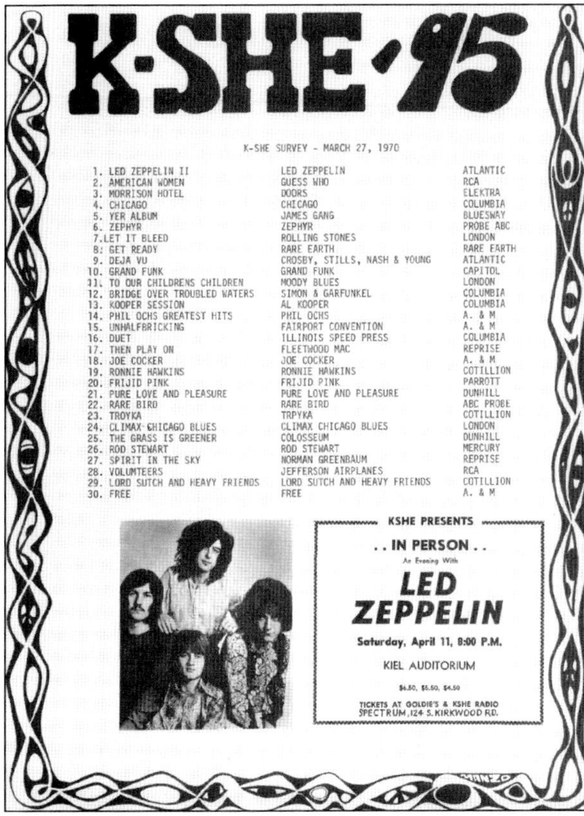

K-SHE·95

K-SHE SURVEY - MARCH 27, 1970

1. LED ZEPPELIN II	LED ZEPPELIN	ATLANTIC
2. AMERICAN WOMEN	GUESS WHO	RCA
3. MORRISON HOTEL	DOORS	ELEKTRA
4. CHICAGO	CHICAGO	COLUMBIA
5. YER ALBUM	JAMES GANG	BLUESWAY
6. ZEPHYR	ZEPHYR	PROBE ABC
7.LET IT BLEED	ROLLING STONES	LONDON
8: GET READY	RARE EARTH	RARE EARTH
9. DEJA VU	CROSBY, STILLS, NASH & YOUNG	ATLANTIC
10. GRAND FUNK	GRAND FUNK	CAPITOL
11. TO OUR CHILDRENS CHILDREN	MOODY BLUES	LONDON
12. BRIDGE OVER TROUBLED WATERS	SIMON & GARFUNKEL	COLUMBIA
13. KOOPER SESSION	AL KOOPER	COLUMBIA
14. PHIL OCHS GREATEST HITS	PHIL OCHS	A. & M
15. UNHALFBRICKING	FAIRPORT CONVENTION	A. & M
16. DUET	ILLINOIS SPEED PRESS	COLUMBIA
17. THEN PLAY ON	FLEETWOOD MAC	REPRISE
18. JOE COCKER	JOE COCKER	A. & M
19. RONNIE HAWKINS	RONNIE HAWKINS	COTILLION
20. FRIJID PINK	FRIJID PINK	PARROTT
21. PURE LOVE AND PLEASURE	PURE LOVE AND PLEASURE	DUNHILL
22. RARE BIRD	RARE BIRD	ABC PROBE
23. TROYKA	TRPYKA	COTILLION
24. CLIMAX CHICAGO BLUES	CLIMAX CHICAGO BLUES	LONDON
25. THE GRASS IS GREENER	COLOSSEUM	DUNHILL
26. ROD STEWART	ROD STEWART	MERCURY
27. SPIRIT IN THE SKY	NORMAN GREENBAUM	REPRISE
28. VOLUMTEERS	JEFFERSON AIRPLANES	RCA
29. LORD SUTCH AND HEAVY FRIENDS	LORD SUTCH AND HEAVY FRIENDS	COTILLION
30. FREE	FREE	A. & M

KSHE PRESENTS

.. IN PERSON ..

An Evening With

LED ZEPPELIN

Saturday, April 11, 8:00 P.M.

KIEL AUDITORIUM

$6.50, $5.50, $4.50

TICKETS AT GOLDIE'S & KSHE RADIO SPECTRUM, 124 S. KIRKWOOD RD.

MANZO

Don Corey was the overnight voice of KSHE from 1968 to 1973. (Kathy Corey.)

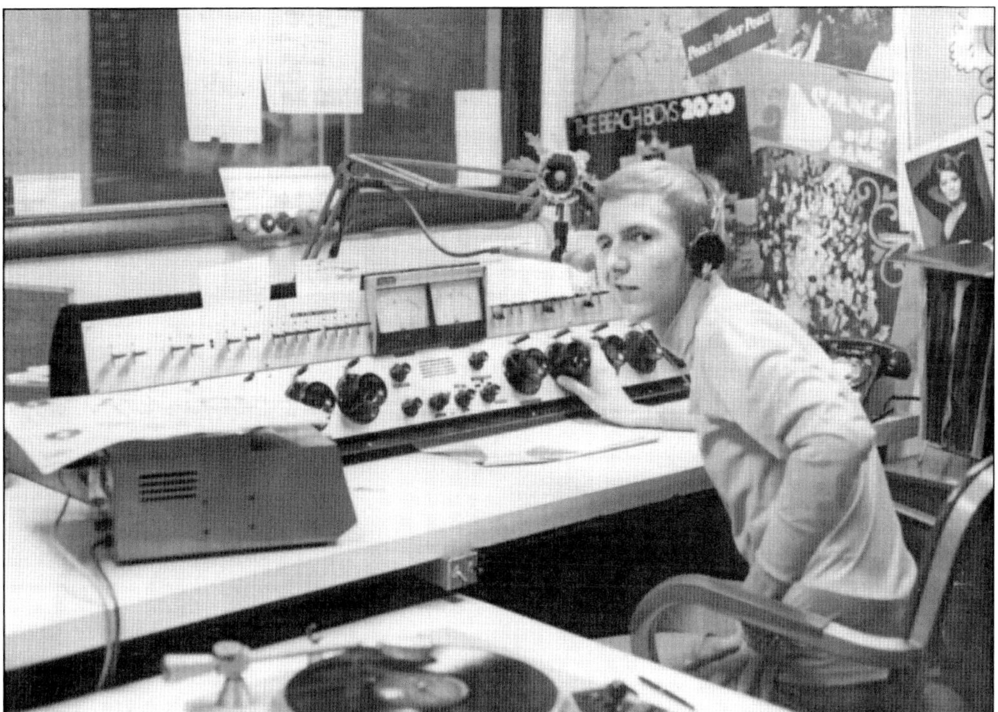

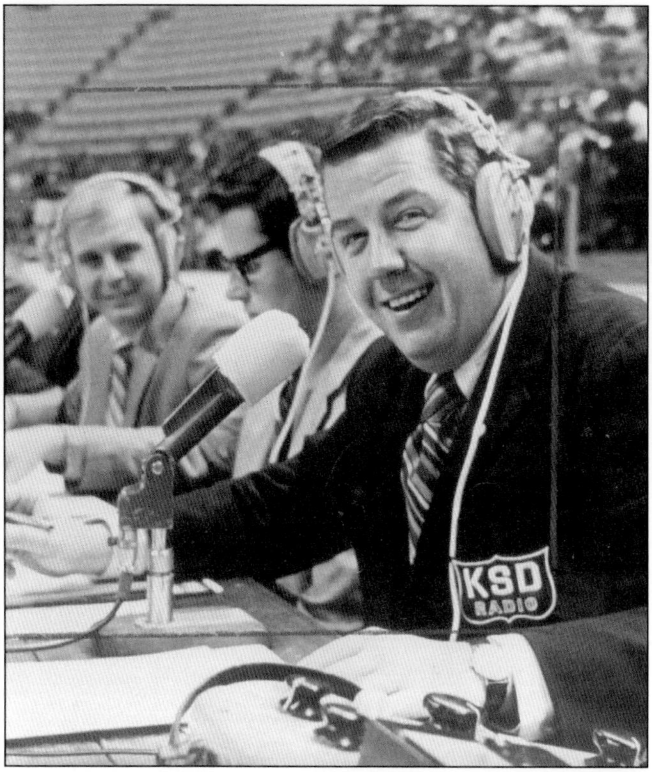

St. Louis television was continuing to develop, carrying live broadcasts of sporting events with local appeal. KSD-TV's Jay Randolph is shown (right) courtside at a basketball game with Ron Jacober (far left). (St. Louis Media Archive.)

Music programs were also seen on television. KSD-TV pioneered a dance show, *The St. Louis Hop*, in the 1960s. KDNL featured local DJs Jim Gates (left) and Bernie Hayes from 1970 to 1972. (St. Louis Media Archive.)

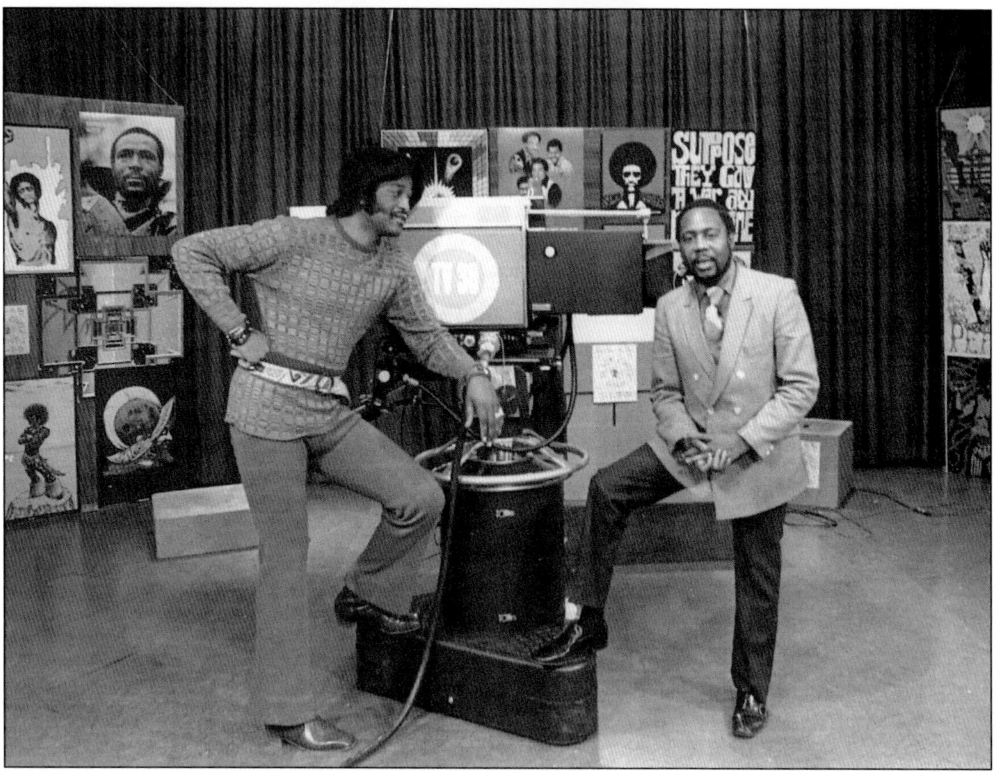

In the 1970s, KMOX general manager Robert Hyland was cementing the reputation of his station as the "sports voice of St. Louis." (St. Louis Media Archive.)

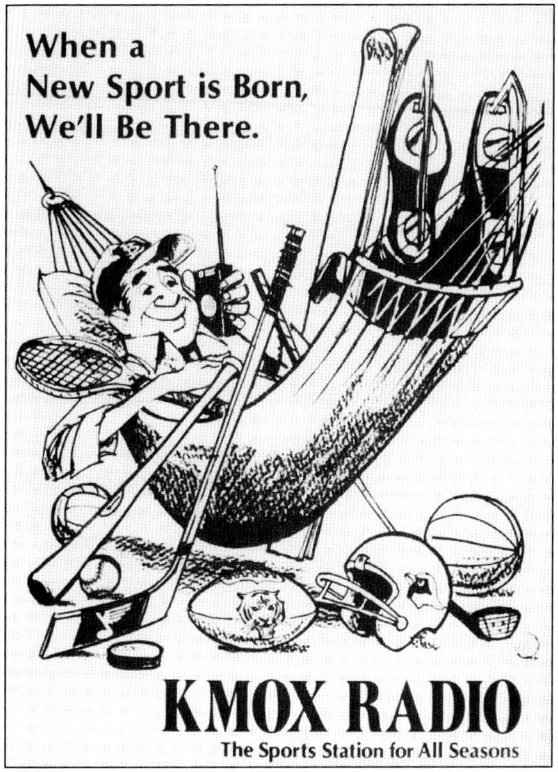

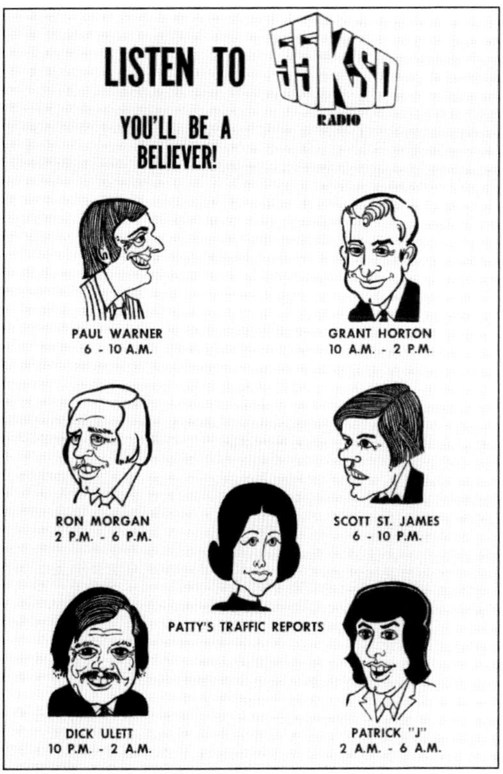

Pulitzer's KSD was still enjoying success by playing "good music" and hiring a strong, personable announcing staff. (Dick Ulett.)

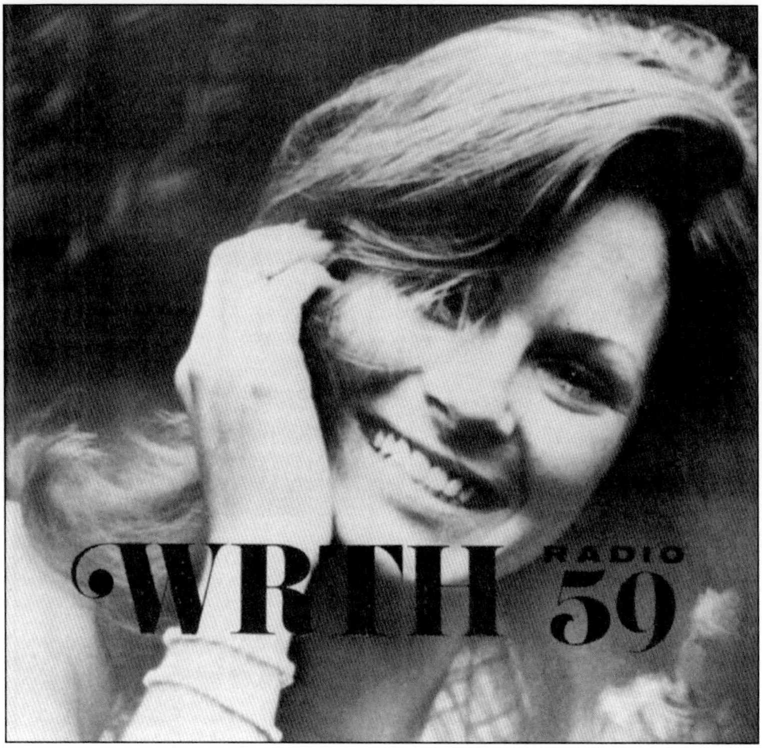

In the late 1970s, WRTH was still competing with FM stations, but frequency limitations and higher expectations for sound quality from listeners soon doomed "beautiful music" on the AM band. (St. Louis Media Archive.)

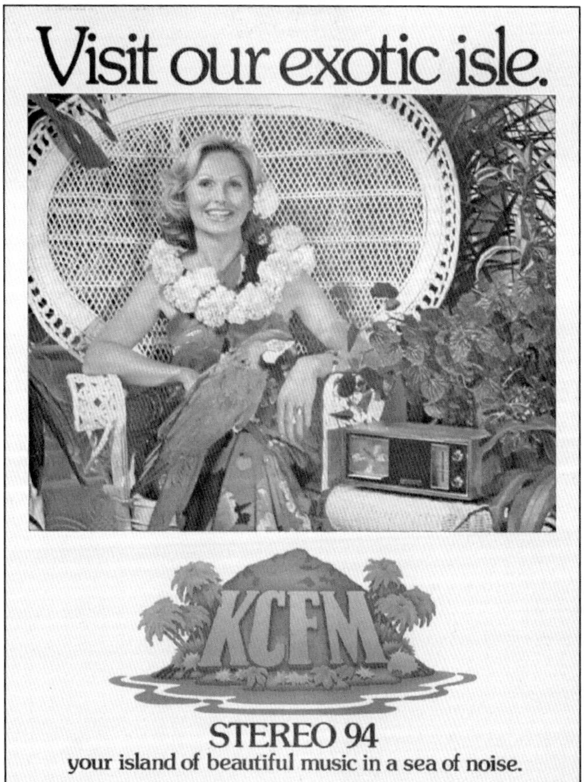

The FM dial truly came of age in St. Louis in the 1970s. KCFM, which had been playing "beautiful music" for many years, developed a higher profile. (St. Louis Media Archive.)

KSLQ became a powerhouse by playing the day's popular music on FM, in part because FM frequencies produced a much better sound than its formatic competitor on AM, KXOK. (St. Louis Media Archive.)

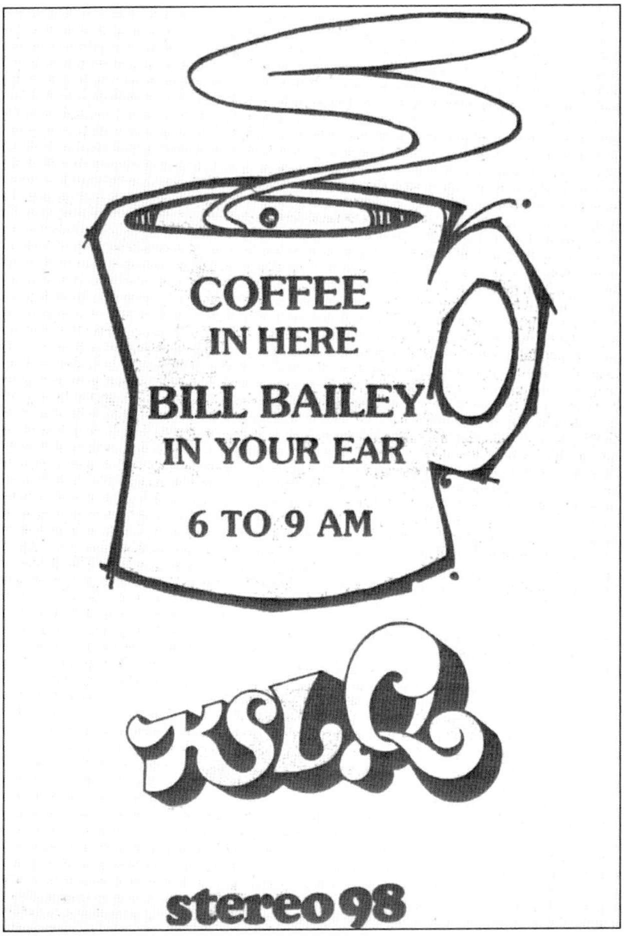

With high-energy announcers like "Young Bobby" Day, KSLQ captured the market's young music listeners while KXOK's popularity faded away. (Bobby Day.)

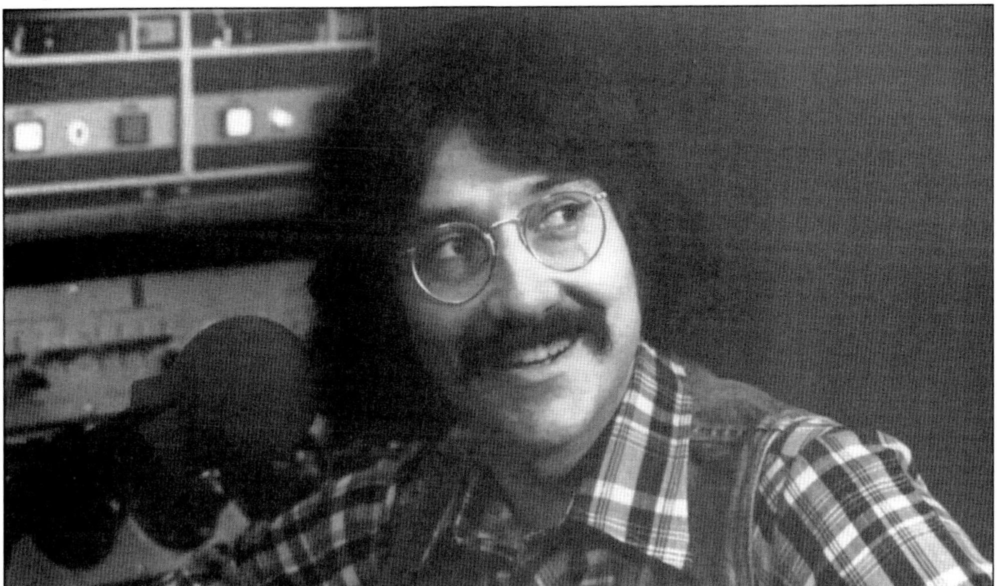

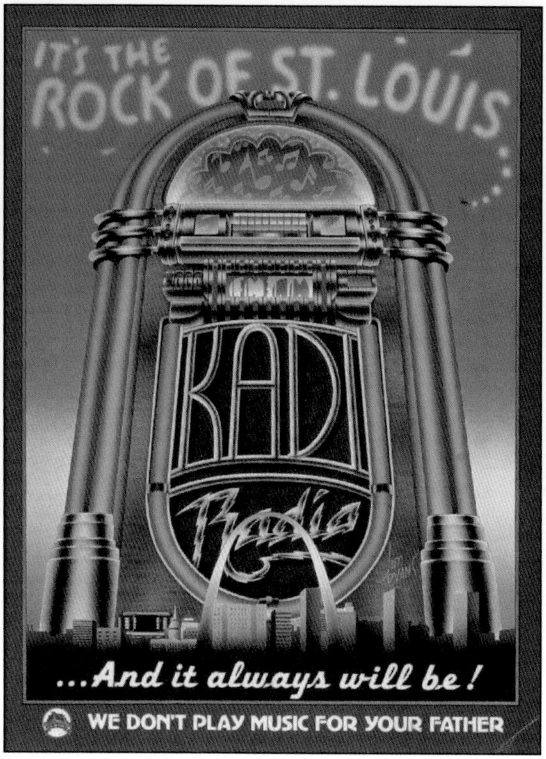

There was continued expansion of musical variety on the St. Louis FM dial through the 1970s. KADI-FM played much of the same music as KSHE but shied away from the very hard-rock album cuts. (St. Louis Media Archive.)

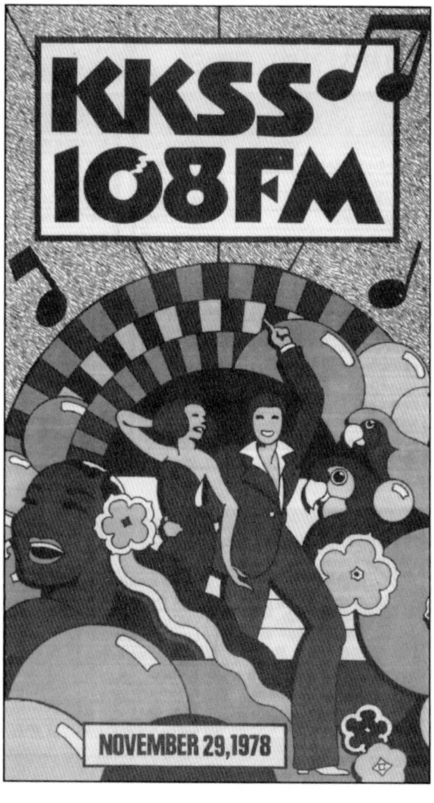

KKSS began as more of a pop-music station, evolving into disco/dance and finally moving to a format featuring black artists. The station's name was changed to KMJM. (St. Louis Media Archive.)

Many viewers have fond memories of the program *Newsbeat*, featuring John Auble (left) and Dick Ford, on KSD-TV in the late 1970s. The two seemed perfect partners who spotlighted light news features about the St. Louis area. (St. Louis Media Archive.)

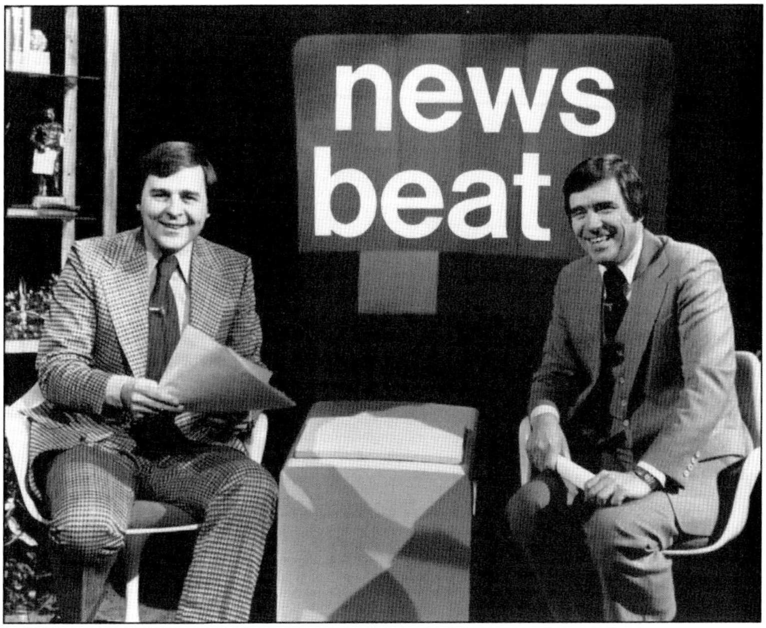

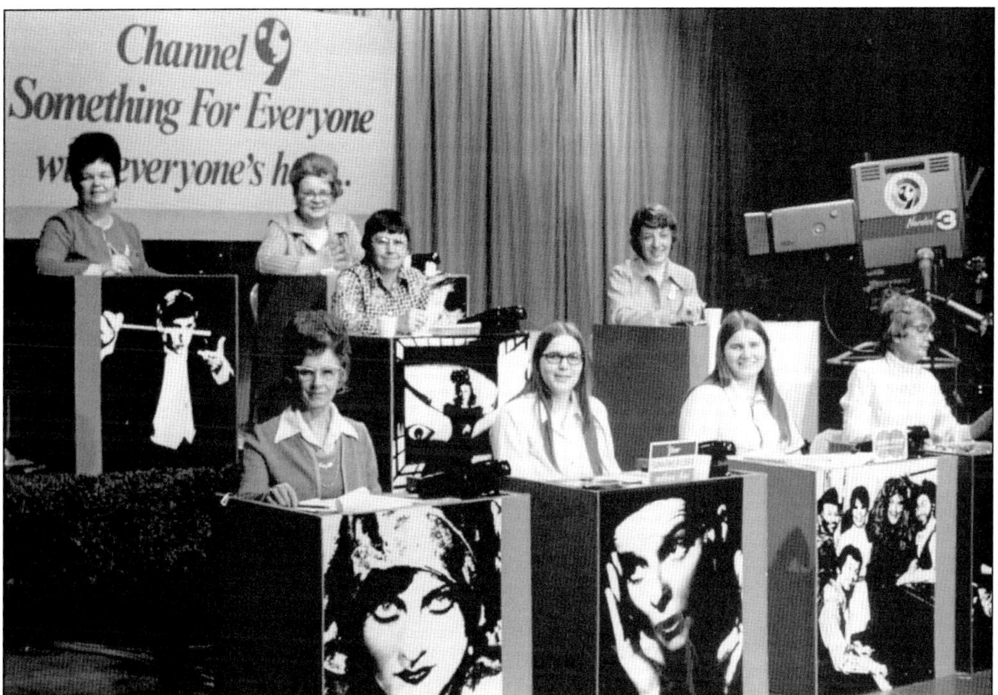

KETC-TV remained active in the market as a public-television station. Just as other public-television stations did around the country, channel 9 conducted regular fundraising auctions on the air. (KETC-TV archives.)

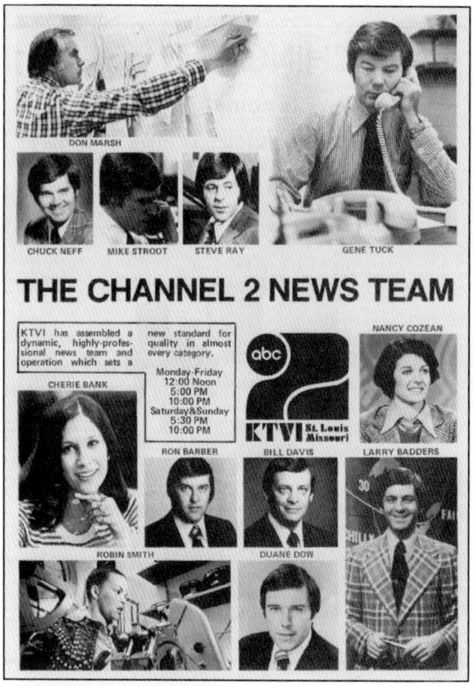

As the 1970s came to a close, television stations were still placing heavy emphasis on their newspeople, as seen in this advertisement for KTVI. (St. Louis Media Archive.)

KPLR's news team in the mid-1970s included, from left to right, Bob Plager, Gil Engler, Christine Buck, Nancy Scanlon, Bill Thomas, Maggie Linton, and Gentry Trotter. (KPLR-TV archives.)

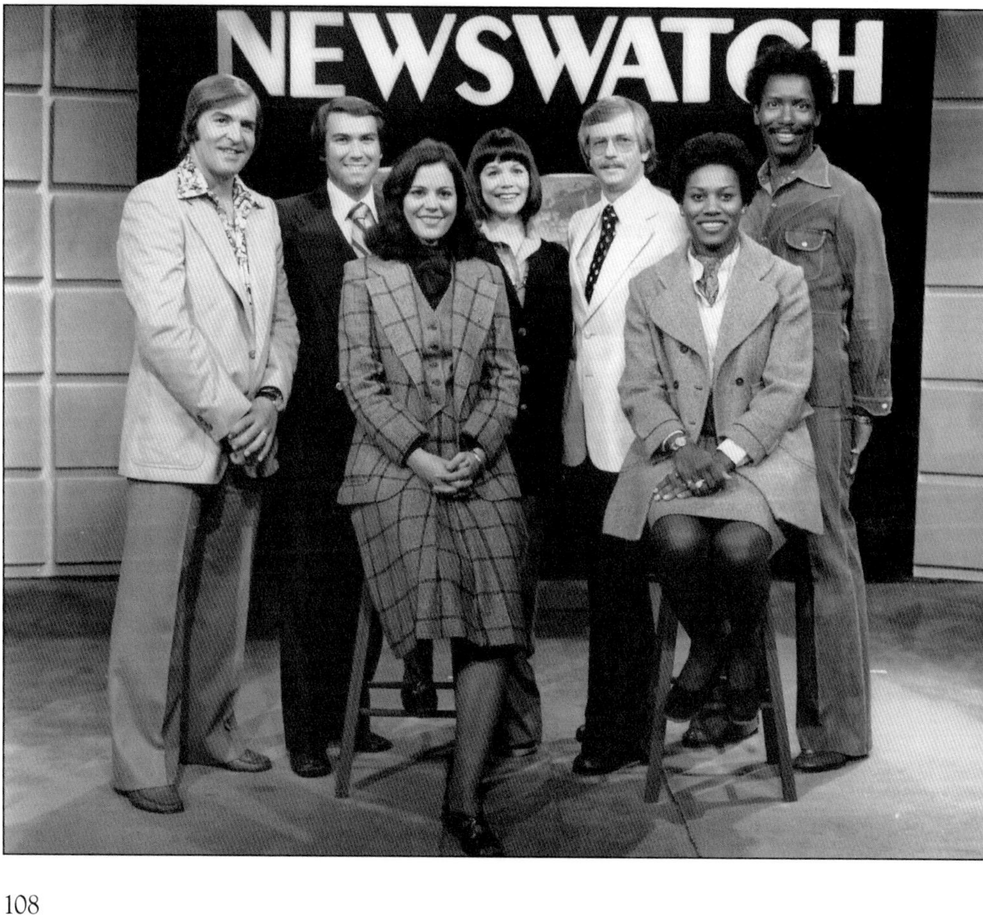

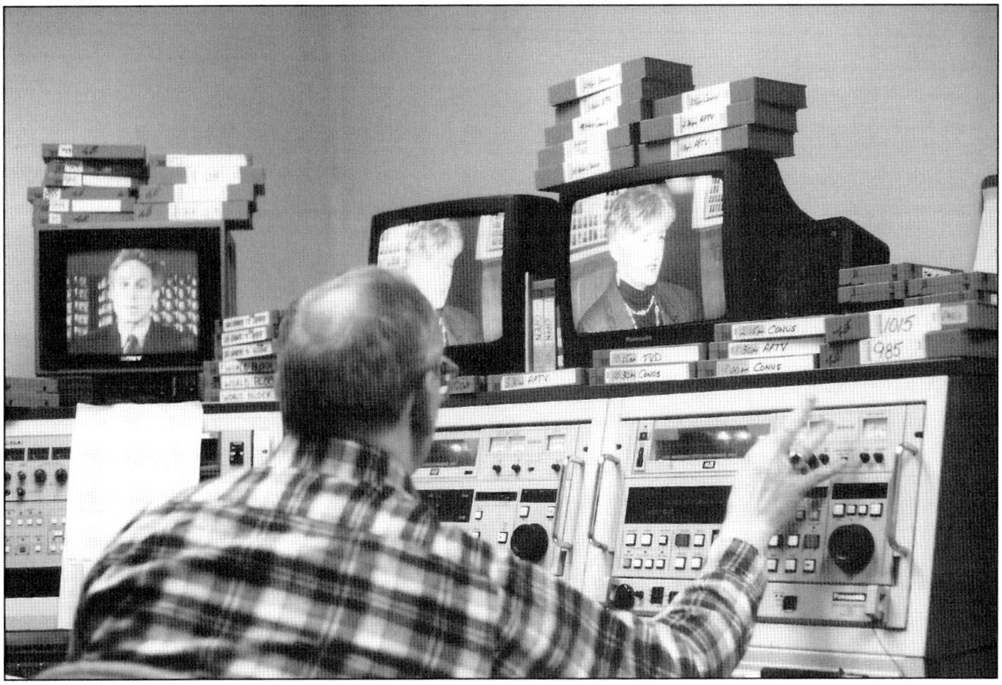

Behind the scenes at KPLR, engineers like Bob Kirschnik staffed videotape-editing stations to help produce news broadcasts. (KPLR-TV archives.)

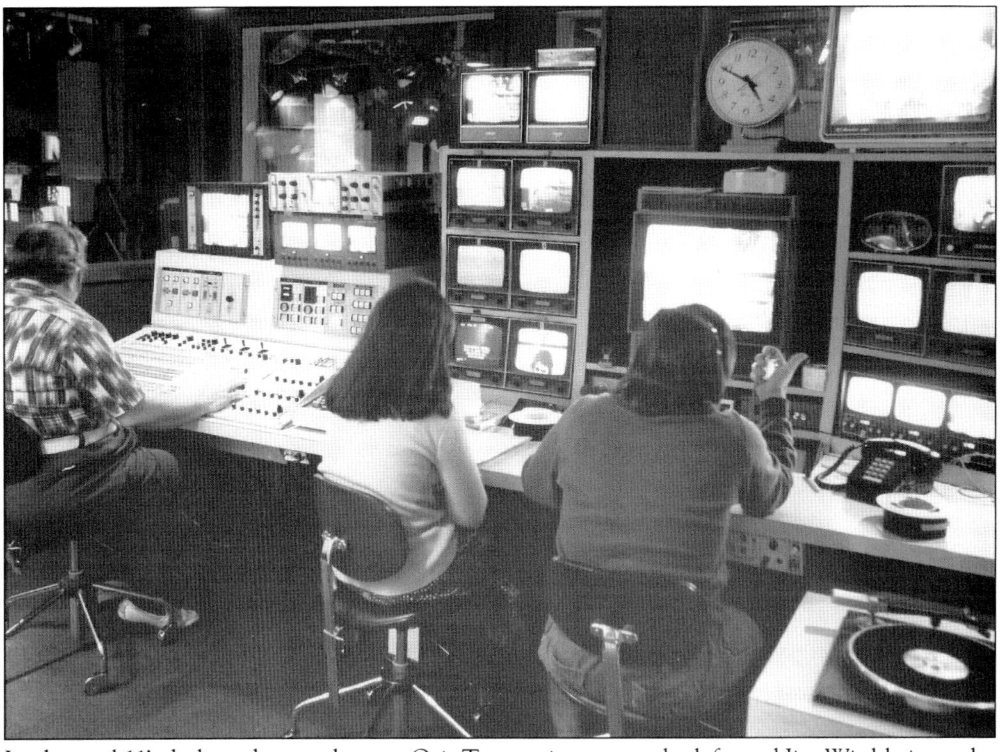

In channel 11's darkened control room, Otis Townes is seen on the left, and Jim Winkle is on the right; the woman's identity is not known. (KPLR-TV archives.)

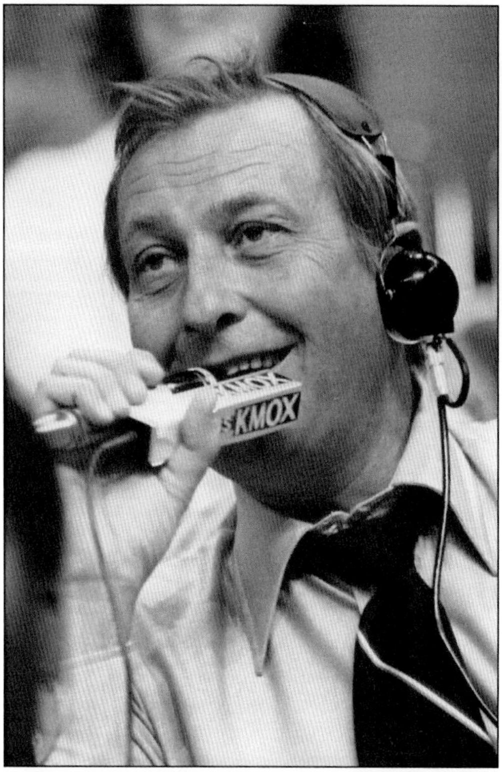

The staff at KMOX in the late 1970s and early 1980s was tops in the market, drawing the largest audience and the biggest paychecks. Bob Hardy wore many hats, including those as morning news anchor and host of the popular afternoon *At Your Service* program. (St. Louis Media Archive.)

John McCormick was known affectionately as "the man who walks and talks at midnight." His program had listeners in almost every state as well as Canada and Mexico. (St. Louis Media Archive.)

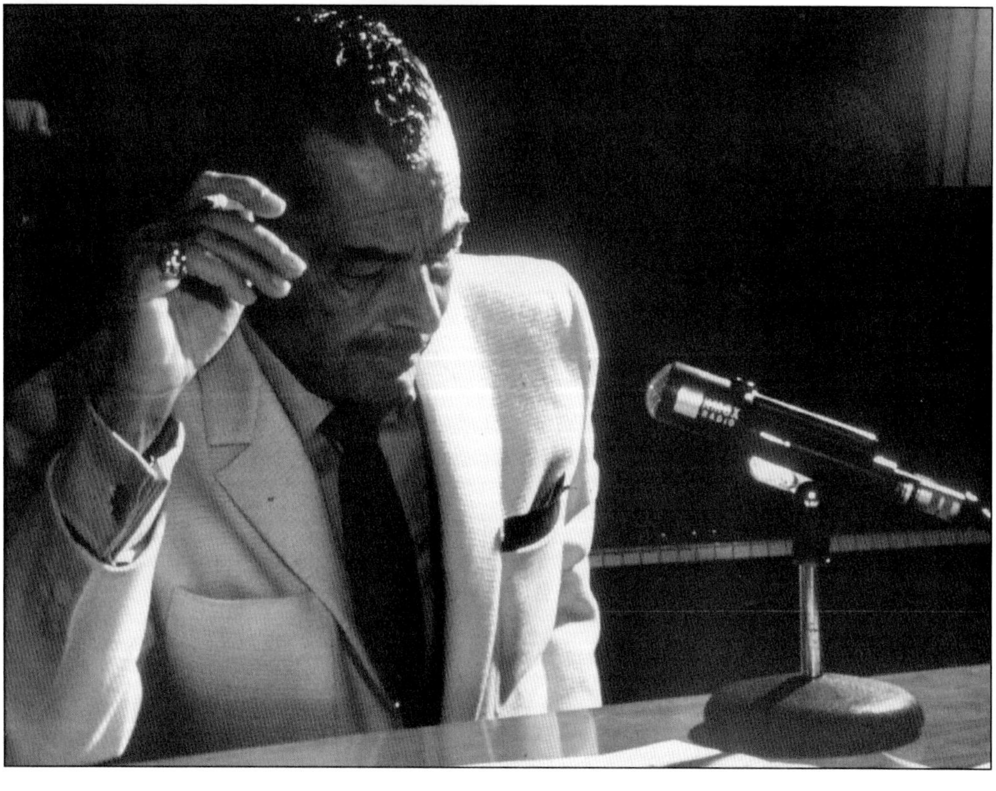

Anne Keefe is seen in the KMOX newsroom with Jeff Rainford. The *At Your Service* program she hosted was among the station's most entertaining and informative. (St. Louis Media Archive.)

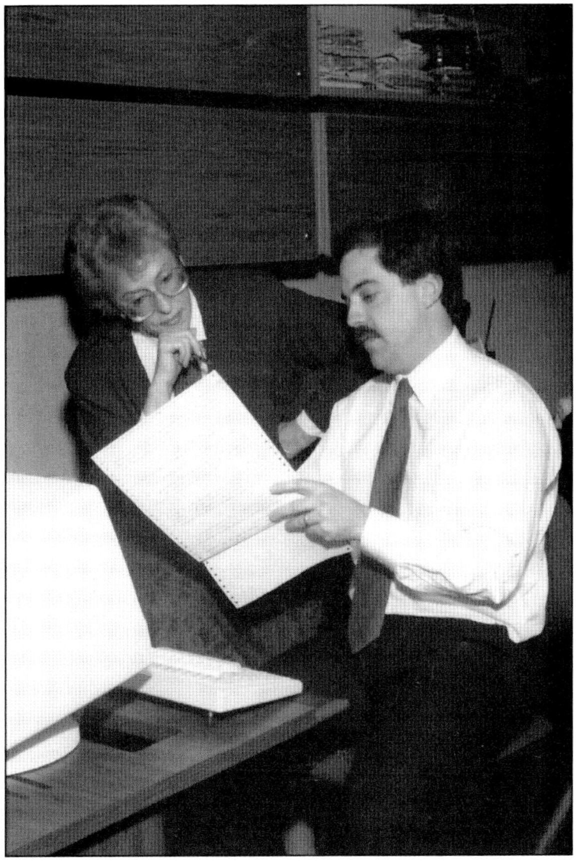

Regular traffic reports on KMOX were provided by Don Miller and Sue Matheis. At one time, they flew in two separate helicopters and broadcast their reports each morning and afternoon. (St. Louis Media Archive.)

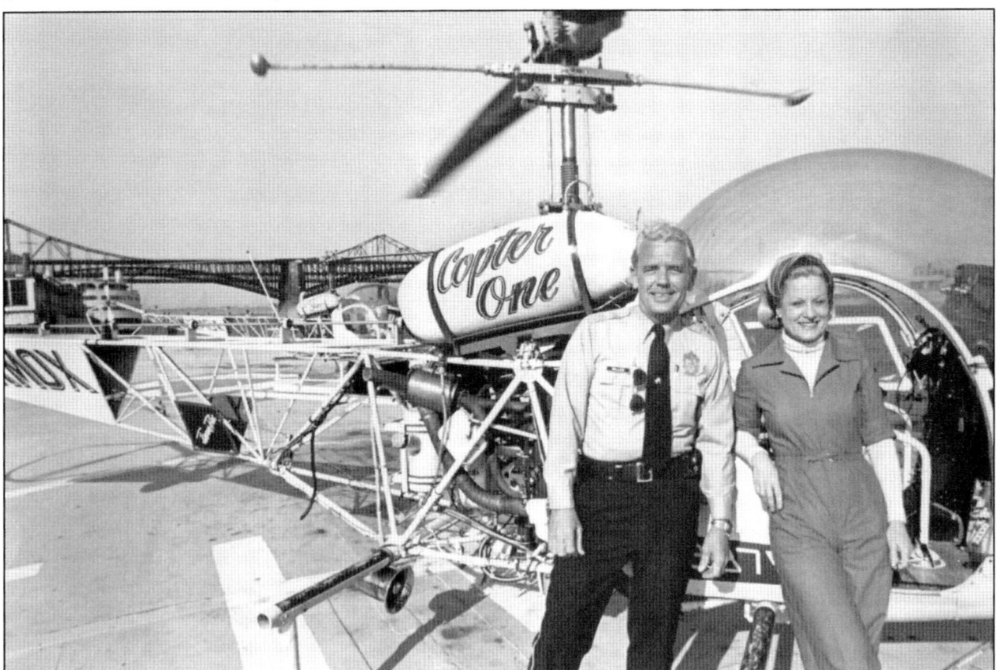

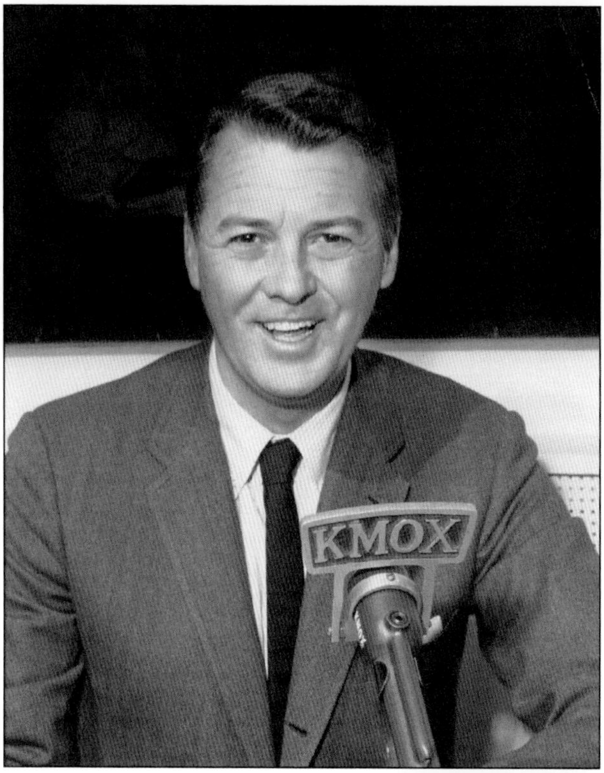

Robert Hyland, the CBS regional vice president, is the man credited with creating the KMOX powerhouse. (St. Louis Media Archive.)

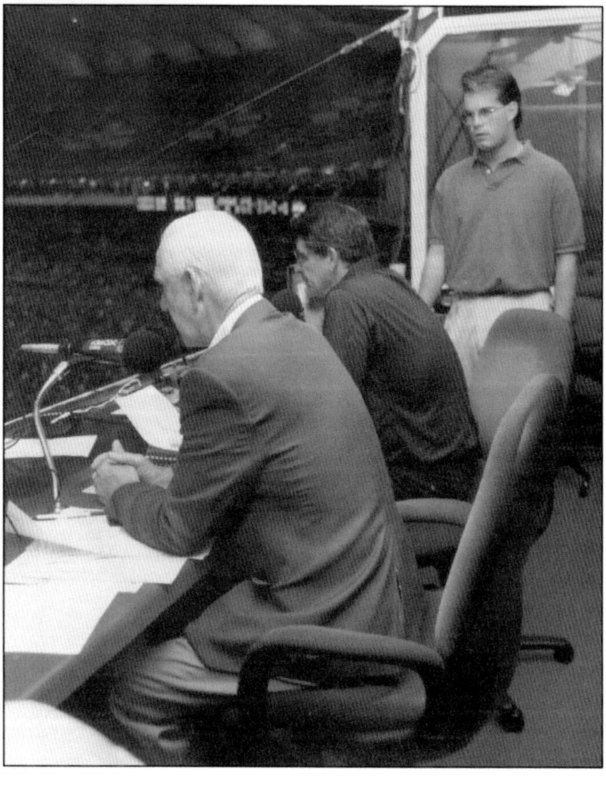

In the Cardinals broadcast booth at Busch Stadium, Jack Buck (left) and Mike Shannon are bringing the action to listeners while Joe Buck (right) observes. (St. Louis Media Archive.)

Even though KMOX, as a news/talk radio station, captured the largest number of listeners, there were still plenty of music choices on the radio. Dr. Jockenstein held court on KATZ. (St. Louis Media Archive.)

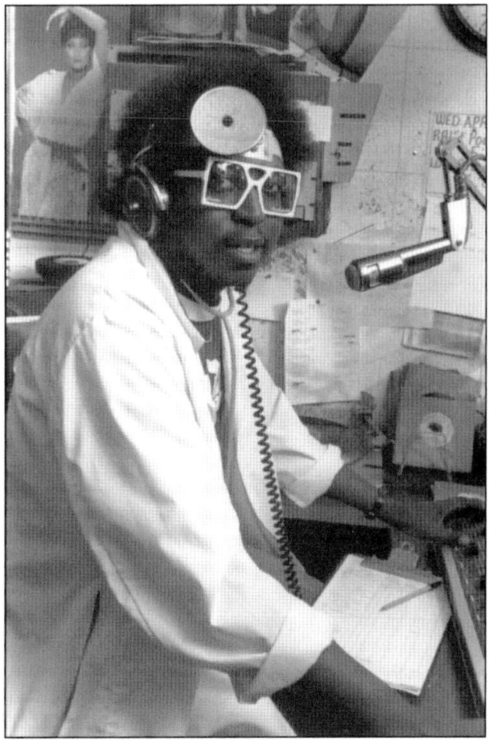

Ron Morgan, a veteran of several popular music–format stations, was heard mornings on KHTR in the late 1980s. He is pictured here behind the mic in February 1988. (St. Louis Media Archive.)

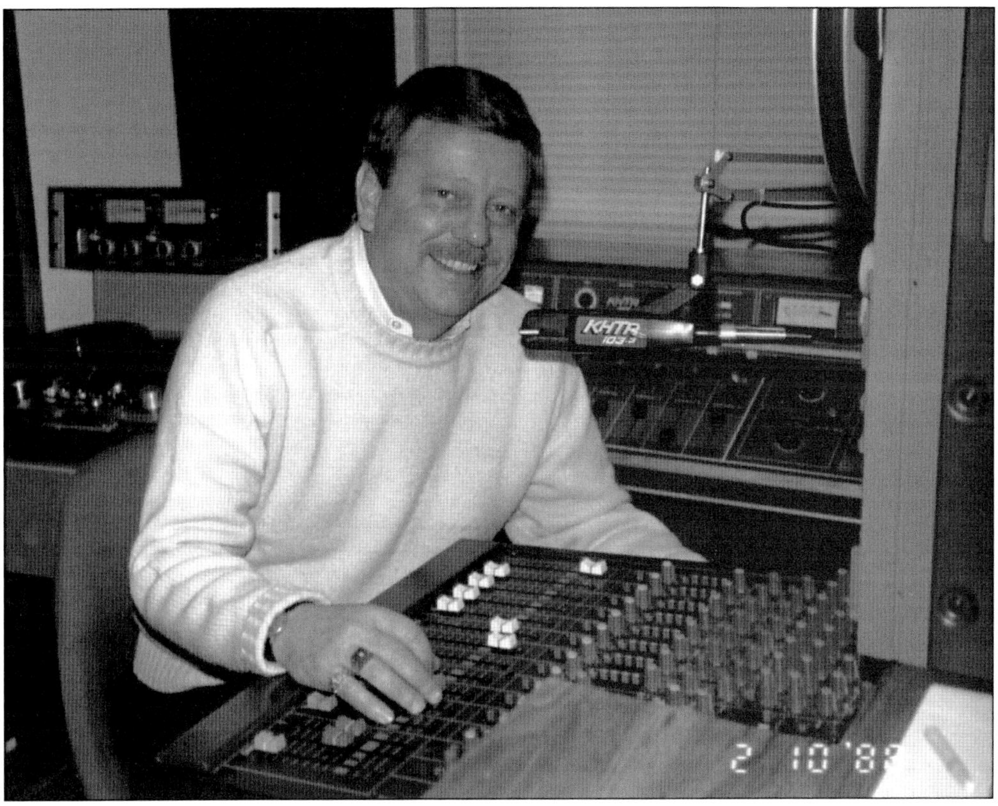

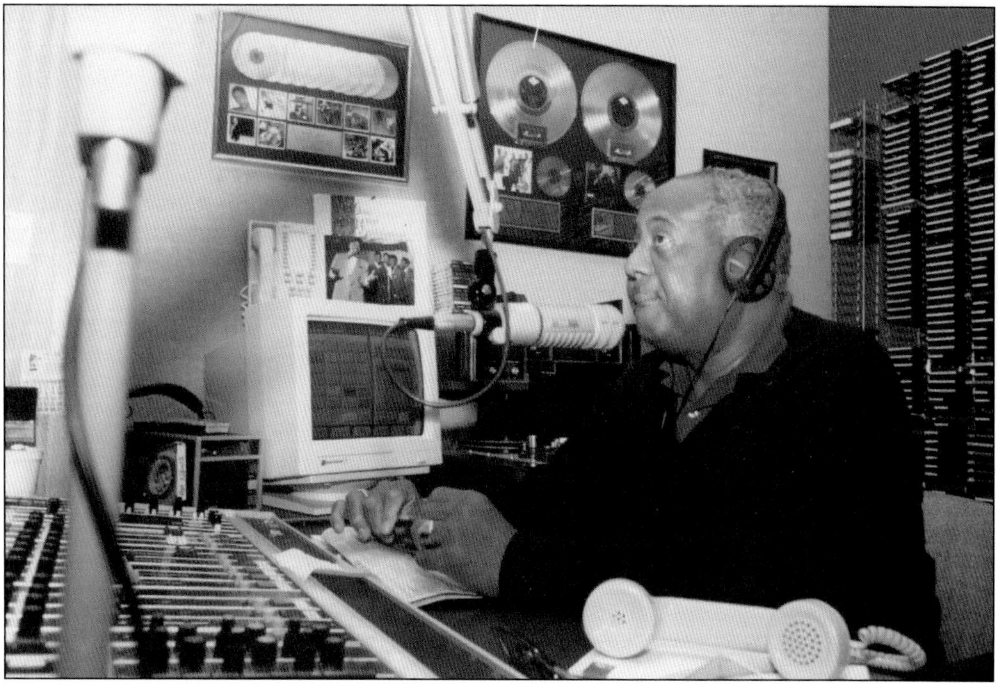

Bernie Hayes's combination of musical knowledge and social commentary could be heard on KATZ. (St. Louis Media Archive.)

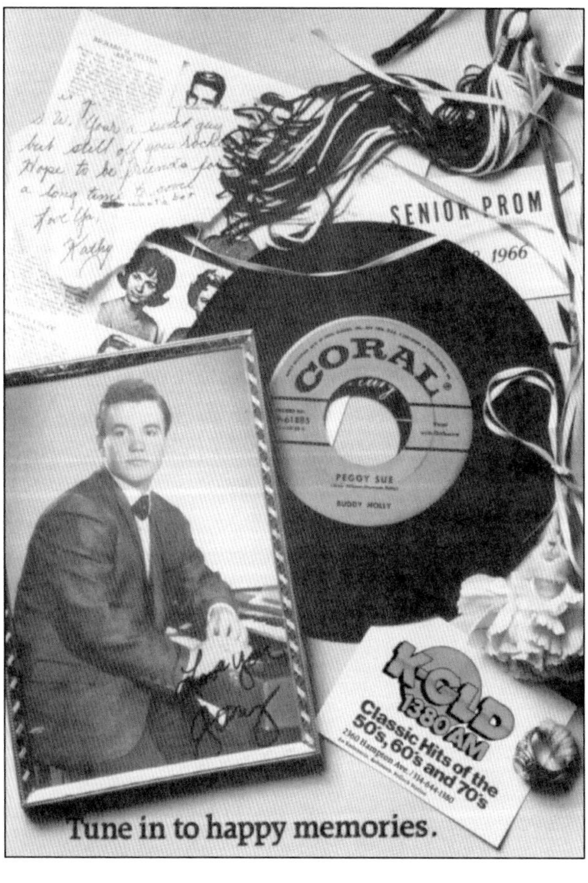

Market veteran Gary "Records" Brown was long associated with the "oldies" radio format. He was the driving personality behind the development of oldies station KGLD. (St. Louis Media Archive.)

WEW, one of the market's first radio stations, has retained its call letters since the beginning. In the 1980s, the station featured big-band music. (St. Louis Media Archive.)

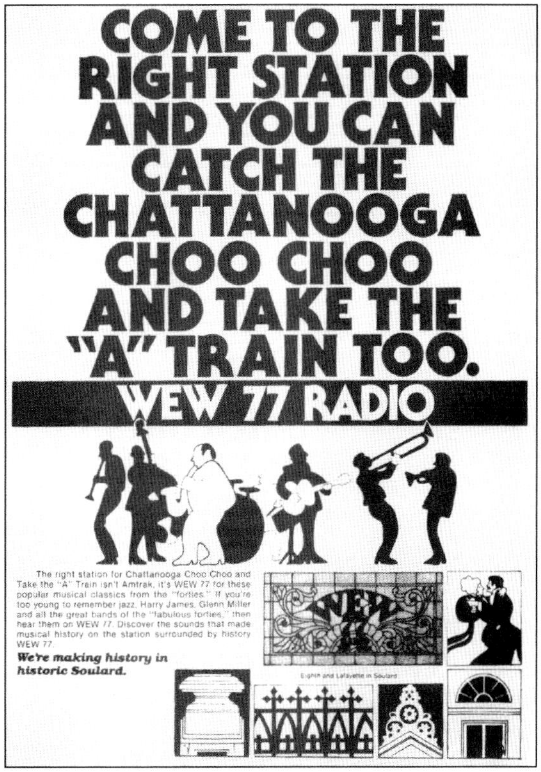

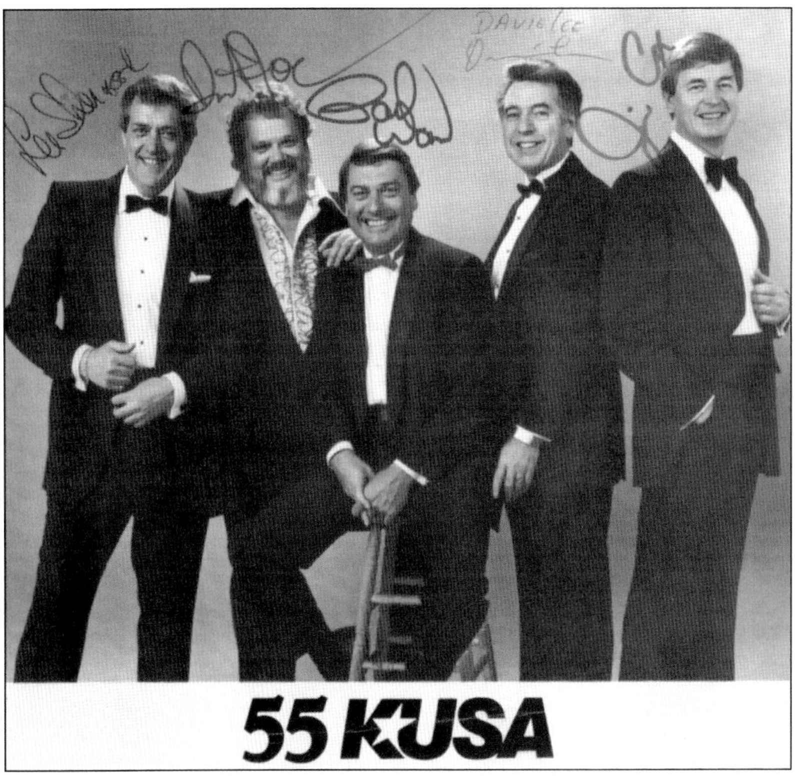

KSD, the other station that signed on in March 1922, changed its call letters to KUSA in the 1980s and featured country music. (St. Louis Media Archive.)

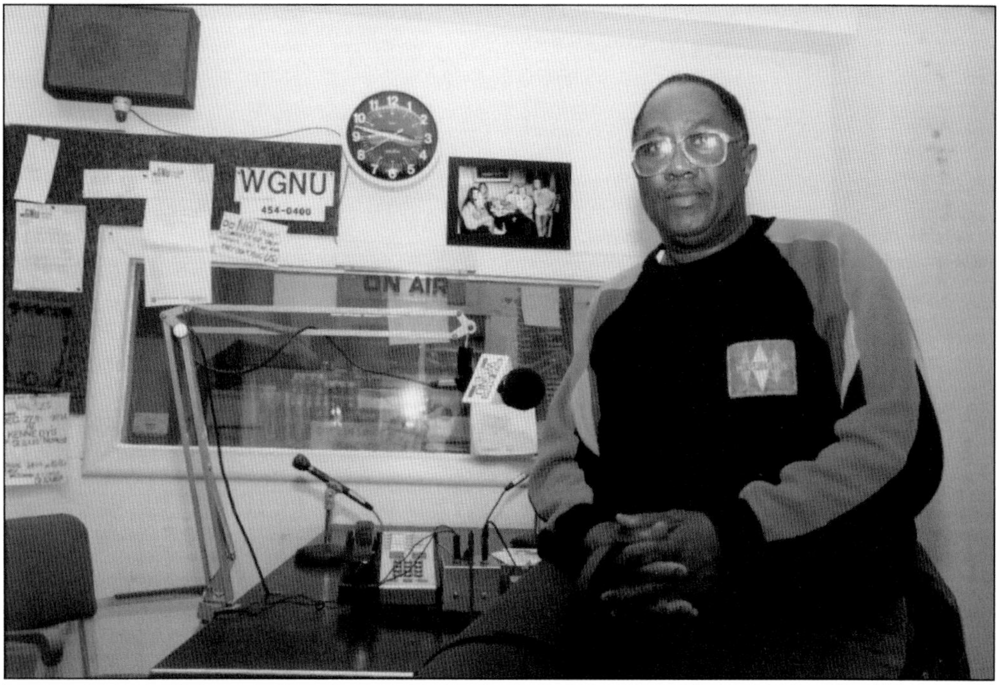

Richard "Onion" Horton found a local following for his brand of talk show, which was often acerbic and confrontational, on WGNU. (St. Louis Media Archive.)

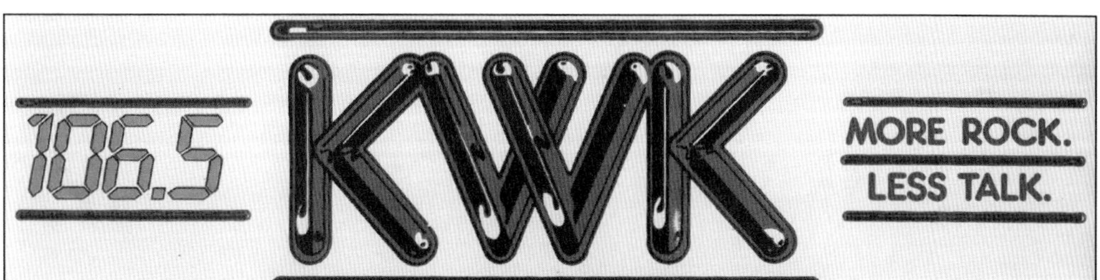

There were many changes in radio in the 1980s and beyond as owners changed formats and call letters with increasing regularity. KWK was advertised as being at 1380 AM and 106.5 FM, although the true name of 106.5 was WWWK. (St. Louis Media Archive.)

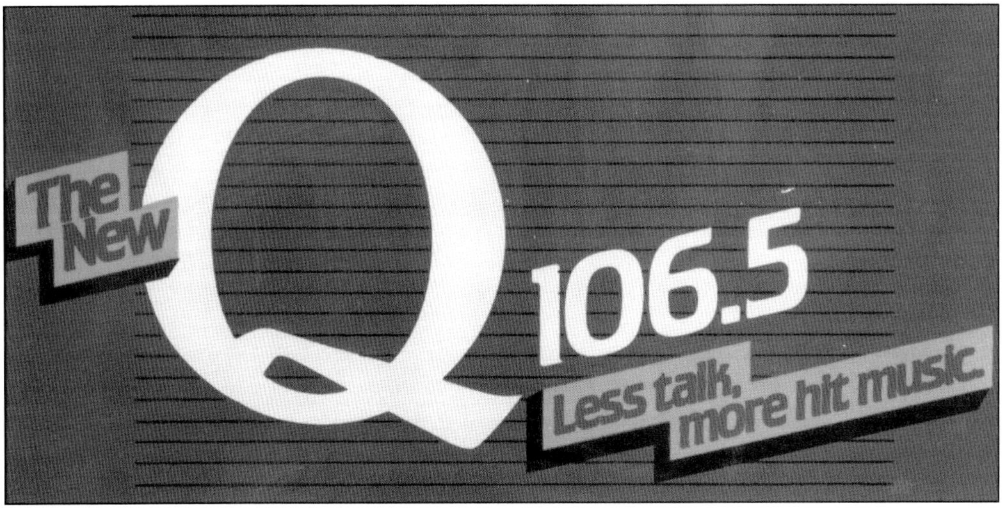

In 1990, KWK-FM became WKBQ. There was no detectable change in the musical selection the station played. (St. Louis Media Archive.)

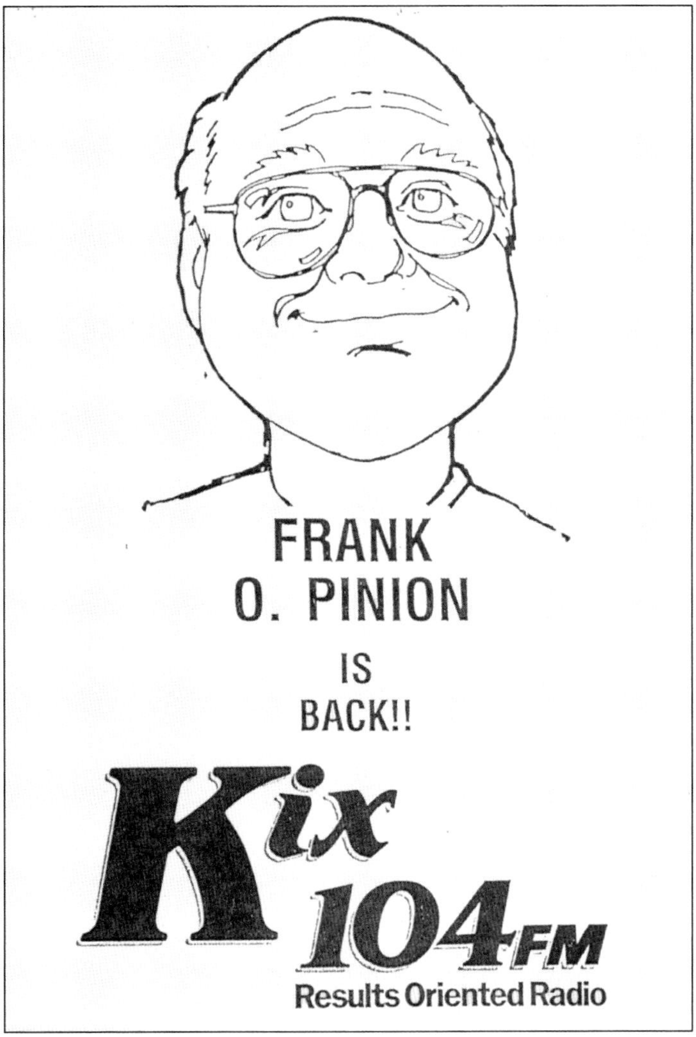

WKKX, which played country music and called itself "Kix," featured personality Frank O. Pinion from 1987 to 1992. (St. Louis Media Archive.)

WIL-FM bounced through a few formats, including "good music" and all news, before settling on country music. (St. Louis Media Archive.)

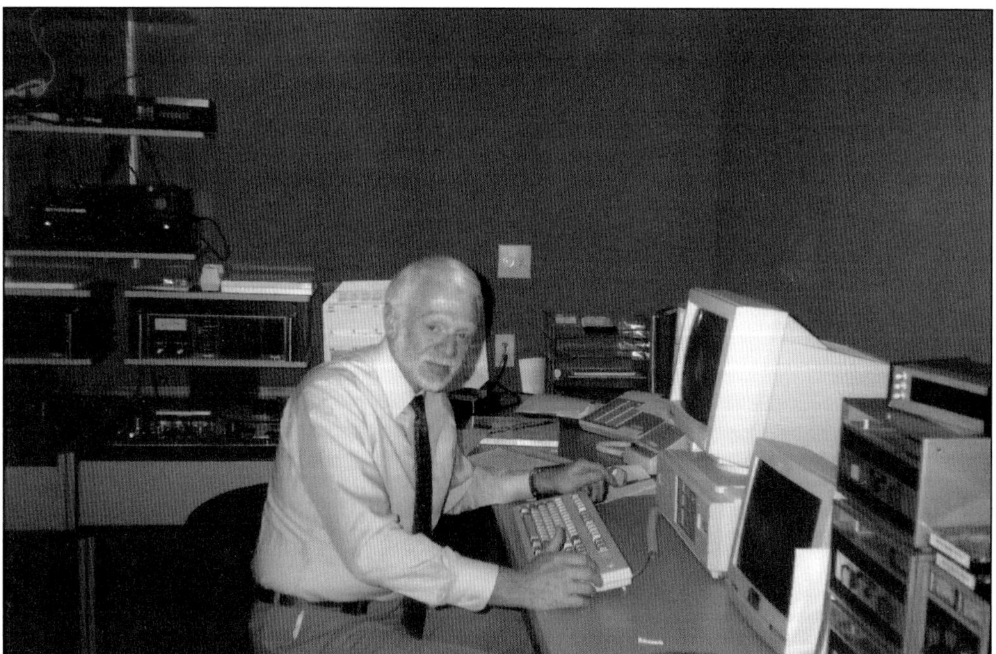

Newsman Gene Hirsch was a mainstay on WIL-AM and FM from 1960 until his retirement in 1994. (St. Louis Media Archive.)

Community radio returned to St. Louis over a decade after KDNA signed off. KDHX was supported by listener donations and underwriting and provided programming not heard on other stations. (St. Louis Media Archive.)

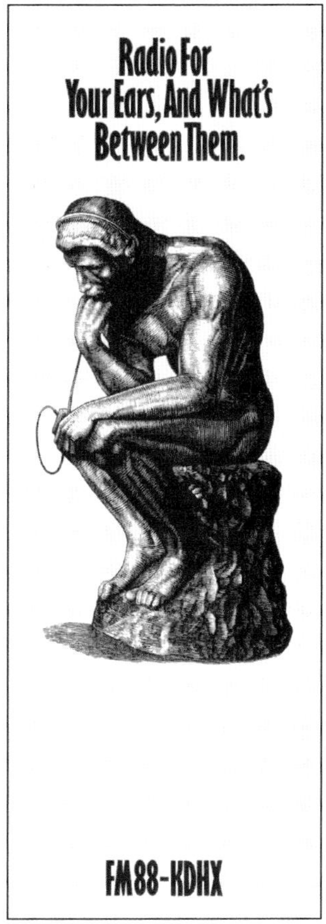

KPNT, owned by a large corporation, portrayed itself as an anti-establishment radio station. (St. Louis Media Archive.)

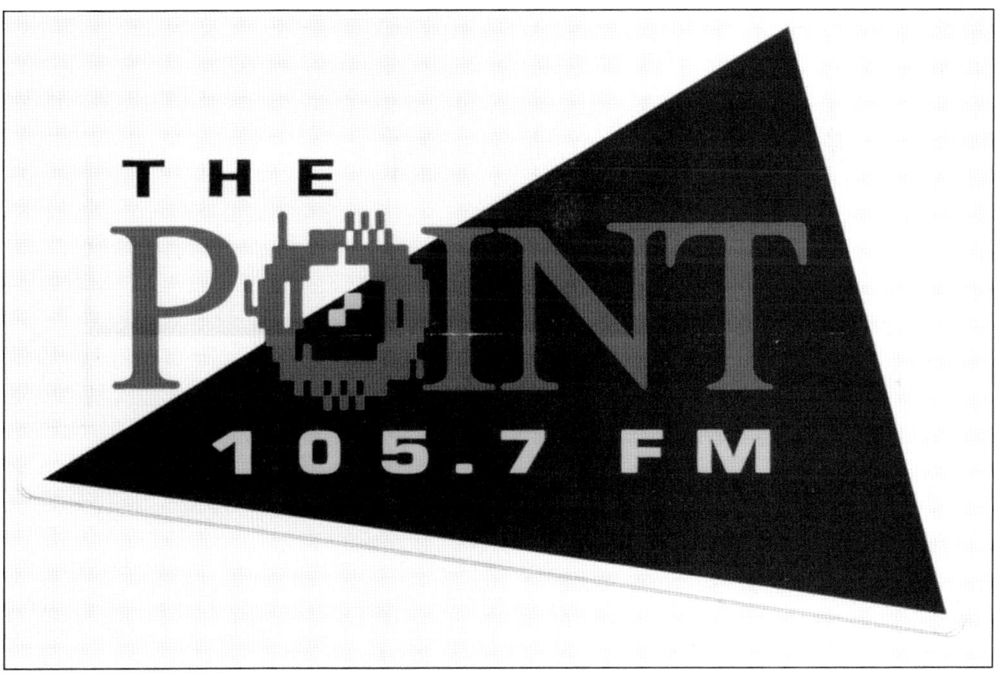

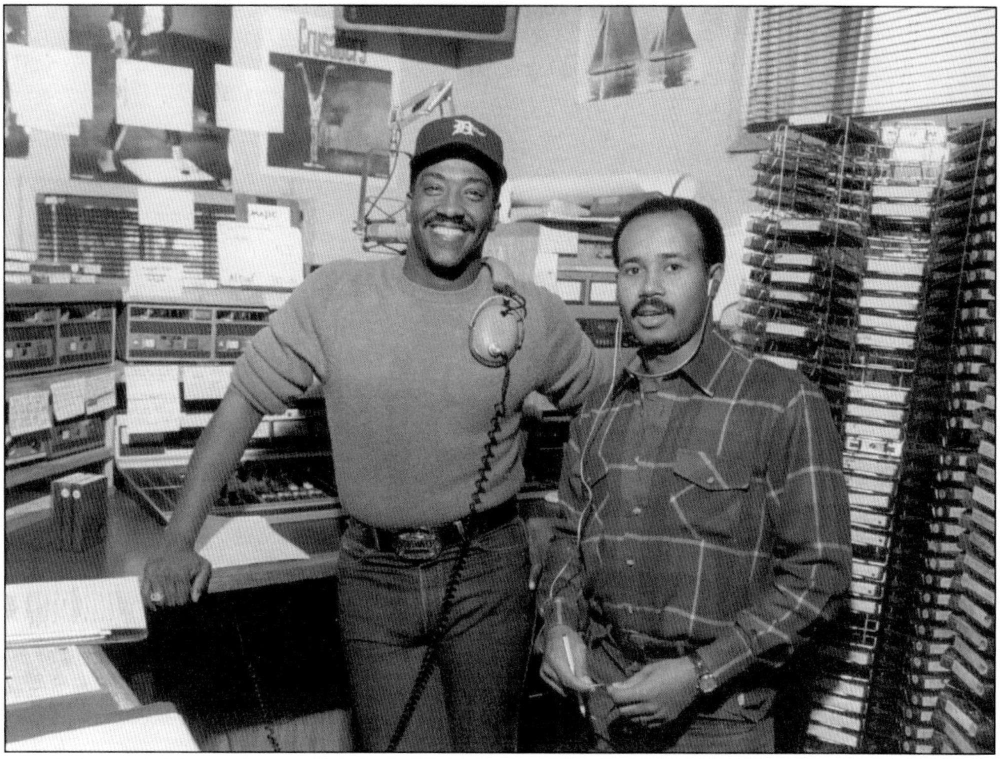

Doc Wynter (left) and Kevin Woodson were two popular local personalities on "Majic," KMJM. (St. Louis Media Archive.)

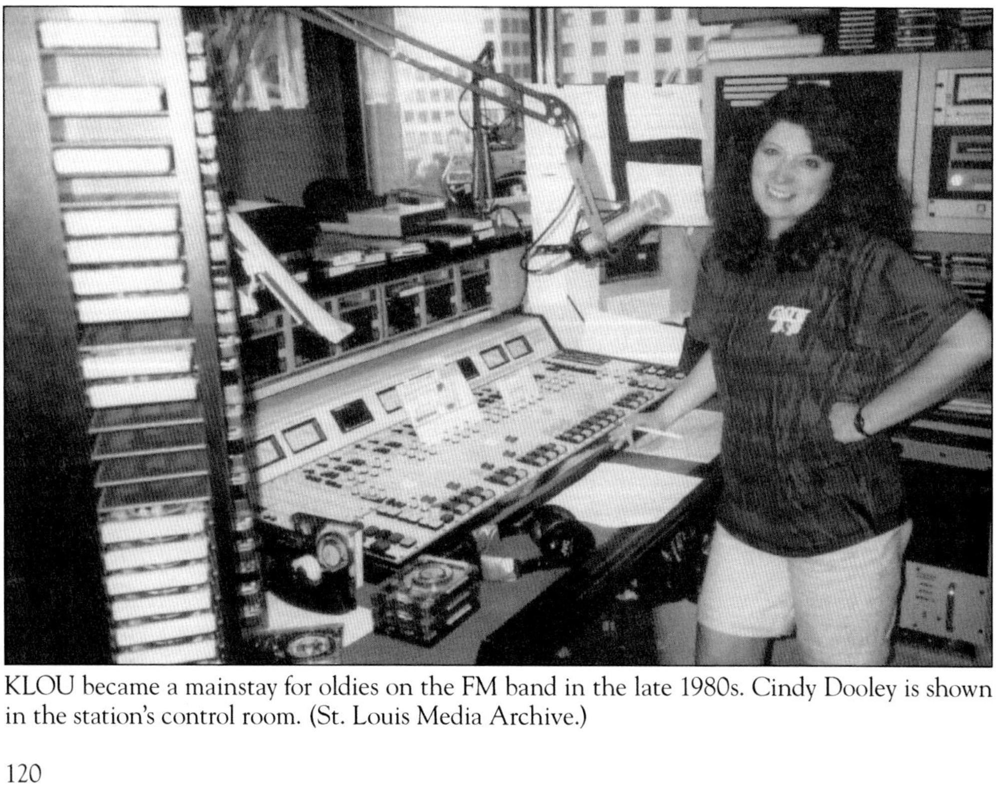

KLOU became a mainstay for oldies on the FM band in the late 1980s. Cindy Dooley is shown in the station's control room. (St. Louis Media Archive.)

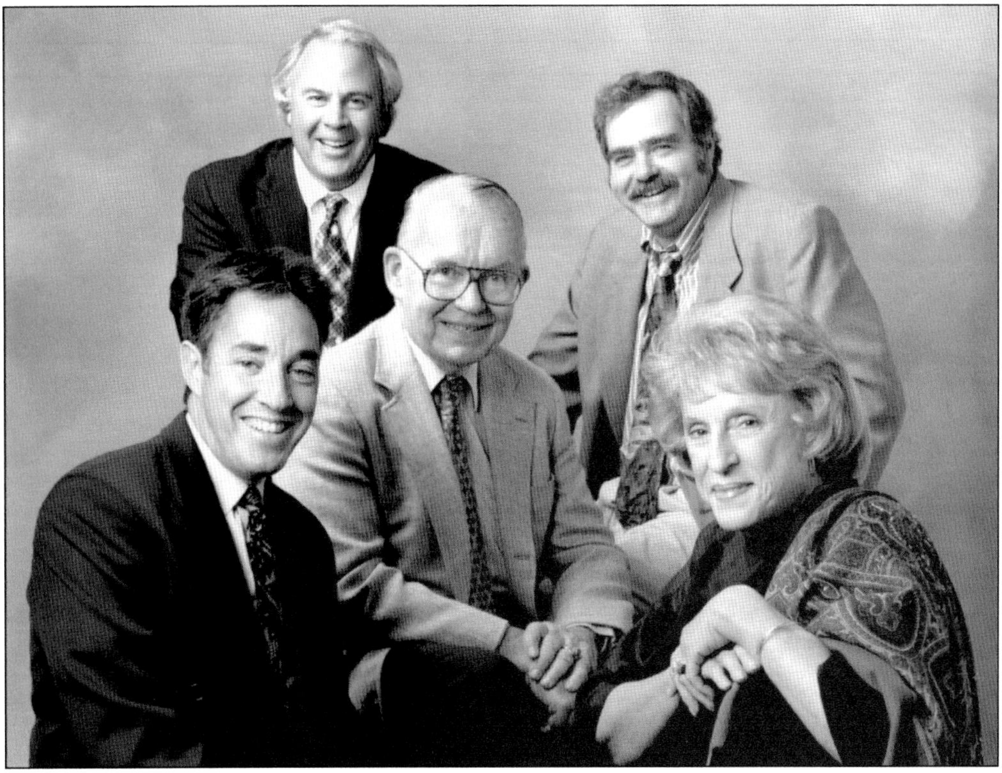

St. Louis media professionals (clockwise from the bottom left) Ray Hartmann, Mark Vittert, Bill McClellan, and Anne Keefe joined host Martin Duggan (center) for *Donnybrook* on KETC. (KETC-TV archives.)

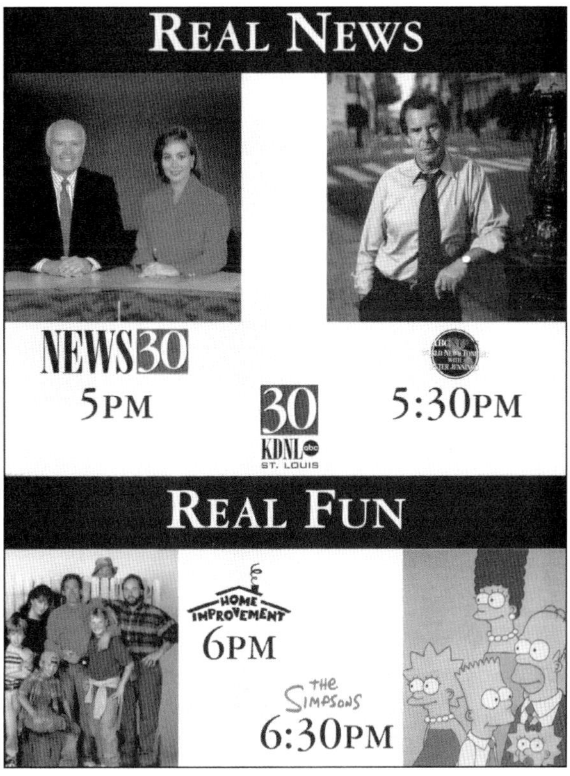

For a brief period in the late 1990s, KDNL-TV produced a local news broadcast, but it was dropped by the station's owners due to low ratings. (St. Louis Media Archive.)

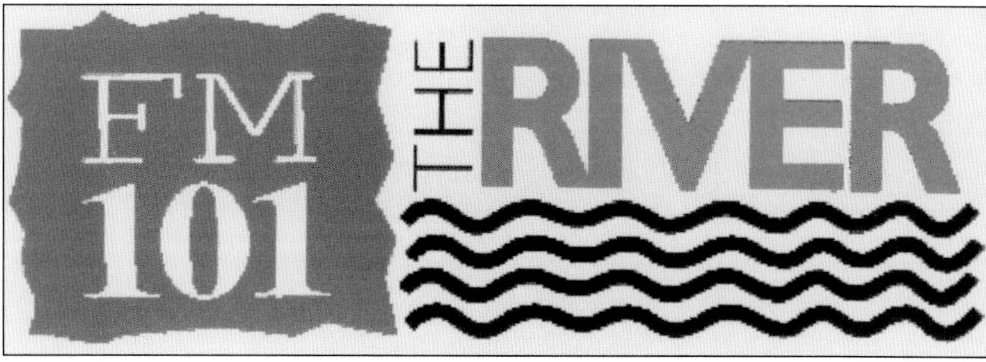

WVRV-FM, known as "The River," survived with its popular music format for 10 years. (St. Louis Media Archive.)

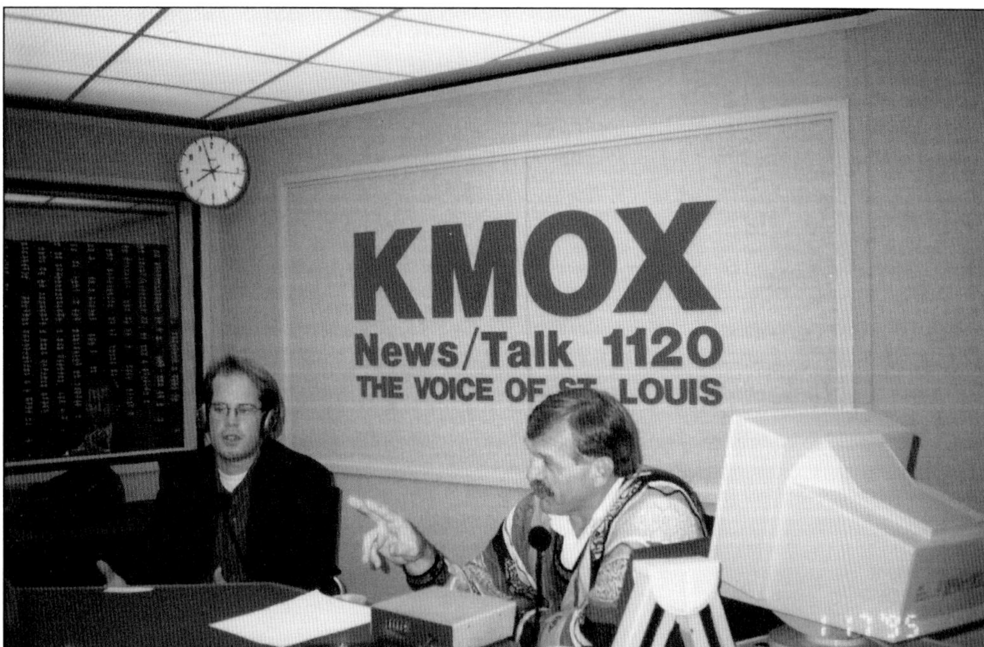

At KMOX, the talk became less local and much more political, but sports talk remained a constant. Joe Buck (left) and Dan Dierdorf are seen hosting *Sports Open Line* in January 1995. (St. Louis Media Archive.)

KEZK's music format evolved from soft, easy-listening music to soft rock. (St. Louis Media Archive.)

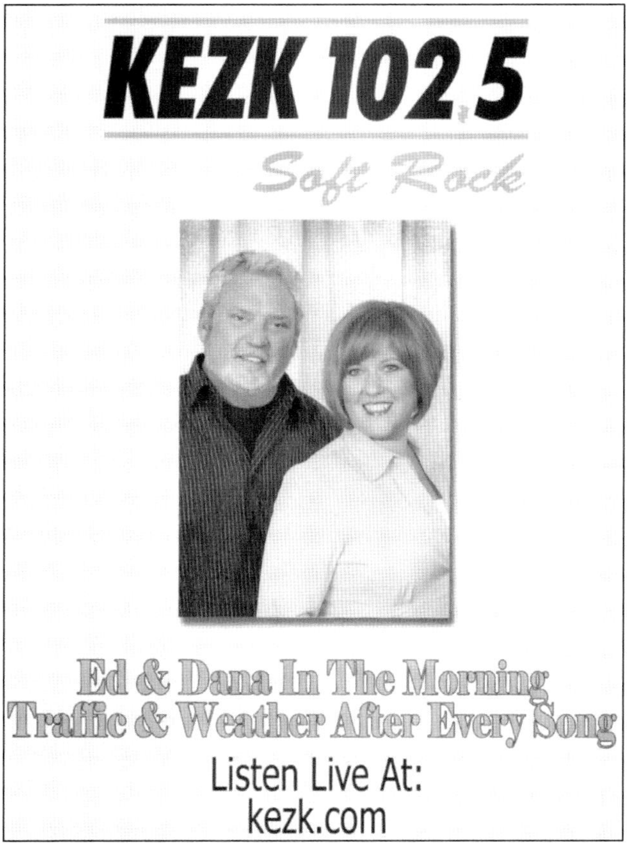

KWMU, the public station at the University of Missouri—St. Louis, has been a strong National Public Radio affiliate. Over the years, limited local programming has been offered with hosts like *Post-Dispatch* columnist Greg Freeman. (KWMU archives.)

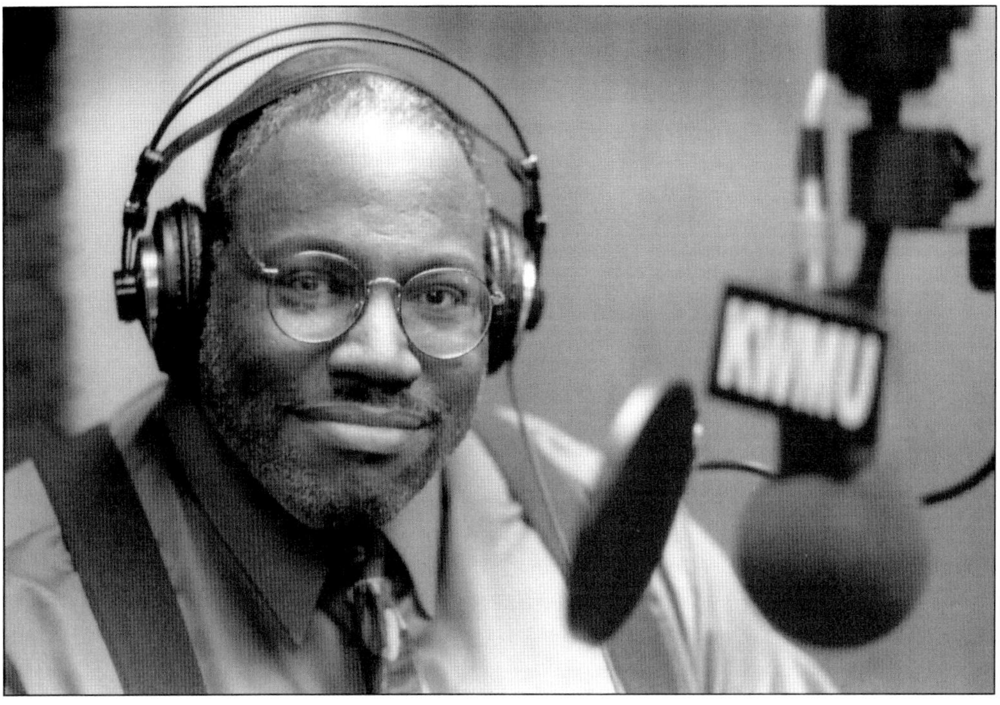

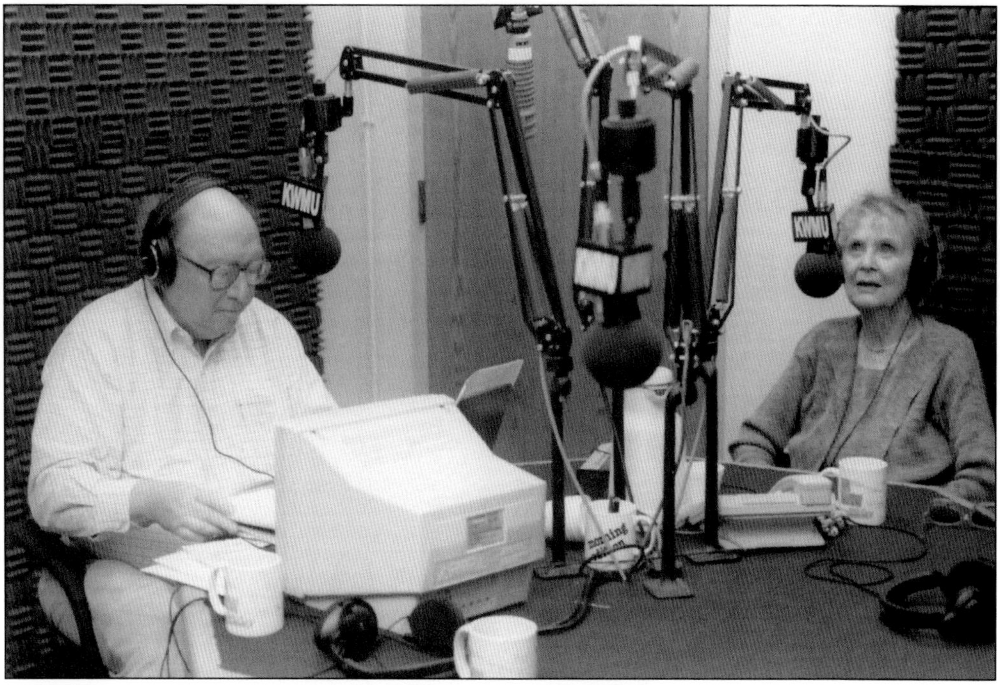

Long-time St. Louis food and arts critic Joe Pollack (left) hosted a local KWMU interview program. The woman in the image is unidentified. (KWMU archives.)

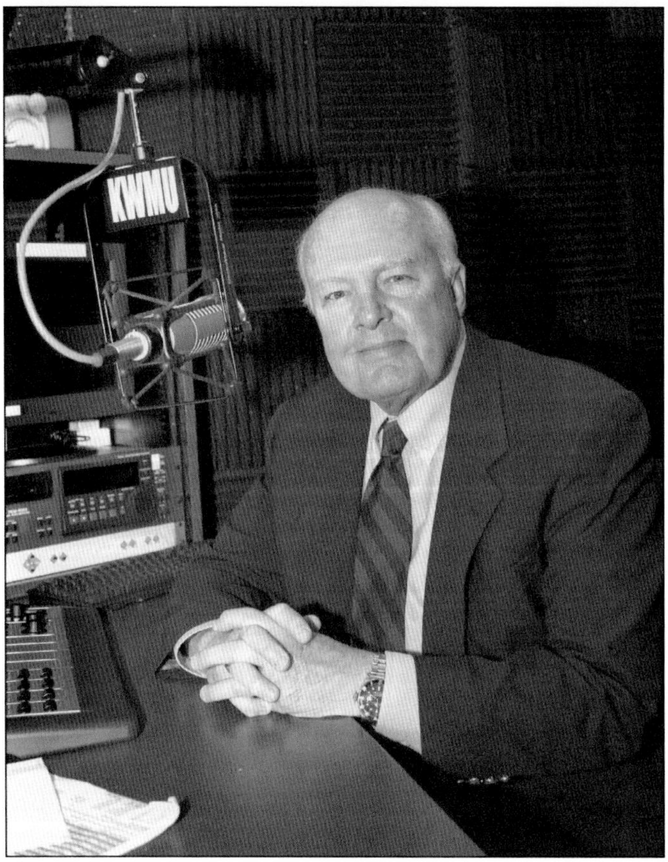

Respected broadcast journalist and former television newsman Don Marsh also had a regular KWMU interview show. (KWMU archives.)

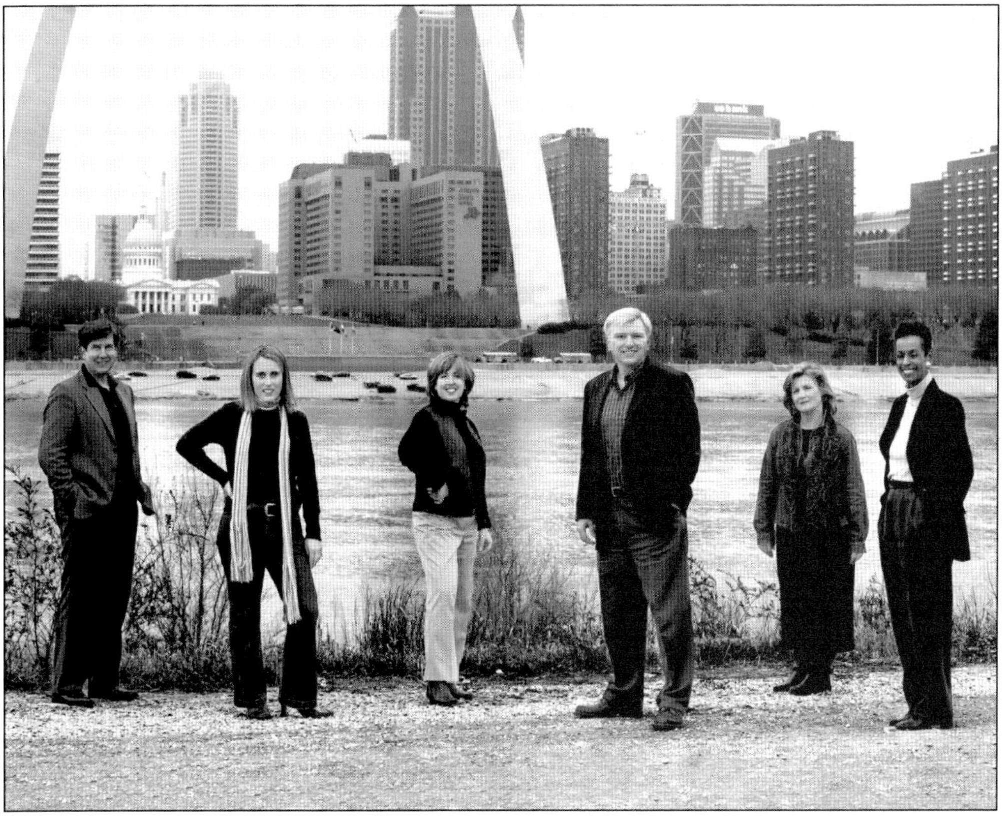

The *Living St. Louis* program on KETC, which debuted in 2004, won many awards. Pictured from left to right are producer/reporters Patrick Murphy, Anne-Marie Berger, Margie Newman, Jim Kirchherr, Jennifer Roller, and Ruth Ezell. (KETC-TV archives.)

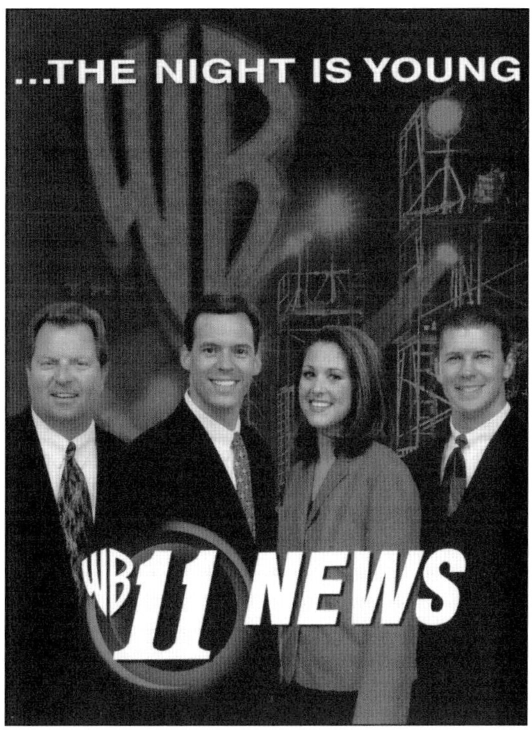

The channel 11 news team in 2000 consisted of, from left to right, Rich Gould, Dave Erickson, Kathryn Jamboretz, and Garry Seith. (KPLR-TV archives.)

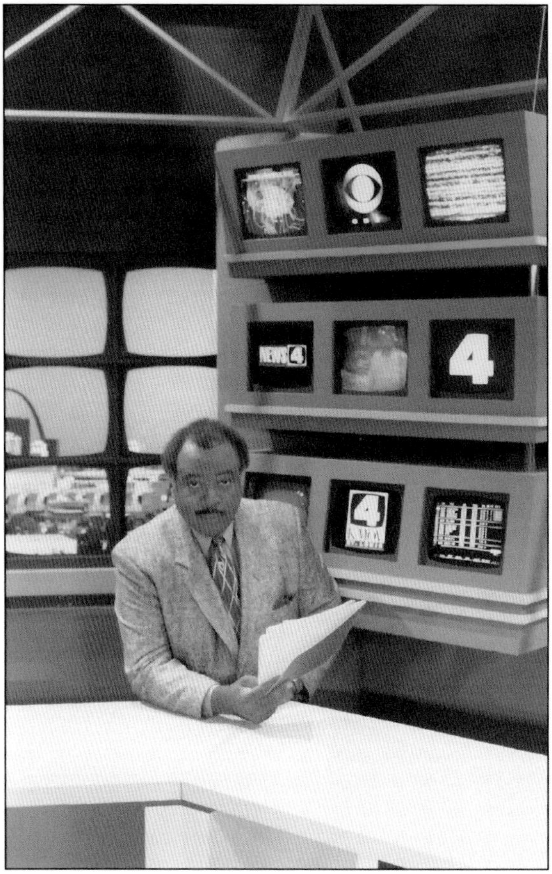

Julius Hunter was seen as a news anchor on channels 4 and 5 over a 36-year period. (St. Louis Media Archive.)

Christine Buck joined KPLR's news staff in 1977, remaining with the station's news operation for well over 30 years. (KPLR-TV archives.)

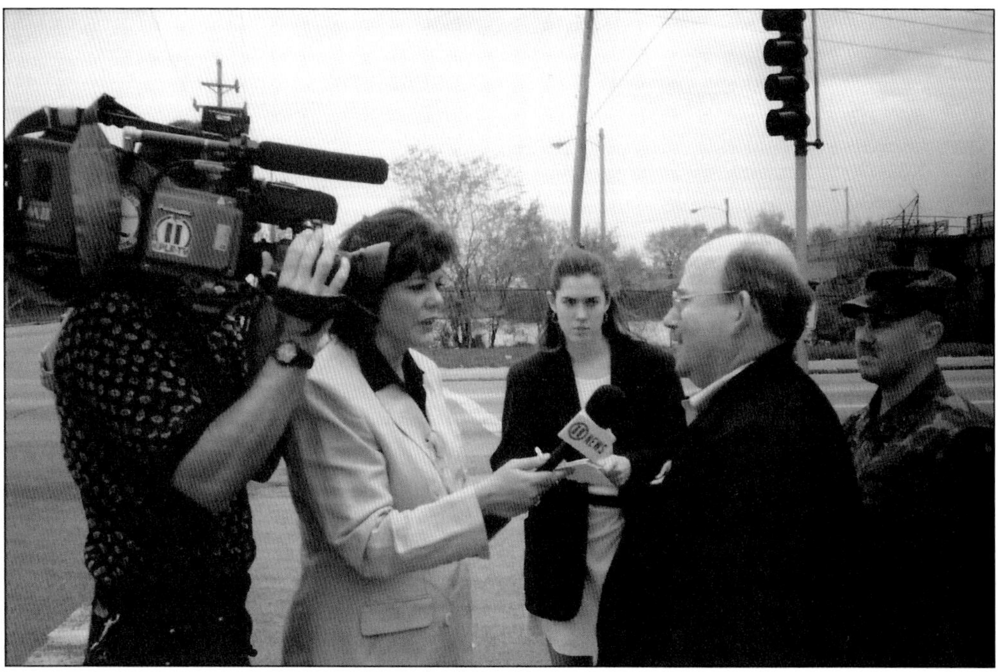

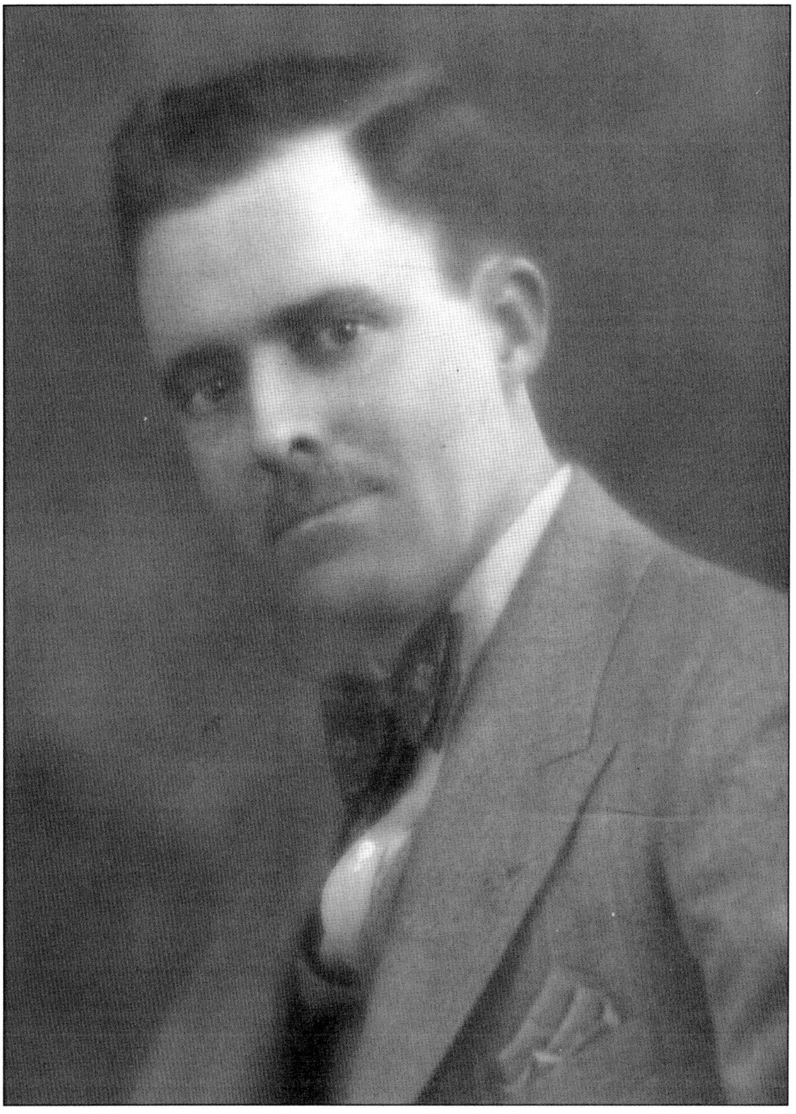

An argument could be made that this man started it all. His name was William E. Woods, and he, along with partner Lester Arthur "Eddie" Benson, handcrafted the first radio transmitters in St. Louis. The pair broadcast the results of the presidential election in November 1920 as the voting totals became available, and Woods's voice was probably the first heard in a broadcast from St. Louis. Later, Woods was licensed to build and run his own radio station in suburban Webster Groves, but he limited his broadcasts to playing music on Sundays. He retired to Florida, where he finished out his years. (Sue Batterson.)

St. Louis Media History Foundation

The St. Louis Media History Foundation was formed to accumulate and preserve media history and artifacts. Working in conjunction with area institutions such as the St. Louis Public Library Media Archive, the foundation continues to promote the storied past of media in the St. Louis area. Visit our website at www.stlmediahistory.org

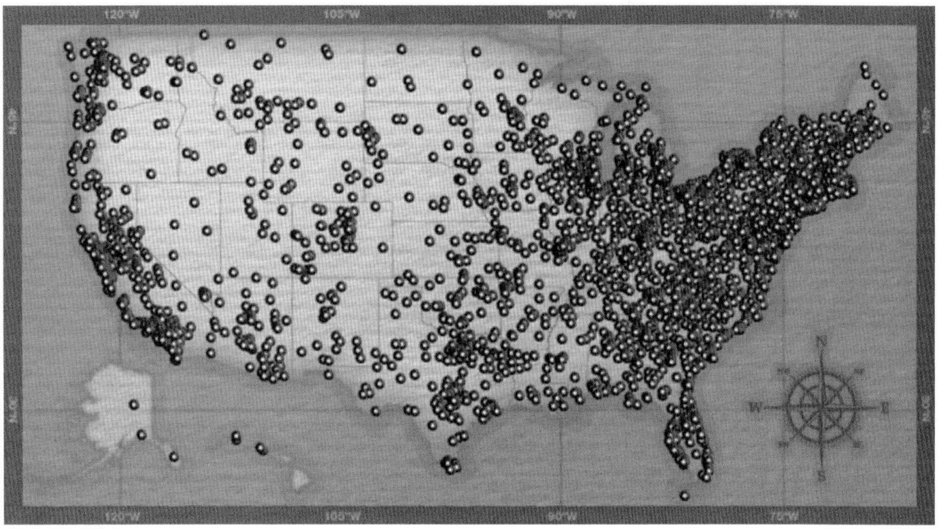